Real Parents,
Real Children

Real Parents, Real Children

Parenting the Adopted Child

ﾐ ﾐ ﾐ

HOLLY VAN GULDEN

AND

LISA M. BARTELS-RABB

CROSSROAD · NEW YORK

1994
The Crossroad Publishing Company
370 Lexington Avenue, New York, NY 10017

Library of Congress Cataloging-in-Publication Data

Van Gulden, Holly.
    Real parents, real children : parenting the adopted child / Holly
van Gulden and Lisa M. Bartels-Rabb.
        p.   cm.
    Includes bibliographical references and index.
    ISBN 0-8245-1368-1
    1. Children, Adopted—United States.   2. Adoptive parents—United
States.   3. Parenting—United States.   I. Bartels-Rabb, Lisa M.
II. Title.
    HV875.55.V36   1993
649'.145—dc20   93-27784
                                                              CIP

To my parents, Nancy and Norman van Gulden,
whose life experiences as parents,
through adoption and birth, inspired me and
provided the basis for much of my work.
—Holly

David, Jonathan and Zora:
Thank you for enduring the process!
—Lisa

Special thanks to Lucille Soli,
without whom we never would have met.
—Lisa and Holly

Contents

Section I

1 · Parenting Is Parenting—Or Is It?   3

2 · Bonding: The Love Question   13

3 · Grief and Loss   30

4 · Identity and the Adopted Child   53

5 · Pregnancy Without a Due Date:
Preplacement and Postplacement Stress   70

6 · On Moving Children   88

Section II

7 · Growing Up Adopted: The Developing Child   105

8 · Early Infancy: The First Six Months   112

9 · The Older Infant—Separation and
Individuation: Six to Thirty-six Months   124

10 · The Preschool Years: Three to Five Years   164

11 · Middle Childhood: Six to Ten Years   191

12 · Adolescence: Eleven to Eighteen Years   212

13 · School and the Adopted Child   241

14 · Adoption Issues in Adulthood   252

15 · On Being Family   257

Bibliography   263

Index   269

Section I

1

❦

Parenting Is Parenting—
Or Is It?

The concept of adoption is nearly as old as human history. The Judeo-Christian tradition gives accounts of adoption going back to Moses' rescue from the reeds by Pharaoh's daughter. Adults want children, children need parents. The equation seems so easy, but like any other human relationship, adoption presents its own unique array of complex emotions, needs, and interactions.

Parenting an adopted child is, for the most part, the same as parenting any other child. Obviously, adopted children need love, discipline, education, food, clothing, shelter, and all the other things all children need to grow into healthy adults. Parenting adopted children, however, *is* different from parenting birth children in some very unique and critical ways. In an effort to assert and advocate for adoption as a valid and beneficial resource for children in need of permanent families, adoptive parents and professionals in the field of adoption have historically de-emphasized—even denied—the differences between parenting adopted children and parenting birth children. As adoptive parents, we feel the need to assert that these are *our* children: We are not second best or second rate. We are our children's real parents and they are our real children.

Indeed, adoptive parents and the institution of adoption provide first-class solutions to the needs of many children who do not have safe, legal, permanent homes and families of their own. Yet in making this assertion, we often overlook a crucial difference, and that is: Whatever happened, whenever it took place and for whatever reasons, children in need of placement and those who are already adopted have become separated from their birth parents and their genetic roots. This is the child's issue even before placement, because it happens before placement. Parents adopt the issue with the child, whether the child comes to the family as an infant unaware of what has happened, or as an older child with memories and the experience of separation. Even open adoption, which resolves some of the issues stemming from this separation, does not offer a perfect solution; after all, knowing one's biological parents is not the same as being raised by them.

To varying degrees this issue of separation is lifelong, weaving in and out of each stage of life, sometimes in the forefront of self-identity, sometimes resting quietly beneath other life issues. This loss, which must be grieved for and resolved, can impact the adopted child's sense of identity and ability to trust and form relationships with other people. Even if denied or covered up, the impact of this separation is as unalterably a part of the adopted child as one's gender or race. Different children feel and grieve the loss to different degrees, but all adopted children must come to terms with it—whether in a healthy or an unhealthy way—at some point in their lives. The difference between parenting a child born to the family and parenting a child who joined the family through adoption is in the following:

- recognizing the impact of the child's experience of separation from her birth parents, whether she actually knew them or not, and the permanent change in destiny, even if for the better, from the life the child would have had;
- helping the child understand and come to terms with these issues and his feelings about them;
- helping the child find appropriate ways to express her feelings;
- learning how to deal with problematic or unhealthy manifestations of these issues;
- recognizing and coming to terms with our own unresolved issues, especially those related to our childhoods and fertility or infertility; and
- accepting the child's unique genetic endowment and the lack of a genetic connection to ourselves.

The Desire to Parent: Choosing Adoption

Whether through procreation or adoption, the desire to raise children stems from the same spectrum of reasons. In either case, there may be numerous healthy or unhealthy factors motivating the adult to parenthood. The factors that lead one to choose adoption over procreation, however, are unique. For many, procreation is not an option. For single adults, adoption offers a viable way of becoming a parent and having a family without compromising one's sexual ethics or moral principles. Other couples and individuals feel compelled to care for children who are already born and in need of families, rather than give birth to a child who would be geneti-cally "theirs."

Perhaps these issues do not distinguish adoptive parents from birth par-ents in big ways, but each has the potential for creating situations birth parents do not necessarily face. For example, infertile couples not only face all the ramifications and emotions surrounding their inability to conceive, they are also put in a position whereby the only way they may have a child is to place themselves "at the mercy" of attorneys, adoption agencies, birth parents, legal systems, and sometimes even the laws of foreign nations. For these couples, the decision to have children is no longer one made in the privacy of one's bedroom—or wherever; adults choosing to build a family through adoption, whether privately or through an agency, must first gain the approval of numerous other people.

Single people who choose to adopt may find themselves admired for their courage and commitment, or challenged regarding the wisdom of their decision. Like all single parents, they are also confronted with the issue of providing their children with role models from both sexes. When faced with the difficulties of single parenting, adoptive parents may find themselves surrounded by family and friends willing to go out of their way to help; or they may find themselves faced with an attitude of "You brought this on yourself; it's a problem you chose, so you deal with it." Sometimes the empathy and support for single adoptive parents can be even less than that shown single birth parents, because they are not "victims of circumstance," such as death of a spouse, divorce, abandonment, or unintended pregnancy.

Gay and lesbian couples and individuals who adopt face additional chal-lenges. Perhaps one of the greatest of these is that even when a couple can demonstrate that they have been together for some time and that their lives are as intertwined financially and otherwise as any heterosexual married couple, they cannot legally become a two-parent family. Only one of the partners can be the legal parent of an adopted child, leaving the other partner with no legal parental rights. They may also find people questioning their fitness to raise children, or questioning just how much "difference" children can tolerate. While gay and lesbian birth parents face the same issues, they are often intensified for adoptive parents.

Regardless of family structure and composition, some adoptive parents are also faced with extended family who do not recognize their adopted children as members of the family, particularly if they are of different ethnic heritage. If a child proves to have extensive medical problems or, even more so, behavioral problems, people are more likely to advise adoptive parents to "abandon" the child, saying that he isn't *really* theirs anyway. Rarely are birth parents given similar advice.

The History of Adoption

A formal system of legal adoption was established in the United States around the turn of the twentieth century, primarily to meet the needs of infertile upper-class couples. But from the time of Moses, formal and informal adoptions have taken place as a way of meeting the various needs of children, birth parents, and adoptive parents.

Even today, in many cultures, communities, and families, informal arrangements to raise children are not uncommon. Grandparents raise the children of their teenage sons and daughters. Aunts and uncles step in to raise nephews and nieces when the children's parents have died or are chronically ill. Parents arrange for one or more children to live with another family in the community because they are unable to feed them. The reasons are as myriad as the children and parents involved.

Historically, minority cultures and lower economic groups have been less likely to turn to the legal system to sanction their adoptions. Prohibitive costs and fears of the system—and of the majority peoples running them—tend to keep them away. Yet informal "adoptions" did and still do take place in these communities. In most cases, such informal arrangements within extended family or the community are based on meeting the child's needs for a home with capable, caring parents.

Adoptions have also taken place with the interests of the parents (birth and/or adoptive) as the primary motivation. In India, tradition has it that if the elder brother and his wife are infertile, a younger brother with several sons may turn over one of his younger sons to the older brother to ensure a family heir.

Adoption in America has undergone many changes over the years. In each era, people truly believed they were protecting all members of the adoption triad: adoptive parents, birth parents, and child. Despite the good intentions, however, the system has not always worked well for all individuals. For adults who grew up in adoptive families, understanding the historical era in which they were raised can be an important step toward healing old wounds. Each change in the system attempted to address a different need, but it also raised new issues that society and families were not always prepared to address.

One of the first large-scale adoption movements took place during the 1800s as the United States forged westward. To reduce overcrowding in East Coast orphanages, children were placed on trains and sent west. Communities along the train lines were notified when the "orphan train" was coming so that families wanting children could meet the train and select from the children aboard. Parents were required to make a minimal commitment of providing food and shelter for any children they adopted, and when the children reached the age of majority, sending each of them off with a change of clothing. While this system presumably led to loving homes for many of these children, it also paved the way for exploiting children as cheap sources of labor.

Of course, in addition to the orphan trains, informal adoptions were occurring within communities and families. The legal system of adoption was established in the early 1900s primarily to protect families, particularly in the area of inheritance. It also protected adoptive parents from the stigma of infertility. The system of sending women away for several months while they were expecting protected both women who were pregnant out of wedlock and infertile couples who were adopting.

At that time, children were still seen as chattel. Society on the whole did not recognize the "rights" of children, nor did it see that children had any special needs. This began to change with the passage of the Fair Labor Standards Act in 1938, which outlawed oppressive child labor, particularly in manufacturing and mining.

Wartime makes both orphans and temporary orphans; it also leads people to open their homes to children for both informal and formal adoption. This was true during World Wars I and II, at the same time that traditional closed adoptions were taking place. The Korean War, however, added a new twist to this situation. In any war-torn country, local women inevitably have children fathered by occupying troops, whether through rape, prostitution, or loving relationships. When this happened in Korea, the Korean-American children were rejected by Korean communities because of their mixed race. Though the response to children of mixed race has historically been a problem in almost all countries (consider the response to "mulattoes" in this country), white Americans were particularly incensed by this reaction because it was a rejection and debasement of themselves. While there were certainly Korean–African-Americans born out of the war and adopted by African-American families, white Americans, as the majority race, were entirely unaccustomed to such rejection. Ironically, though Americans were appalled by stories of the treatment of these children in Asia following both the Vietnam and Korean wars, the United States did not offer citizenship to the Amer-Asian children. In fact, it was the only Western nation participating in these conflicts that failed to offer citizenship to the children their troops fathered with local women.

The resulting movement to adopt Amer-Asian and Korean war orphans brought an old question to the forefront: Should adopted children be told they are adopted? This was the first move toward openness about adoption. Children of obviously different racial backgrounds from their parents could not be lied to. The consensus turned toward telling children about their adoption, but no further. Amer-Asian and Korean children were told about

Korea, its culture, and the war, but were given no real facts about their personal genetic heritages. Throughout this period, the term *transracial adoption* was reserved for the placement of African-American and Native American children into white homes. Yet the adoption of Asian children by white Americans was obviously transracial, as well.

In the early 1960s, two movements arose: transracial domestic adoption (African-American and Native American children into white homes) and a parent-initiated movement to adopt "hard-to-place" children. This movement was based on social justice, but not on reality. Many well-intentioned parents adopted these children with the expectation—reinforced by agencies—that with lots of love the children would do just fine. When reality proved different for some of these children, parents were left with nowhere to turn for help in dealing with the problems.

Increasingly in the late 1960s and into the 1970s, placement itself was no longer assumed to resolve all problems within the triad. The first center in the United States to provide postadoption services was founded in 1968 by the Children's Home Society in St. Paul, Minnesota, as a response to this and many other needs. For the first time, help was available for all members of the adoption triad.

Eventually, the question of identity for adopted children came to be recognized. While most parents today accept that it is wise to tell children about their adoption at the earliest age, many adoptive parents remain uncomfortable discussing their children's birth parents and genetic heritage. In the 1960s and 1970s, the adoption community stressed the importance of cultural, racial, and ethnic identity. This often proved more difficult in domestic transracial adoptions than in international adoptions, where the child's ethnic heritage had the appeal of being exotic.

The move for greater openness swelled in the 1980s, as birth parents sought more say in how and with whom their children were to be placed. The number of adopted children and birth parents searching for each other increased dramatically, and more adopted individuals knew their birth parents. Similarly, prospective adoptive parents—especially white parents seeking white infants—opted for open rather than closed adoptions because that was where the children were, and some recognized the benefits of openness for the children. Agencies responded to this trend by developing their own open placement programs, in part to compete with private placements, but also to better meet the identity needs of the children.

Types of Adoption

With each new era, new forms of adoption came into being to better meet the needs of all involved. Today, the decision to adopt is just the first step.

From there the question becomes *how* to adopt. Here are some of the options available:

Open versus closed adoption. In traditional closed adoptions, the adopted child and the birth parents have no contact with one another following placement. The adoptive parents may be given their child's family medical history and some background information on the birth parents, but this is not always the case. Though many children and birth parents years later may seek each other out, traditional closed adoptions provide no ready means for them to locate each other.

The system of closed adoption was intended to protect the birth mother's privacy and enable her to start life anew; to protect the adoptive parents' ability to raise their child without interference from the birth parent; and in some cases, to protect the child from information about his or her roots that was believed to be potentially detrimental. Closed adoption also enabled families to maintain a pretense that the child was genetically "their own," protecting the parents from the stigma of infertility and the child from challenges against his or her rights of inheritance within the adoptive family.

Open adoption was established to help avoid many of the identity pitfalls present in closed adoptions, while maintaining a sense of security for the adoptive parents and helping the birth parents deal with their loss of a child. In open adoption some degree of contact is maintained between the adoptive family and the birth parent. The amount of contact varies widely, from a mere exchange of cards and letters, all the way to "adopting" the birth parent as a member of the extended family. This type of adoption is broken down further by direct-contact openness and third-party openness. In third-party openness, letters to and from the birth parent and the adopted child or his family are sent first to a third person, such as a lawyer, who then lets the person to whom it is addressed know that the letter is waiting. This allows the addressee to choose an emotionally convenient time to receive it. Sometimes only first names are used, protecting each member of the triad from undesired intrusion by other members. Adoptive families and birth parents can decide to adopt a system of third-party openness at any time; it does not have to be established at the time of placement.

Private versus agency adoption. Adoption agencies are designed to protect the interests of children in need of placement by finding them appropriate homes with appropriate parents. They also provide birth parents a means of placing children in adoptive homes without having to do an unwieldy search alone. Many agencies offer support services for all members in the triad.

Some prospective adoptive parents, however, opt for private adoptions arranged through a lawyer, physician, or even directly with the birth parents or their families. Private adoption is usually more expensive than adoption through an agency, but some prospective parents feel that avoiding the red tape of agency adoption is well worth the extra expense. It also offers them a way of maintaining a greater sense of control in the matter, while avoiding a sometimes lengthy screening process. Often, white prospective parents desiring to adopt white infants find it easier to locate and adopt children through private sources than through agencies.

Same-race infant adoption. In many respects, same-race infant adoptions are the least complicated. In fact, throughout this book this type of placement is used as the "baseline" to illustrate the impact adoption by itself has on the child. For our purposes, infants are children under one year of age, and preferably under nine months.

Preferential adoption. This is the term used to describe adoptions by parents who already have genetically related children or who are capable of conceiving and giving birth but choose to adopt instead.

Older child adoption. In general, any child over the age of one is considered an older child. This age cutoff has been gradually moving to younger and younger ages because of the complexities and difficulties these children have been shown to experience. We consider the cutoff between infant and older child adoptions to be between six and twelve months because the onset of stranger anxiety and other developmental tasks often makes the transition to a new family more difficult even for older infants.

Sibling-group adoption. Sometimes siblings are placed for adoption together. Placing siblings in different homes from one another creates an additional injury for children, who already must deal with the separation from their birth parents. In some cases, however, separate placements with continued contact between the brothers and sisters may provide the best opportunity to meet the special needs of one or several children in the family. This exception aside, most professionals in the adoption field hesitate to separate siblings, even though finding a home for them together can be difficult. Sibling-group adoptions have been traditionally categorized as special needs adoptions.

Interracial or transracial domestic adoption. This is adoption in which the adoptive parents and the adopted child come from the same country but are of different races or from different ethnic backgrounds that have maintained unique cultural identities within the wider society.

International adoption. This term is self-defining. An international adoption is one in which the child comes from a country other than the one in which the adoptive parents live. Often this type of adoption requires approval from both domestic and foreign courts.

Special needs adoption. This classification includes:

- children who have physical or mental disabilities, chronic or otherwise serious physical illness, or developmental delays;
- children who have had multiple foster or institutional placements; and
- children who have been neglected or mentally, physically or sexually abused.

Of course, this is a simplified picture of adoption. In addition to potential variations within each of these forms, prospective parents today are faced with an array of complicated hybrids, such as surrogate parenting, as well as high-tech solutions to infertility, such as in vitro fertilization and artificial insemination using donated sperm.

Adoptive Parenting Is Different

Though the term "special needs children" is used in a very specific way in adoption, we believe all adopted children have special needs—needs that children raised by their birth parents do not face. In the 1980s, a statistically higher percentage of adopted individuals sought inpatient and outpatient mental health services, both as children and adults. It is normal for adopted individuals to struggle with issues surrounding their genetic heritage, who their birth parents were, why the birth parents could not or chose not to parent them, and what all this means about themselves. By understanding how your child understands, interprets, and feels about adoption and why, you can do much to help him or her through these struggles. And that is what this book is about—helping parents help their children and helping them identify when they need to turn to professionals.

We believe the information in this book will also be useful for professionals working with adoptive families. While the clinical information is couched for the most part in lay terms, techniques for helping children and families can easily be applied in clinical practice as well as by families themselves. Of course, this does not mean that once parents have read this book they will never need professional help. We encourage families to seek the help of professional family therapists, social workers, psychologists, or psychiatrists when needed. Self-help is fine and good, but just as you wouldn't fill your own cavities, diagnose your own physical illnesses, or perform surgery on yourself or your children, when a serious or potentially serious psychological or emotional issue arises, it is often best to consult a professional before things get worse.

2

Bonding: The Love Question

Whether awaiting an adoption or the birth of a child, one fear is common among expectant parents: Will my child and I be close? Will we bond? Pick up almost any book for new parents and you're sure to find a section on bonding. With the exception that many books for new birth parents emphasize the importance of togetherness in the first few hours and days of the baby's life (which, by the way, birth parents, too, are not always able to enjoy, especially when medical complications arise), the basic concepts are the same for all parents. But when adoption is added to the picture, the fear of not bonding takes on a new dimension. Spoken or unspoken, the new question becomes: Can I love an adopted child the same as I would a birth child?

You need not be embarrassed or feel guilty if this question has run through your head. It's a natural fear, one that nearly all adoptive parents experience at one time or another. After all, how do you suddenly love someone who has no connection to you, whom you've never met before? Would you walk up to a stranger on the street and invite her to live with you and be a part of your family? Probably not. Yet in many ways adoption isn't as far from that as we'd like to believe. Though you will not have a genetic tie to your child, you can still have a deep emotional connection with him. And your chances of accomplishing the latter are improved immensely if you can accept and feel comfortable with the absence of the genetic tie. Expectant parents today seem less able than in the past to speak openly of their fear of not loving an adopted child. While some therapists suggest that less talk is a sign that people are less afraid, we believe the opposite is true.

As people delay having children, the discovery of infertility brings a greater sense of desperation. The closer to forty a woman is when infertility is discovered—whether her own or her partner's—the less time there is to resolve the problem, leaving the couple or individual with fewer choices. Rarely is the initial diagnosis that nothing will work, but with the biological clock ticking away the right solution may not be found in time. And the greater the chance of never having a birth child, the more intense the fear of not being able to love an adopted child.

Society and science also contribute to parents' fears about their capacity to love. Increased tensions between economic and racial groups and greater questioning about the role genetics—as opposed to environment—plays in determining who a child will eventually be only add to parents' fears. In the early 1980s, twin studies conducted by Thomas Bouchard, Ph.D., at the University of Minnesota, put a real scare into adoptive parents. The studies explored personality traits of identical and fraternal twins reared together and apart, and found genetic links for eleven personality traits previously thought to be influenced primarily by environment; those traits are as follows:

- extroversion;
- conformity;
- anxiousness (worry);
- creativity;
- paranoia;
- optimism;
- cautiousness;
- aggressiveness;
- ambitiousness;
- orderliness; and
- intimacy (Wellborn 1987, 62).

Other studies have found that some traits, such as friendliness, anxiety level, shyness, curiosity, engageability, and flexibility, persist over the course of a lifetime, regardless of what life—i.e., environment—might hold (Neubauer and Neubauer 1990, 39). The idea that personality might be genetically inscribed sent chills of fear through the adoption community. Did this mean that adoptive parents really could not shape and mold a child? If so, how could they be certain that the children they adopted would be people they could get along with and love?

Fortunately, nothing is entirely black and white. After many years of studying twins, Bouchard has concluded that no more than 50 percent of one's personality is inherited from one's parents, and even that 50 percent is divided between both parents (25 percent from the mother and 25 percent from the father). In *Nature's Thumbprint: The New Genetics of Personal-*

ity, Peter Neubauer, M.D., and Alexander Neubauer, a father-and-son team, conclude that personality is a result of both nature *and* nurture. "What is endowed at birth," they write, "is not a set of traits but a range of expression. The range is set by human evolution and the individual's inborn variations, and it accommodates flexibility. Our genetic programs allow for, and cannot thrive without, environmental influence" (1990, 22–23). In fact, this point is supported by studies of adopted children, which have shown that in some ways "they remain close to their biological parents, revealing the relative strength of heredity, and [in other] ways they mold to their adoptive parents, revealing the influence of imitation, identification, and adaptation to the environment" (Neubauer and Neubauer 1990, 23).

Though these recent findings on genetics dashed the idealism of the 1960s and 1970s when it was widely believed that adoptive parents could, like the mythological Pygmalion and the George Bernard Shaw comedy of the same name, shape and mold a child into someone they could love, adoptive parents can and do influence how their children express their endowed traits.

Finding an Answer

Whatever the reason behind the fear of not being able to love an adopted child, the fear itself needs to be discussed. But where can you bring it up? If you talk about it with the adoption agency, will they let you have a child? If you are adopting privately, who is there to ask? The physician? The attorney? The birth mother? Perhaps not knowing who to turn to in itself is why very few people bring it up. Some agencies, but not all, raise the issue directly. Support groups for adoptive parents can help you in your struggle to find an answer. If you are uncomfortable with group settings and you don't know anyone who has adopted, network among your friends to find someone who has. Ask the adoptive parents you find what love for an adopted child is like, what it feels like.

Many people move into adoption without ever acknowledging that these fears and doubts exist. It sometimes becomes a family secret. Sometimes it isn't even expressed between husband and wife. So the first step is to admit that the fear is there and understand that it is normal.

Next, ask yourself if you can love—that's the root question. After all, what's the real difference between an adopted child and a birth child? Admittedly, you won't see *your* nose go on for generations, and there will be issues unique to raising an adopted child. Your child may develop habits you cannot identify as coming from anyone else in the family. And these habits may be pleasing or irritating. But when they are irritating and cannot be assigned to someone else in the family ("You bite your nails just like your father") they can become divisive. One response would be to tell the child, "I bet your birth mother drove her mom crazy doing that." But, in the end, your ability to love remains the essential question.

While no one ever knows for sure whether they will love an adopted child before that child is in their home and part of their family, you can make a pretty fair prediction by understanding your needs.

- Can you accept differences? Your child will be different from you, even in a same-race adoption.
- Does your desire to parent stem from a need to form a loving relationship with a child whom you then set free, or from a need to fulfill unmet expectations in your own life (you never became the doctor you always wanted to be)? All parents must eventually let go of their children, and having children solely to live vicariously through them is never healthy.
- Or does your desire stem from a need to re-create yourself? All of us have that need. Even people who choose not to parent have a desire to leave something behind, whether it's their art, their literature, or their work. But all parents should understand that their children will be unique individuals, unlike themselves in any number of ways.

For adoptive parents, these issues can be particularly difficult. First you face the loss of birth children you always hoped for, and then you are called on to resolve these issues before you even have a child. But if either of the last two is your primary reason for wishing to adopt, adoption is probably not appropriate for you at this time. That's not to say you should *never* adopt. In the future, if you are able to work out those needs, meeting them in other ways, or if their importance diminishes, then adoption may be right. There is no such thing as "never" because people can and do grow.

Bonding and Attachment

We've talked about how you may feel toward your child, but what about how your newly adopted child will feel about you? When we begin to talk about the two-way tie between parent and child we are talking about *bonding* and *attachment*.

The terms *bond* and *attachment* are often used interchangeably by many professionals and in literature on the subject. A healthy parent/child relationship is actually composed of three different parts: trust, usually referred to as the bond; positive interaction; and claiming and belonging. Like a

Things to Consider Before You Adopt

Below are some emotional factors from the parents' side that can make for rough going in an adoptive family. All are just twists on what can happen in birth families. Often, women experience these feelings sooner and possibly more acutely than men, for whom these issues may not arise until the child is older. Regardless of who feels them more strongly, parents need to recognize them when they occur. These issues can have a real impact on the family if no one is aware they are happening.

- Infertility unacknowledged as a loss.
- Fear of failing to love the child.
- Fear of failing to meet the child's needs.
- Fear that the child will not meet your need to have someone be like you. This fear is seldom expressed before adoption and often does not arise until the child begins to express herself as an individual.
- Inability to deal with the child's statement that you would love a birth child more than you love him.
- Fear that the child will love her birth parents more than she loves you.
- Not understanding that it is natural to feel ambivalent about the child's birth parents—sometimes feeling gratitude, sometimes empathy for their loss, and sometimes fear or a sense of competition.

three-legged stool, the absence of or marked deficits in any of these three areas can create instability in the parent/child relationship.

A bond is the initial tie of trust the child has in his parent. The bond is established when the bonding cycle, which involves repeatedly meeting the infant's needs, is successfully completed on an ongoing basis, primarily during the first six months of life. Once a child has bonded with one caregiver, such as a birth parent or a foster parent, the bond can be transferred to another caregiver: an adoptive parent. The bonding cycle establishes trust; once a child has learned in infancy to trust one person, he has the capacity to trust others, as well. Because the bonding cycle focuses on trust rather than affection, the cycle can fail for reasons beyond the parents' control, despite their love for their child. Chronic illness in infants, a high threshold for discomfort, or the inability to express need are some examples. Love for the child is not the issue; completing the bonding cycle by returning the child to a relaxed state is.

While many people associate bonding with love, such emotional and psychological ties are actually the attachment that develops from the bond and continues to change as the child matures. Kennell, Foos, and Klaus (1976, 25) define attachment as "an affectional bond [or link] between two individuals that endures through space and time and serves to join them emotionally." In our analogy of the three-legged stool, attachment is represented by two of the legs: positive interaction and claiming and belonging.

Bonding and attachment can also be compared to a thick elastic bungee cord. The bonding cycle, completed successfully over and over again, "hooks" the bungee cord in place, holding the parent and child together. The hooks on either end provide the bond; the cord in between is the attachment. As the child matures, the cord, or attachment, gradually becomes longer and thinner, stretching to accommodate the child's growing independence. Life events also affect attachment. At various times, such as a mother helping her teenage daughter prepare for a big dance, the cord springs back, momentarily thickening as it contracts, drawing the parent and child closer. At other times, such as when a two-year-old's mother is hospitalized for several weeks, the attachment is stretched thin. A strong affectionate link between parent and child gives the relationship the elasticity it needs to weather temporary separations and stresses. Such affection and elasticity are key to healthy attachments.

During childhood and adolescence, the cord of attachment is vertical, with the child dependent on the parent for support. In healthy relationships, the attachment eventually becomes horizontal as the child reaches adulthood and moves from a dependent position to an equal plane with the parent. In many families, attachments eventually move again to a vertical position, this time with the child in the caregiving role and the older parent in the dependent position.

Because of personality differences, attachments are different for each parent/child relationship. For some the cord will always be longer and thinner, or shorter and thicker when compared with that of other parents with children of the same age. Even within a family, a parent may have a closer attachment with one child than with another, or a child may be closer to one parent than the other, even when the "love" for each child or parent is the same.

Can You Bond with an Adopted Child?

In recent years, a school of thought has developed that children truly bond only with their birth parents. The theory stems from the work of Bourguignon and Watson, who define bonding as "the unique tie between child and biological parent, primarily the mother," and attachment as "the psychologically rooted tie between two people that permits them to have affectual significance for each other" (1987, *After Adoption*, 12).

While this theory may provide comfort for adoptive parents experiencing serious difficulty attaching with their child by reinforcing that the parents are not necessarily the root of the problem, we believe that for most it is very disturbing. As Bourguignon and Watson point out, there is a "primal bond" between birth child and birth parent that begins before the child is born and persists regardless of separation. Children inevitably wonder about their birth parents, fantasize about who they are, and experience a very real loss at the separation, no matter how young they were at the time.

Yet to say with accuracy that a child can never truly bond with adoptive parents depends on how you define *bond*. There is a "prenatal bond" between birth child and parent, but this is an enhancer to attachment and the child's identity formation, not a basis for bonding. If the womb experience were the primary foundation for bonding, then birth fathers, too, could never truly bond with their children. It would also leave us seeking to explain how birth mothers can fail to bond with their babies. What makes the bonding cycle work and what can cause it to deteriorate are the same for mothers and fathers, for genetically related and adoptive families.

While it is erroneous to say that children never bond with adoptive parents, it is equally misleading to imply that adoption never impedes this process. Children moved after the age of six months, the primary period in which bonds are established, may have difficulty transferring the bond established with the first caregivers to the "new" parents. This problem often goes unrecognized and untreated, in part because an attachment can develop even in the absence of a bond. Failure to transfer the bond, however, leaves the child with only limited trust for the adoptive parents and an incomplete sense of security. A number of factors, which we will discuss later in this chapter, can hinder this transference, leaving only attachment—healthy or unhealthy. When this happens, the goal is to maximize healthy attachment and, wherever possible, to promote trust and bonding. Unfortunately, some children may never bond with adoptive parents because of past traumas or a lack of bonding in the first six months of life. This, however, is not true for all adopted children. In dealing with problems that arise, families and therapists need to thoroughly understand bonding and attachment so they can realistically identify whether the barriers to the relationship can be overcome and, if so, to what degree.

Most adopted children and their parents can bond and maintain healthy attachments. All children need assistance from family or professionals to sort out who they are, why their birth parents couldn't take care of them, and where they belong. Children adopted after the first six months of life generally need more help because they must transfer the hooks or learn trust for the first time, instead of "growing" them from the very beginning with their adoptive parents.

The Bonding Cycle

The bonding cycle has gone by many names: the *arousal-relaxation* cycle, *first-year-of-life* cycle, the *trust* cycle, and the *love* cycle. The bonding cycle works like this: You and your baby are both *relaxed*. He is sleeping, contentedly playing or babbling, and you are sitting back enjoying a book and a cup of coffee (let's pretend!). But before long, he *feels a need*. He may be hungry, cold, too warm, in need of a diaper change, lonely, or wanting to be rocked, so he fidgets or starts to cry. You begin to feel tense, but don't respond immediately, hurrying to finish the page you are reading. He cries louder and more intensely, reaching the *strong arousal stage*, sometimes called displeasure or rage reaction. At this point you intervene, picking the baby up, changing his diaper, feeding him, or doing whatever else he needs, thereby *satisfying his need*. Once satisfied, the baby quiets, the tension leaves your body, and you both return to *relaxation*, ready to begin the cycle anew as soon as another need arises.

Repeated fulfillment of the bonding cycle teaches the infant to relax between episodes of need by teaching him to trust that his needs will be met in the future, specifically by one or two significant caretakers. He learns to associate his parents' or caretakers' look, smell, touch, rhythm, and voice with fulfillment, and will be comforted in strange environments by their presence. This trust is the foundation of the bond between parent and child that grows into the affectionate relationship known as attachment.

The bonding cycle also defines for the child his environment. If his needs are consistently met, he learns not only to trust Mom, Dad, or a specific caretaker, but people and the world in general, enabling him to form relationships. If his needs are not sufficiently met or met only after prolonged distress, the child learns not only that his primary caretaker cannot be trusted, but that the world and other people are untrustworthy as well.

This is not to say that parents must rush to immediately meet all of the baby's needs. If a child never feels need, he will never realize it is his parent who comforts him. It's like the old question about why there is evil in the world: without evil we would not appreciate good. According to Fahlberg, "If a parent consistently meets the child's needs before he is uncomfortable or protects the child from any stimuli that would disturb him, the [bonding] cycle is disrupted" (1979, *Attachment and Separation*, 15). If a child is kept from feeling discomfort—if he is always fed before he is hungry, or changed before he notices he is wet—he will not associate relaxation and satisfaction of need with his parent. And this association is the essence of bonding.

Successful completion of the bonding cycle is based on the child's dependence on the parent to fulfill his needs. For this reason, though equally effective in adoptive families as in birth families, the cycle does need to take place during infancy, primarily the first six months. Ideally, when older infants and children are adopted, they transfer this bond from their birth parent or other primary caretaker to their adoptive parents; they rehook the bungee to the adoptive parents, and together, parents and child develop the cord, or attachment, between them. A child adopted at an older age may trust her parents differently than a child who bonded with her adoptive parents in early infancy. For example, an eight-year-old who was malnourished prior to adoption may never trust anyone for food, but may trust her parents to share her emotions. In the end, a fully transferred bond is of no less quality than an original bond; however, some older children may complete only a partial transfer of trust to their adoptive parents. A small percentage of older infants and children placed for adoption never developed a bond with previous primary caregivers during early infancy, leaving them with no sense of trust to transfer to adoptive parents.

Parents' actions play a crucial role in the bonding cycle, yet parents are not necessarily to "blame" if bonding does not occur. A chronically ill infant, for example, may have difficulty bonding if her parents are unable to relieve her pain. Likewise, a baby who is unable to readily sense discomfort will not regularly experience the relief his parents provide. And even the most attentive parent may find it difficult to meet the need at hand in a timely fashion if all of the baby's cries sound alike. In cases such as these, love for the child is not the issue; completing the bonding cycle by returning the child to a relaxed state is.

Building Attachment

Attachment is built through mutually positive interactions, in conjunction with the parent's claiming of the child and the child's feeling she belongs with the parent and fits as a member of the family. Before a healthy attachment may grow, a bond, or trust, must first be established between parent and child, or, in the case of older infants and children, transferred from a previous caregiver to the newly adoptive parents. Once the bond is present, the parent can successfully initiate a cycle of mutually positive interactions by smiling, praising, and playing with the child, and through other signs of affection, to which the child will respond positively by smiling, giggling, or playing in return. Eventually the child learns to initiate the process, too. While the bonding cycle builds the infant's trust, the positive-interaction cycle builds self-worth and self-esteem, and may be used throughout childhood. The positive-interaction cycle enhances the bonding cycle by helping parents to relax in the knowledge that their baby loves them in return.

Both parent and child need to know how to elicit smiles and laughter from one another. Perhaps the most rewarding aspect of the positive-interaction cycle is that it teaches the child how to make Mom and Dad smile, too. As Fahlberg points out, "There is some evidence that these sorts of social interactions between [parent] and child contribute more to the bonds between them than do the kind of interactions that occur around meeting the child's physical needs" (1979, *Attachment and Separation*, 17).

In addition to finding joy in each other's presence, parents and children need to feel they fit together as family. In genetically related families, the family member who is most different from the rest often becomes the "black sheep." Such individuals, as well as other family members, fail to find enough shared traits to allow them to comfortably claim one another as family. In adoption, we use the term *claiming* to refer to the parents' ability to feel that the child is their own, while accepting the child's uniqueness. Belonging is used to refer to how well the child feels he fits into the family; a child may lack a sense of belonging even if the parents have a strong sense of claiming if he feels his uniqueness sets him too far apart from the rest of the family.

Enhancers and Inhibitors

All relationships are surrounded by factors that either strengthen them or add stress. In adoption, these enhancers and inhibitors may be historical (occurring before the placement) or day-to-day, and can affect the development or transfer of bonds, the growth of attachments, or both. Some enhancers and inhibitors, such as physical appearance, come as a package deal with the child or the parent, while others—particularly the parents' actions—may be controlled. In either case, once identified, inhibitors can often be counteracted by changing behavior or consciously adding enhancers.

The first thing to remember is that even if things go—or have already gone—awry, don't get caught up in guilt and blame. Therapies exist to help create bonds and nurture attachments, so find a professional to help you and your child attach, and do it soon; in general, the younger the child, the easier it is to build attachments and bonds.

Past bonds. Perhaps the strongest single enhancer to bonding in adoptive families is if the child has formed a healthy bond in the past. Again, bonding teaches the child trust, and once learned, the child should eventually be able to transfer that trust to her adoptive parents, barring other complications. Age, however, plays a strong role in this process. The optimal time to move a child is before she reaches six or seven months of age. Infants develop stranger anxiety to one degree or another at about this age, and this anxiety commonly remains strong until the child is two or three. If a child must be moved during this time, adoptive parents need to be sensitive to the child's fear, grief, and loss at the separation from the previous caretaker, and be willing to work carefully with her to resolve these issues. (We will talk more about how to recognize and help your child deal with grief and loss in the next chapter.)

Trauma and loss. Past traumatic events, such as moves from one foster home (or the birth parent's home) to another, hospitalization, neglect, abuse, or a significant loss, can inhibit bonding by eroding the child's trust or creating grief. Because developmental stages affect how children interpret and respond to life events, the impact of such events will vary depending on the child's age at the time of occurrence. Furthermore, a single issue may reappear each time the child enters a new developmental stage.

Personalities. The personalities of both the parent and child can either enhance or inhibit attachment formation, depending on compatibility. There are no absolute tests or rules to delineate what personality types will be most successful together in a family. It all boils down to what kinds of people you get along with—and this could be different in your role as parent than it is in your social life—and vice versa for your child.

For example, for Mary and her ten-year-old daughter, Agnes,* personality differences were a major sore spot. Mary and her husband were outgoing, athletic people. They were boisterous whether having fun or disagreeing with each other. Agnes came to the family at age four, a shy, easygoing child who sometimes just needed quiet time alone. Looking back on Agnes's first years in the family, Mary says she simply did not "like" her daughter. She didn't understand Agnes's quietness, and frankly, it got on her nerves. The personality clash between the two inhibited attachment. They had, however, formed the hooks of trust. Mary met Agnes's basic needs and Agnes accepted her "mothering." But because of the personality clash and Mary's unmet expectations of her new daughter and their relationship, the attachment that should have grown between them was not developing. The almost total absence of positive interactions left Agnes feeling rejected, and Mary felt embarrassed and ashamed because she did not like her daughter. Over time, the lack of attachment would have eaten away at the existing bond. Counseling focused on helping Mary understand her daughter's personality, on validating her dislike, and on modifying her

---

*Name has been changed.

expectations. Mary and Agnes were both encouraged to look for activities and interests the two could enjoy together, and for ways to decrease negative interactions. The two eventually developed an attachment as well as a bond, but it took several years of therapy.

Positive interactions. Knowing how to evoke positive reactions from one another enhances bonding and attachment. Agencies sometimes try to prepare parents in this respect by giving them a list of interactions or cues—songs, looks, games, rhymes, stories, hugs—that make the child happy. But interactions that work for one caregiver don't necessarily work for another. The old cues may, in fact, anger or sadden the child when they don't come from the right person. Often, too, a child will realize his parents were told what makes him smile and will refuse to respond because to do so would be to betray that other caregiver. Rather than relying on what has worked for others, it is probably better, though not necessarily easier, to find something special between the two of you.

Children, too, need to know how to please their parents. Things can go awry if behaviors that brought praise and smiles in the child's former home are unacceptable in yours. A child who is trying to please the only way he knows how will feel rejected if his attempts are met with scolding rather than the accustomed laugh or smile. Just as adoptive parents need to learn new ways to evoke positive reactions from their child, the adopted child needs his parents' help to find ways to please them.

Eight-year-old Anne,* for example, had a repertoire of funny faces that drove her adoptive mother crazy. When she first came to the family, she repeatedly performed her "talent" before her parents, company, classmates, and even the therapist. She made not one face, but a full series with never one left out. There was the gorilla and the monkey, the rolled-back eyelids, pushed-in nose, and pulled-out ears—the type of faces boys make more often than girls. After each "performance" she would wait for the laughter and praise, but all she got was scolding. Her mother was appalled to see her very attractive daughter making such faces. The school noticed there was a problem when Anne performed her routine for the talent show.
ings, and even at church, in her country of origin. It was her "talent" and had always evoked laughter and praise from her birth family; she kept waiting for the same reaction in her new home. In therapy, we played with the routine, making the faces back and forth at each other. While her mother could never bring herself to make the faces back at her daughter, the two were eventually able to play with the mother's dislike. The mother

---

*Name has been changed.

was able to replace the scolding "Don't make ugly faces!" with a joking "Ooo, yuck!" As the tension between mother and daughter decreased and as Anne was no longer deprived of the pleasure of positive responses from her mother, she gradually performed her routine less frequently. With this inhibitor diminished, the two were then able to work on other inhibitors in their relationship and to build positive interactions and enhancers.

Claiming and belonging. A child's physical appearance can contribute to attachment. While attractiveness is usually an enhancer, some children use good looks and superficial charm to distance adults. A child's physical appearance also plays a role in attachment to the extent that the child looks like her adoptive parents. A child who can identify how she is like her parents—if not by looks, then by talents, abilities, behaviors, or common interests—is able to internalize or claim her adoptive parents. Parents can strengthen the attachment by identifying for the child—and themselves— how she is like them.

Distancing behaviors. A child who is still grieving the loss of his former parents or who feels he is betraying them if he becomes part of a new family may perpetually repeat negative behaviors to distance himself from his adoptive parents and family. Distancing behaviors differ from negative behaviors aimed at gaining attention. A child who is trying to gain attention will usually respond to behavior modification—praise and rewards for positive behavior, punishment for negative behavior—and eventually overcome his need to repeatedly act out. But, if he is trying to distance himself, increased attention for positive behavior will most likely exacerbate the situation, leading him to act out with greater frequency and intensity.

Poor personal appearance—clothes and hygiene—is one way children distance themselves. A child may ruin brand-new clothes or just manage to stay perpetually dirty, often to the point that neighbors, school bus drivers, and teachers begin to believe the family is impoverished or neglecting the child. While teens are known for choosing outrageous clothes, makeup, and haircuts to establish their identity, in younger children this is usually a sign that they are still struggling with grief and trying to distance themselves from family.

An example of more severe distancing behavior is that of the older child who plays on the family's weak points, forms intense antagonistic relationships with one or more family members, or abuses a sibling. Attempts at traditional behavior modification alone will not work. Positive reinforcement for good behavior intensifies the negative behavior, and punishment for bad behavior only accomplishes the child's goal of preventing closeness at all costs. The task then is to figure out why the child needs to distance herself from others, to identify factors blocking attachment and transfer of trust, and then to find a way to resolve those issues. If your child seems to be exhibiting severe distancing behaviors, it would be wise to check in with a professional counselor.

Feelings about the adoption process. On the parents' side, several factors can inhibit bonding. First, a difficult adoption process or one filled with bad experiences can affect how parents feel about their new child, just as a difficult pregnancy can affect birth parents' feelings for their baby. Parents need to acknowledge any anger, hurt, or frustration over the adoption process. Talking about it openly with someone—a spouse, friend, relative, agency personnel, or therapist—can help parents separate the bad experience from their feelings for their child.

When a planned adoption falls through, whether for legal reasons, the birth mother's change of heart, or death of the child en route, prospective parents need adequate time to grieve their loss, just as birth parents do following miscarriage. Physicians generally advise couples to wait anywhere from three months to a year before attempting another pregnancy after a miscarriage, not only because the woman's body needs time to fully recover, but also because the waiting period allows the couple time to grieve. Adoptive parents need this time also. Even if you had never met the child you were to adopt, you probably knew specifics about him—his name, his age, or what he looks like—and had already developed an image of who he was. Such images can be as strong as if you had actually known the child. Telling an adoptive parent that there will be other children to adopt is as helpful as telling parents whose child has just died that they can always have another. One child can never *replace* another.

The elation parents feel on the day their child finally arrives in their home is seldom shared to the same degree by the child. Adoptive parents are often upset and hurt if the child they have so longed for finally arrives and clearly does not want to be with them. For the child, the move to a new home can be traumatic. He may not run to you with hugs and kisses the first day, or even for several days or weeks afterward. This doesn't mean you should not celebrate your child's arrival; by all means do, but be sensitive to your child's feelings, and don't expect too much right away.

Great expectations. Unrealistic expectations on either side of the relationship can also inhibit attachment. Parents and children alike create images of each other and of the life they will have together. Children may envision parents who never punish, give them everything they want, and let them do as they please, who look a certain way, or who already have a specific number of brothers and sisters for them. Parents may imagine sharing experiences they love—and the child enjoying the experience equally—or a child with specific talents, intelligence, interests, and future. If either parent or child cannot let go of their expectations and accept the realities of the family as it is, there will be friction in the relationship.

Daily life. We've talked about some of the large-scale enhancers and inhibitors, but both also come in smaller, day-to-day sizes. Daily inhibitors for parents can include financial stress, job stress, or even an argument between spouses. Such stressors are inevitable from time to time, but daily enhancers can often counteract the inhibitors and help parent and child to grow a good relationship anyway.

One of the strongest enhancers is spending time with your child on a regular basis. Find something special you both like to do: read to her, go to McDonald's once a week, have a special time to talk together, establish an enjoyable bedtime routine, or do whatever works for you. Find a code word, a look, or a private joke you can use repeatedly throughout the day to remind your child of your love. Make it brief, something that only takes a few seconds. Such brief moments can reinforce your relationship with your child throughout the day until you can focus your attention more directly on her.

When Attachment Goes Awry

So far we have assumed that all attachments are good and healthy. But before we move on, we need to discuss unhealthy attachment—a strong, emotional, and psychological connectedness that is void of affection on the part of at least one of the parties involved. Other names for unhealthy attachment include *attachment disorder, unattached,* and *unbonded.*

One of the mistakes often made in counseling victims of sexual abuse, in particular, is the failure to acknowledge the victim's emotional and psychological connection to the perpetrator. This connection may be based on fear, hate, past love for the person, or a variety of other emotions. It is one of the factors that keeps many battered women from leaving their partners. Likewise, a child who is physically, emotionally, or sexually abused will still have an attachment, though unhealthy and destructive, with the abuser. If the abuser is a parent, the mixture of emotions may be particularly confusing for the child. Children often blame themselves for the abuse, feeling they must have done something to cause it. Or they may feel guilty for hating the abuser, especially if that person is the child's parent. Children who have been abused need help acknowledging their attachment to their abuser and understanding that the attachment is unhealthy before they can break free and move on to healthy attachments.

Past abuse, however, is just one of the reasons children have difficulty forming healthy attachments with adoptive parents. The enhancer/inhibitor model is designed to help you sort out not only your current life with your child, but also how your child's history, as well as your own, affect your relationship. The ultimate goal is to find ways to increase enhancers and virtually eliminate or counteract all inhibitors. But of course, such perfect scenarios rarely exist in reality. Given who you are and who your child is, you may not be able to fully counteract some inhibitors. A child who has been severely abused or neglected, for instance, may never be capable of trusting his adoptive parents to the extent they would like, or to the degree to which children are typically capable. So once you've looked carefully at the current and historic enhancers and inhibitors in your relationship, you need to identify what levels of attachment and bonding are realistically possible between you and your child. Will she be able to trust you and to what degree? Are there support and counseling resources available to your family to help you build healthy relationships with this child?

In addition to setting goals, you also need to understand your current relationship. We often hear parents say, "Our therapist told us Joe is unattached, but I know there is something between us. How can this be?" Or on the flip side: "The counselor told me that the strongest, most intense relationship in my life is with this kid I hate. He has abused my daughter. I'm in court constantly. How can that be my most intense relationship? We don't have a relationship."

Attachments between parent and child can be based on the child's pathology, with the pathology hooked into the parent's need to help her. Whenever another person consumes a large portion of your thoughts, your time, your emotional energy, there is a relationship. It may not be fulfilling, positive, or healthy, but it's a relationship—an attachment—all the same.

Some degree of attachment can also exist in the absence of a bond. The hooks aren't there, but the cord is, and both parent and child are just hanging on. The cord may fall from their hands at times, but it is still present and can usually be picked up again later. Lack of bonding, however, can inhibit the quality of the attachment and will certainly negatively impact the child's ability to accept authority at home and elsewhere. When children come with traumatic backgrounds or traumatized interpretations of past events that may not appear traumatic to the external world, their very neediness drives them to hang on to somebody. They may hang on out of negative needs—for instance, the need to take rage and anger out on other people—or their strongest need may be to hurt others. Even so, they still need a connection, good or bad, to other people. Such attachments may be unpleasant for parents and difficult to break or change.

For many years, adoptive parents were told, or believed, "Just love her and she'll come around." We only wish it were that easy. Without addressing the underlying problems for the unhealthiness of the attachment or for the lack of bonding, love alone will not do the trick. When you adopted your child, you were prepared and willing to love her—perhaps you already did; perhaps you still do. But while love enhances bonding and attachment, it cannot cure psychological problems. With professional guidance, identify where the problems are, which ones can be solved, and which ones cannot. Look for ways to build the best possible relationship with your child given the realities of who you and she are. Keep in mind that even Father Edward Flanagan, the founder of Boys Town, did more than just love the children he worked with.

3

❀

Grief and Loss

*I*f we were to rank human experiences by difficulty, in our society grief would have to be among the top five. *Webster's New World Dictionary* defines grief as "deep and poignant distress caused by or as if by bereavement." It's difficult both to endure and witness. In American culture especially, we often find ourselves at a loss for ways to comfort, or even interact with, people who are grieving. Thus, we avoid the woman whose husband has just died, or speak only superficially to the man whose son was killed a month ago, for fear of stirring emotions we are ill-equipped to handle.

With children, the story is different. We have long been indoctrinated to believe children are resilient, that they quickly forget, because they can change their emotions on command and smile within minutes of crying. And then as adults we go through years of therapy to resolve the pains of our childhoods; as John James of the Grief Recovery Institute in Beverly Hills so aptly puts it, "Unresolved grief will last a lifetime" (1986, 20).

Perhaps we've painted the picture grimmer than it actually is today. Many things have changed in the last twenty-five years and we must give credit where it is due. For instance, society for the most part recognizes the grief children undergo when their parents divorce. Schools, courts, physicians, and therapists are usually sensitive to the effect divorce has on children. Not so well recognized, however, is the grief children experience when moved from one home to another—including when they are adopted. Frequently, losses in adoption go unidentified or are minimized by families and professionals alike. Often, the benefits of adoption for the child— having a family of his own, being rescued from an abusive home, or joining a family that can economically provide necessities, even luxuries, the birth family never could—are so wonderful that we have difficulty understanding how an adopted child could be anything but happy.

As parents, the joy of bringing a child into the family can make us forget that, for the child, adoption also represents losing his or her birth family. It's often scary for adoptive parents to think of their child as having deep feelings for her birth parents. Yet even if a child is adopted immediately after birth, on some level, at some time she will grieve this loss. To understand how this can be we must first understand loss.

Loss is the permanent or temporary removal of an important object, person, or event, or failure to achieve a coveted goal. Awareness of lacking something others have can also bring feelings of loss. It doesn't matter that a teenage girl has never gone to prom before; classmates are going and she is not, so she grieves for the loss of an event: the prom. It doesn't matter that the seventh-grade boy is vying against eighty other boys for fifteen positions on the basketball team; when he doesn't make the team along with sixty-five others, he grieves for the lost coveted goal and the many events—basketball games, pep rallies, and so on—in which he looked forward to participating. It doesn't matter that the sixty-year-old man has had a very successful career in management for the last thirty years; he never made CEO and is grieving for the coveted goal he knows he will never achieve. And it doesn't matter that the adopted six-year-old girl doesn't really remember her birth mother or that she has wonderful adoptive parents, whom she loves dearly; there are no pictures of her as a baby, as there are for her brothers and sisters, and her mother can't tell her stories about when she was pregnant with her, like she tells her other children, because she never was.

Loss is always a personal crisis. Each loss we experience forces us to redefine who we are. Not attending the prom, trivial though it may sound, forces the young woman to see herself differently than if she had attended. She may feel bad about herself because she didn't attract a date. She may feel like the odd-person-out even if only some of her friends attended. Grieving the loss may take no more than a few days or even months, but in some respect her self-image has changed from what it would have been had she attended. Likewise, the boy who didn't make the basketball team (the only intermural sport at his school) had envisioned himself a good athlete until then, but now he must reassess who he is as a young man. If he cannot be a jock, what new image will he find for himself? Likewise, the adopted child's interpretation of what her birth parents' decision not to raise her means about herself is bound to, in some way, alter her self-image from what it might have been if this were not the case.

Loss may also be a traumatic interpretation of a nontraumatic event. Even if you cannot relate to some of the examples above, for the individuals experiencing those events the loss is nonetheless real. In the same respect, you may not understand how a child adopted at birth can grieve for birth parents she's never known. But loss is not temporal; it can be projected into the future for years to come. Thus, a child adopted at birth may later feel acute sadness, anger, or yearning for "what should have been": "My birth parents *should have* found a way to keep me."

Likewise, a child who is adopted when she is older will grieve even for a birth family that gave her nothing but abuse and bare sustenance. For such children the "should have" statement may be "My birth family should have been different—not abusive [or whatever else necessitated the child's removal from the home]—so I could stay with them."

The thing to remember is that "should haves" focus on the loss, not on present circumstances. Your child may feel that her birth mother should have kept her, and at the same time have no regrets about being your child. Such apparently conflicting feelings can be difficult for parent and child alike.

Feelings about "what would have been" are perhaps less acute than those surrounding "should haves." They are more often the melancholy felt as time goes by, even after the grieving is done. A child adopted at birth may fantasize about what life would have been like with his birth family. Or if the child has memories of her birth family, a particular situation may recall past events or traditions, making the child feel sad for what would have been but is not.

Perhaps an easier way to understand how an adopted child might feel this way is to look at an adult example of a woman whose husband has been dead several years. Enough time has passed that she has already worked through the grief process. On their anniversary, however, she lies in bed remembering how he used to let her sleep in on that day and then bring her breakfast. While she is remembering past anniversaries, she also imagines that her husband is walking through the bedroom door, smiling as he nears the bed with her breakfast on a tray, orange juice splashing over the edge of the glass (because he never was very good at carrying trays) and a red rose in the crystal bud vase. That's how it would have been if her husband were still alive. But he's not and she is sad—not with the heartrending sadness of grief, but sad all the same.

Even if their marriage was never as wonderful as the image above, the woman might envision the same scene, picturing how things would have been if her husband had only changed or lived long enough for the two of them to resolve their marital problems. Her sadness then stems from the *lost opportunity* for a better relationship with her husband.

With change comes loss. Even if a child is not old enough to cognitively experience the loss when it occurs, his life is forever different—for better or worse—from what it would have been had his birth mother been able to parent him. In some way, he is a different person now because he was raised by someone else. A child in an adoptive family will have different relationships than she would in her birth family for the mere fact that her family is comprised of different people. She may play out her role as daughter in the same fashion, but interactions with her parents will be different as they react to her in their own individual ways. For the child, adoption represents not only a loss of birth family, but also loss of the person he would have been had he remained with his birth family. Again, he may be a much better person because of his adoptive family, but that's not the issue. The issue is the unknown possibility.

Losses in Adoption

Adoption brings a loss to all members in the adoption triad: child, adoptive parents, and birth parents. According to family-systems theory, what affects one member of a family has an impact on the entire family. This is why it is important to understand the losses adoption represents for each member of the triad. The objective in looking at these losses is not to make you feel bad about adoption. Rather, by better understanding the losses involved, you will be better equipped to help yourself and your child work through issues as they arise, and in doing so, build a healthy family.

The Child
The loss experienced by adopted children centers as much on self-identity as on the lost relationship with the birth parent. The child's life is forever different from what it would have been.

Lack of a genetic tie to family represents another poignant loss. This can be as great an issue for the child as it is for the adoptive parent. Adoption means growing up with no one around to point to and say, "I look like that person." Even in same-race adoptions, the likelihood of a child having physical characteristics—beyond perhaps hair, eye, and skin coloring—like those of Mom, Dad, Aunt Ella, or Uncle Joe are slim. Yet sharing physical traits is an important anchor for a sense of belonging. Even if, as in an open adoption, the child knows her genetic relatives, knowing and living with are still two very different things.

Being adopted means feeling different; and feeling different from others is a loss. Remember what we said earlier: lacking something others have can be a loss. Even at as young as three and four years old, adopted children understand that their family story is somehow different from those of other children. For very young children, the loss lies more in not having the same story than in not having their birth family. Often three-year-olds who have had "heavy pregnancy exposure" (virtually every other woman of child-bearing age they see is pregnant) begin walking up to strange women and asking, "Are you that lady?" All the three-year-old knows is that babies come from women and that some woman other than Mommy gave birth to her. But the child's search is not actually for the person who gave birth to her as much as it is for the character missing from her story, the one who would make her story the same as that of the other children. It isn't until later—six to eight years old—that children begin to internalize the story and assess what it means for their self-identity. The loss that stems from being different—from not having come into the family in the way most children do—is a "should have been" the child will reprocess each time he or she reaches a new cognitive level.

An important, though controversial, point to make here about children and loss is that children *do* grieve. The debate centers on whether children possess all the cognitive and emotional elements believed to be requisite for fully realizing, experiencing, and processing (or grieving) a loss. But, as Rando writes in *Grief, Dying, and Death*:

> Intellectual debate may rage ad infinitum about the child's ability to classically mourn; but what is undeniable and incontrovertible is that children, even young infants, will have dramatic and long-lasting reactions to the separation from a loved one. They experience intensely painful responses that adults must understand, legitimize, and help them through. (1984, 155)

Some adults who were adopted as infants say they have never experienced a great sense of loss or feelings of grief for their birth parents and that therapists and others make too much of adoption as a contributor to "problems" in their lives. Some adopted children, particularly those who come to their families before six months of age with a history of healthy bonding and attachment, will quickly and with little struggle resolve the losses of their adoption, while others wrestle with these issues throughout childhood and even into adulthood. Each child's personality plays a large role in how he or she will be affected by the birth parent's inability or decision not to parent. Remember that what is an acute loss to one person may be easily handled by another.

Whether the loss should be easy or difficult, however, is not for someone else to decide. Only the person experiencing the loss should determine how painful it is—even if that person is a child.

The following are points to remember when addressing adoption as a loss for your child:

- Don't ignore or deny your child's feelings of loss and grief because you or other family members find them uncomfortable or believe they are unwarranted.

- Help your child identify his feelings, but don't make more of the loss than your child is actually experiencing. Avoid indoctrinating the child that he *should* or *will* feel a certain way—sad, angry, fortunate, or whatever. Instead, reinforce that the feelings he *is* having are normal and OK.
- Remember, not every problem adopted children face is related to adoption. As a normal part of growing up, adopted children will act out, have fussy days, misbehave, have difficulties in school or with other children, have sad days, and so on, the same as children who are raised in their birth families. It is when such problems go beyond the norm or follow patterns that coincide with anniversaries related to the adoption or the birth family that parents need to be aware that adoption-related grief may be the underlying issue.

The Adoptive Parent
It's difficult to think of adoptive parents as doing anything but gaining through adoption. But adoption represents losses even for them. Many of the inhibitors to bonding and attachment discussed in the last chapter are also losses: the absence of a genetic tie, of shared talents, habits, mannerisms, and of the sense of immortality in knowing that a piece of you will go on for generations through your offspring. Even if you already have six children by birth and then adopt six more, there is still a loss with each adoption. You consciously chose not to create another child that looks like you, and each adopted child takes a slot that could potentially have been filled by a birth child.

A majority of adoptive parents today, however, have faced infertility. When infertility is an issue, another layer of loss is added to the picture. First, there is the loss brought on by the infertility itself. The biggest factor in this loss is the realization of how much you wanted a loving relationship with a birth child. Second, deciding to adopt, for many people, symbolizes abandoning all hope of having a birth child. For the sake of the adopted child and the family as a whole, parents need to recognize and work through their feelings about their infertility. If one or both parents are stuck in any of the phases of grief, attachment with the child may be inhibited—if not now, then perhaps later when he becomes an adolescent.

Even when parents have already dealt with their infertility, talking about it again during preadoption counseling can bring all the old sadness to the surface. Such resurgence of emotion should not be misinterpreted as a sign that the loss is still unresolved. Grief is not a one-time thing, never to be felt again. After a loved one dies, the pain doesn't end with the funeral. It's natural to long for that person occasionally, even years later. The same is true for other losses.

If, however, you or your partner are infertile and have not resolved your feelings about it, find a support group or a therapist to help you. Infertility raises far more issues than simply not being able to bear children. It can affect your sexuality, your marriage, your sense of control over your life. We find that people who are aware that infertility is a loss that brings much pain have fewer problems with it in the long run than those who deny the pain.

Another major loss for adoptive parents is one that is fairly well recognized in genetically related families, but often overlooked in adoptive families. No matter how or at what age a child joins the family, the parents' relationship with each other undergoes changes, and the time available to attend to each other and the relationship is diminished. When a baby is born, birth parents are told by the pediatrician, the obstetrician, even the diaper service, to take time together early on and regularly, without the baby. Unfortunately, we often forget to remind adoptive parents to do the same thing.

While changes in the marital relationship, particularly in the first year after a child joins the family, affect both men and women, men usually are affected more acutely. Even today, women remain the primary caretakers in most families, and in the hustle and bustle of making sure the child's (or children's) needs are met—that they are changed, bathed, fed, comforted—time available to share with one's husband understandably becomes scarce. Even an older child who doesn't require the constant care infants demand still needs considerable attention to help her adjust to her new home, school and neighborhood, to build attachments, grieve, and in general to feel safe and part of the family. Other children in the family, too, may need special time and attention to help them with feelings about having a new brother or sister. Fathers who are involved in caring for their children may not feel quite as shortchanged; but even so, relationships with one's children cannot replace, for either parent, the relationship with a spouse.

Take time out as a couple. Hire a baby sitter once a week or arrange for the children to spend a few hours with their grandparents while the two of you stay home together. Make sure you have time to talk about topics other than the children. And when you do go out, avoid the trap of making every date serve a dual purpose of time out together and time out with friends you've been meaning to see.

The Birth Parent
At times, empathizing with our children's birth parents is the last thing we feel like doing. Yet, because children need to be able to picture their birth parents—birth mothers in particular—as people with emotions and both good and bad points, understanding the birth parents' loss is important.

The loss itself is obvious: it is the loss of the child, her relationship with the child, seeing the child grow, and knowing and being a part of who he becomes. Placing a child for adoption is almost always a difficult and painful decision.

That's not to say that the child should not or will not feel angry even though he understands what his birth mother probably went through. Even if you believe—or know—that the birth mother was callous in her decision, passing that belief on to your child serves no positive purpose. Adopted children derive part of their self-definition from what they know or believe to be true about their birth parents. If all they believe about them is negative, they will look for those negative traits in themselves; and if they look hard enough and believe strongly enough, they will inevitably find them.

One way to explain to your child why her birth mother could not parent her is to explain that she probably faced very difficult circumstances. If you know what those were and if your child is old enough to handle the information, then tell her. A general guideline is "If they are old enough to ask, they are old enough to know." (Sometimes, however, children never ask. When they don't, parents still need to provide the information.) This doesn't mean you must provide details the child cannot yet understand. For instance, a preschooler probably will not understand the concept of involuntary termination of parental rights no matter how you try to explain it. A preschooler, however, could understand a simplified explanation such as, "Your birth mother was very young when you were born. She wasn't old enough to take care of a baby and didn't have anyone who could help her."

Above all, don't lie. If you don't know the answer, however, it is OK to speculate, saying something like, "Maybe your birth mother loved a boy and became pregnant. Maybe she wasn't old enough to take care of a baby. Or maybe she was very poor and couldn't buy food for you. But it must have been very hard for her when she decided she would have to let someone else take care of you." The word *maybe* is a gift from the English language for those of us who don't know the answers.

Sometimes adoptive parents, in their zeal to humanize birth parents, overempathize. Well-intentioned statements like "If I were in her situation, I probably would have made the same decision" can come back to haunt you. If you tell your child that his birth mother was very poor and therefore couldn't take care of him, and follow up with the statement above, you may find your child packing his bags if you lose your job or begin to have financial difficulties. A better statement is "Your birth mother had a very difficult decision to make because of her situation. We've thought about what we might do if we were in her shoes and decided we would keep you no matter what." Better yet is to avoid placing yourself in the birth parent's shoes. Say instead, "I think your birth mother lost out in choosing not to parent you. But I'm awfully glad you are my daughter."

A commonly suggested alternative is to tell the child that you feel the birth mother used "poor judgment" in choosing not to parent the child. For young children, "poor judgment" is too abstract and can be difficult to understand, particularly if they have been told the birth parent was probably poor. Poor judgment, poor as in poverty. The two meanings can easily be confused, leading preschoolers in particular to believe that poor people—those in poverty—have poor judgment. This terminology is better suited to adolescents, who will be exploring the judgment their birth parents used in becoming pregnant and in handling the situation once the baby arrived.

Even if you believe that the birth parents' circumstances at the time warranted their decision not to parent *a child*, children hear this message as "They were correct not to parent *you*." Keep in mind that though poverty, youth, single status, drug addiction, and so on are all possible and valid contributors to a decision not to parent, not all single, young, poor, or even drug-addicted parents place their children for adoption. When adoptive parents overidentify with the birth parents' rationale, the child's sense of security in the adoptive family may be weakened.

Talking about birth parents is rarely easy for adoptive parents. In addition to all the emotional issues surrounding the topic, there is also fear of saying the wrong thing and somehow alienating or harming the child. To make things easier, we offer four simple rules. If you keep these in mind when you talk with your child, you'll probably do just fine.

- Be honest.
- Don't make the mistake of simply choosing to say nothing or of forever withholding specific information.
- Don't say too much too soon. Save details your child is too young to comprehend until she is appropriately equipped cognitively, emotionally, and socially.
- Don't load your presentation of information with value judgments. If you devalue the birth parents, your child will invariably feel devalued, too.

The Grief Process

According to James, "We grieve for every life change that occurs" (1986, 120). Change equates with loss, and each loss in our lives requires a reaction. This reaction is the grief process, and even the most insignificant losses take us through, at the very least, an abbreviated version.

Take for example when you lose a favorite $3.95 pen, one you have been writing with for a few months. You like the pen's feel, the way it glides over the paper as you write, the color of its ink, even its click. You always carry the pen in your pocket or purse, and the last hundred or so checks you wrote were written with that pen. One day as you are about to pay the monthly bills, you discover the pen is no longer where you always keep it. You check your other pockets or the other compartments of your purse, patting and reaching into each pocket, or shaking and stirring the contents of your purse. You look around the house and then check your purse or pocket again, thinking maybe you just overlooked the pen or didn't feel in all the crannies. (Rechecking where you have already looked is a form of disbelief and denial, one of the immediate reactions in the grief process.)

As you pick up another pen—one of those ten-to-a-pack stick pens that always skip for a while before writing smoothly—you feel irritated that your favorite pen is gone. You don't like writing with the new one; you even glare at it a little. And as you write out the checks, you continue searching in your mind for where you might have left the old pen.

In a matter of minutes, you yearn, pine, and search for the pen; you have strong feelings about its loss—in this case irritation—and eventually, you experience mild despair as you lose hope of finding it. You finally reorganize your thoughts and feelings, put the loss into perspective, and recenter your thoughts on other things in your life. But even so, a week later a strong desire to retrieve the lost pen or even anger over its loss comes over you again like a wave. Such unexpected waves of "grief" for the pen occur less and less frequently over the next few weeks, eventually dissipating.

The phases of grief are essentially the same no matter what the loss. The duration and intensity of grief, however, depends on how greatly the griever's sense of self is involved. Because a pen has little to do with sense of self, the grief process for a lost pen is short and of relatively mild intensity. Parents, on the other hand, play a large role in their children's—even their grown children's—sense of self, and therefore grief for a parent may be prolonged and acute. Though individuals will grieve more for some losses than for others, comparing one individual's grief to that of another is meaningless. It is unproductive to say, "My pain is worse than yours because. . . ." As James writes, "Each person experiences his or her pain at 100 percent" (1986, 18).

The grief process is comprised of essentially five phases and a final integration of the loss into one's life and identity. The phases are as follows:

- immediate reaction, which includes shock, disorganization, and defense mechanisms;

- yearning, pining, and searching;
- strong feelings;
- despair and hopelessness; and
- reorganization.

These phases are not necessarily sequential, nor are they mutually exclusive; a person may experience more than one phase at a given time. Though the grief process usually follows a general pattern or order, most people vacillate among the various phases until they finally make sense of the loss, accept it, and integrate the entire experience into who they are.

The phases of grief are basically the same for children as they are for adults. Differences arise, however, in how the phases are expressed. Not only do individuals each express grief in their own ways, there are basic differences in expression between men and women, and between adults and children. For example, in yearning, pining, and searching, adults often try to suppress the urge to physically search for a loved one who has died (Rando 1984, 23). It is not unusual, however, for children to search openly, as in the case of the three-year-old adopted girl who approaches strangers, asking, "Are you that lady?"—referring to her birth mother.

Another difference between adults and children is that children repeat the grief process for a single, major loss each time they achieve a new level of cognition. The eight-year-old who has grieved and then integrated the loss of his birth mother, as he understands it in his concrete thinking, will grieve again for this same loss when he develops abstract thinking. This repetition is necessary because each new level of cognition brings a new connotation to the loss with which the child must deal.

Because adults are capable of processing a loss at many different levels, they generally do not repeat the grief process in its original intensity once they have integrated the particular loss. But even after integration, adults may experience occasional resurgences of grief, touched off by an event, smell, sight, taste, sound, or a new loss. These resurgences are like waves: they may come rapidly and strongly after the initial disturbance in the water, but they eventually come less frequently and with less impact.

"Mourning is never really over," writes Siggins (quoted in Rando 1984, 157), "for new life-situations may appear at any time which evoke for the griever aspects of the lost relationship insignificant at the time of bereavement." The need to address all aspects of a loss may also explain why adults and children vacillate among phases during grief; just when you think you are over being angry with your spouse for dying and leaving you to care for the children alone, you realize that, by dying, he or she also took away your best friend, and you are angry all over again.

Grief does not always take place at the time of loss. Adults and children alike may delay, or repress, grief for a later time. According to Rando, "grief may be delayed for an extended period of time, up to years, especially if there are pressing responsibilities or the griever feels he cannot deal with the process at that time" (1984, 60). An adopted child who feels insecure in her present environment or who feels she must take care of and protect her siblings or avoid hurting her adoptive parents may suppress her emotions regarding the loss of her birth parents until she feels safer. Often another loss or an event related to the original one triggers a full grief reaction at a later time.

The Phases of Grief

Before we move on, let's define the basic phases of the grief process. Though we explain below a few key points about children and grief, in later chapters we will look more specifically at how adopted children at each developmental stage interpret the losses of adoption and express grief.

Immediate Reaction: Defense Mechanisms

There are actually three levels of reaction that follow immediately after a loss occurs, all of which act to protect the griever from being overwhelmed physically, emotionally, and psychologically by the loss. An adopted child may experience these kinds of immediate grief reactions either when first removed from her birth family or a foster home and placed with her adoptive parents, or upon learning at a later age about her adoption or some "unpleasant" fact related to it.

The first of these reactions, shock and numbness, can last anywhere from a couple of hours to a couple of weeks. Of all the phases of grief, this is the only one that is not revisited. Shock and numbness are physiological responses to the intense emotions brought on by the initial stun of the loss and protect the individual from being overwhelmed by pain. This psychic shock is similar to clinical (primary) shock following injury. The individual may feel cold and clammy to the touch and have glazed eyes. Other symptoms included dizziness, fainting, nervousness, trembling, twitching, perspiring, chest pain, and a "lump" in the throat (Parkes and Weiss 1983, 294).

Shock and numbness are precursors to the defense mechanisms, particularly disbelief and denial. Defense mechanisms act like Venetian blinds, limiting how much reality the griever must face. Just as a blind filters light, defense mechanisms allow the griever to "see" only as much of the truth as she can handle at a given time. When defenses are down, it is as if the griever is looking through a window with the blind fully raised. Such instances may be times of despair or reorganization. If despair is the controlling factor, the griever views the loss head on, discharges emotions, and then closes the blind again. If the griever is in a phase of reorganization, she is able to briefly look through the fully open window and begin to accept and integrate portions of the loss into her sense of self. At other times, defenses can be so strongly in control that the blind is not only down, but tightly closed.

Disbelief and denial may be used in this way to filter out aspects of the loss that are still too painful for the griever, allowing him time to rationalize how and why the loss occurred. Denial involves a conscious or subconscious choice not to accept the realities of the loss. Disbelief is usually less intentional, but unlike denial it blocks out most of the truth. In order to deny something, you must first recognize its existence.

In a training workshop for Wisconsin state police one officer described a classic example of total disbelief. Part of the state police's job is to be the first to inform family when someone dies in a car accident. The officer described an instance when he had to tell a wife that her husband had just been killed on the highway. The woman had been waiting for her husband to return since 8:30 P.M. He was a very reliable man, rarely late, and if he had to be, he always called. During her wait, the woman had experienced a gamut of emotions ranging from fear and nervousness to anger. She tried going to bed at 11:30 P.M., but could not sleep. At 1 A.M. she heard a knock at the door. She rushed to answer it, only to find a state trooper and a close neighbor. When the officer told her about the accident she screamed and collapsed on the floor. The police officer and neighbor stayed with the woman a while. Just when she seemed to be pulling herself together, she said, "My husband should be home soon. Would either of you like a cup of coffee while we wait?" She had not failed to comprehend the news; at that moment, she simply did not believe it.

During the workshop, the officer wanted to know what to do in situations like the one he described. What do you do? The answer is to respect the defense mechanism and allow it to serve its purpose of protecting the griever from overwhelming pain; don't try to convince her of reality at this time. Over the next hours, she will believe that her husband is dead, though she may not believe all the details about how he died. For instance, she might for a long time deny the accuracy of blood tests showing that he had been drinking the night of the accident.

When a child switches from crying to a happy state following news of a loss—or in the case of adoption, upon being moved from one home to another—he is usually in total disbelief. This often leads adults to believe the child is all right or that he doesn't really understand what has happened. Both interpretations can be problematic. If the child is believed to be all right—in other words, not grieving—he will not receive the support and guidance he needs to work through the grief. He may even become stuck in his disbelief. If, on the other hand, the adults think they haven't gotten through to the child, they may continue to badger him with the news, denying him the defense mechanism's protection from the pain.

In addition to disbelief and denial, grievers will use bargaining as a defense mechanism. Bargaining incorporates strong yearning, denial of the loss's irreversibility, and often a belief on the part of the griever that she somehow caused or was responsible for the loss. The individual promises herself or God to act a certain way, do specific deeds, or make sacrifices in exchange for regaining what was lost. An example of bargaining is the teenager whose girlfriend has just broken up with him. After thinking about it, he concludes that some deficit in himself caused him to lose her. He then strikes a bargain that if he can change himself—dress better, drive a sportier car, act more cool, make the football team—he will get her back.

Children are particularly adept at bargaining, with some able to maintain their side of the deal well into puberty. For adopted children and children in foster care, the bargain often is that they will be "perfect" in order to return them to their birth parents or other significant caregivers. But in other cases, particularly when a child has sustained several major losses (or moves from one home to another) and blames herself for the loss, the deal is to be "perfectly horrible" so she will be sent back to where she came from.

Bargains are attempts at regaining power in the situation, but they also reinforce shame. When the person asks, "Why did this happen?" the answer is often, "There is something wrong with me." For the adopted child, a bargain to be perfect implies that the child feels she is not good enough as she is. If she has promised herself to be perfectly horrible, her negative behavior and the negative responses her behavior elicits from others is likely to reinforce her belief that she is bad.

Disintegration, the fourth category of immediate reactions, usually sets in at about the time shock and numbness begin to wear off, and can continue in conjunction with other phases throughout the grief process. Disintegration refers to the loss of a cohesive sense of self; the individual may feel changed, fragmented, confused, or no longer whole. Individuals in this phase may be disorganized, forgetful, or slower and less proficient than usual at completing tasks. A child who is experiencing disintegration may regress to earlier developmental stages and skill levels, temporarily losing mastery of skills already achieved.

The distinction between disintegration and normal forgetfulness or mistakes is that in disintegration the mistakes often take on a pattern. We all occasionally make mistakes like pouring orange juice on cereal, spraying on air freshener instead of deodorant, or making elementary mistakes on routine portions of our jobs. A person experiencing disintegration, however, might find himself accidentally pouring orange juice on the cereal so often that he eventually just eats it rather than waste more food. And most likely, he will find himself making similarly ridiculous mistakes in other areas of his life as well.

Yearning, Pining, and Searching

In this phase, the primary focus or desire is to reverse the loss and bring back "what should have been." The inability to recover what was lost commonly brings crying, tension, restlessness, irritability, disbelief, frustration, and anger (Rando 1984, 12).

The yearning and pining aspects of this phase are the deep longings that consume the griever's thoughts. According to Rando (1984, 22–23), searching is the active expression of this longing, and involves "motor, perceptual, and ideational components." The griever restlessly, physically searches for what was lost, even if it is a person who has died. Her thoughts will focus on events and places associated with the lost person and on maintaining a clear visual memory of him or her. In addition, the griever's perception of her environment is altered to focus on what was lost. Rando writes:

> The griever develops a perceptual "set" to perceive and pay attention to stimuli that suggest the presence of the deceased and ignore those that don't. Occasionally ambiguous sensory data will fit the image of the lost person and the griever will think he has seen the lost loved one. As well as having the illusion of seeing the person, the griever may also feel a comforting sense of the presence of the deceased or have to restrain impulses to speak to or do things for the absent person. (1984, 22)

The adopted child who never knew her birth parents will create images and fantasies of the birth parent, with little restraint. Some children in middle childhood talk about speaking with their birth parents or make presents to send them, even though they do not actually know who their birth parents are. The "perceptual set" that Rando speaks of can lead school-age children to scan crowds for adults who look like themselves and then to find what they are looking for, whether it is really there or not. For example, a child who is a brunette living in a very blond community may decide that the only other person in the neighborhood with dark brown hair is her birth mother and she will "see" other physical similarities even where there are none.

Finally, Rando points out that unrewarded searching actually makes the loss more real for the griever. The young adult who has initiated a search for her birth parents, which then proves fruitless, is more acutely aware of the loss and, with support, may be in an even better position to resolve the grief for her birth parents because the loss has now been given greater substance. If the search is successful, but the adopted person does not find what he hoped or believed he would in his birth parents, reunification may still not heal the grief unless the adopted person can identify what expectations were not met and then grieve that loss.

Strong Feelings
Strong feelings may be directed toward self or others, and may include acute sadness, anger, guilt, and shame. Children, as well as adults, often choose to be angry to protect themselves from the pain of sadness, guilt, shame, and other unpleasant emotions. When a child is grieving the loss of birth parents, the focal point of her anger may be the birth mother, the birth father, adoptive parents, God, herself, or anyone else she *currently* believes is responsible. Once the anger is expressed and validated in healthy ways, children are freer to move on to the underlying sadness and pain, and thus move closer to resolution.

Guilt refers to feelings of self-reproach for something the individual has *done* to cause the loss. Shame, on the other hand, refers to feelings of disgrace or humiliation for what one *is*. Shame may not be present when the individual is grieving because someone has died, but it frequently arises in adopted children grieving for their birth parents.

Despair and Hopelessness.
This is the phase in which people ask, "Why did this happen to me?" The griever relinquishes the search to recover what was lost, and at the same time is fixated on the idea that things should be different—that is, the way they were before the loss. Other feelings present may be rage, loss of power, depression, a sense of violation, and "a disinclination to look to the future or to see any purpose in life" (Rando 1984, 25).

This stage can be frightening for others to witness, particularly when the griever is enraged. The combination of anger and despair that comprise rage make it especially scary. The griever feels he has nothing further to lose and therefore does little to temper his expression. The griever may even entertain thoughts of suicide as a way to end the pain.

On the positive side, despair and hopelessness can act as a turning point in grief. The person in grief has a choice of staying in the depths of the valley (depression) or moving out and climbing back up by accepting the loss and that they can be OK even in the absence of what was lost. This is the point at which children may sob for long periods of time for their loss, because in their despair they feel there is nothing further they can do: searching didn't work, anger didn't work, bargains failed, there is nothing left but to cry. Unfortunately, sobbing is often difficult for parents to listen to and to respond to supportively. There are no answers parents can give their children to relieve despair; the most helpful thing they can do is to offer comfort with their presence and to let the child know it is OK to cry, even for a long time.

Reorganization
Reorganization is the path to recovery. Like other phases, periods of reorganization may be intermittent and may pertain only to selected aspects of the griever's life. While in this phase, the individual returns to her previous level of functioning. The griever's ability to complete tasks returns to normal, as well as her interest in things other than what was lost. Bit by bit the griever reorganizes her identity or sense of self and begins to look toward the future. For a man whose wife has died, this means that he starts seeing himself as a widower rather than as his dead wife's husband. The child who is adopted when older begins to see himself as the son of his adopted parents, to accept his new last name as his own, and to regain mastery of age-appropriate skills. The ultimate goal of reorganization is full integration of the loss.

Integration

While reorganization is part of the grief process, integration is its resolution. The mourner incorporates the loss and all she has learned from grieving into a redefined self. She now looks to the future rather than dwelling on the past, fully accepting the permanence of the loss and the alterations it has made to her various roles in life. Before integration, a widow may maintain in her mind a continuing relationship with her dead husband (Parkes and Weiss 1983, 99). Once integration has occurred, however, she not only identifies herself as a widow and a single person, she assumes responsibility for the tasks her husband previously handled and carries them out in her own way, no longer obliged to do it as he would have. When individuals achieve healthy integration, they no longer feel devastated by their loss, but are strengthened by the experience and their ability to endure and learn from it.

An adopted child who has achieved integration will finally feel OK about being adopted, no longer wondering what bad things it might mean about him, and accepting that his birth parents' choice was painful to him and them, but also accepting the blessings and opportunities of membership in his adoptive family.

Withdrawal

Woven throughout the grief process may also be times when the griever withdraws from those around him, including those with whom he otherwise feels close. While withdrawal sometimes called detachment—is not usually considered a phase of grief, it is a common and normal response to grief. According to Rando (1984, 268–269), people diagnosed with terminal illnesses gradually withdraw from those around them, maintaining relationships only with those closest to them. But at a point close to death, terminally ill patients withdraw even from those closest to them.

A similar withdrawal is common among children in foster care. Shortly before a move, the child withdraws from the foster parents, even if they have been close throughout the placement. She may isolate herself from the foster family or even friends she has made during the placement. She may be selective in her withdrawal; for example, by being outgoing during play, and isolating herself at times when emotional contact normally occurs, such as during family time or at bedtime.

While withdrawal is often pronounced in anticipatory grief (grief for an impending loss or imminent death), it also occurs in grief following a loss, even if the object of the loss returns. Bowlby (1980, 19–22) describes studies of withdrawal in children aged six months to three years when they are rejoined with their parents following a separation of one week or more. Such reunions are "characterized by an almost complete absence of attachment behavior when [the child] first meets his mother again." Initially, the child may turn away or even walk away from the mother, alternating between tears and lack of expression. This detachment or withdrawal seems to persist to some degree throughout the first three days of reunion. At the same time, the child may respond affectionately to the father.

No matter what the loss, withdrawal allows the griever time alone to process his feelings about the loss. Because loss is seldom processed all at once, withdrawal may occur intermittently throughout the grief process. During times of withdrawal, the grieving child should be supported in ways that are nonintrusive and nonconfrontive. For example, if he decides not to come to the dinner table with the rest of the family, prepare a plate and bring it to him in his bedroom. He should be allowed time to experience or protect himself from emotions, particularly pain, without being called upon to "snap out of it." At the same time, if withdrawal persists overly long—for example, several days for young children, or a week or more for older children and teens—the withdrawal should be gently challenged to prevent it from becoming a constant state. "In infants and children," Bowlby writes, "it appears, defense processes once set in motion are apt to stabilize and persist" (1980, p. 21).

Children may need assistance in coming out of withdrawal. One way to do this is to offer your presence and touch while helping the child identify her feelings. Hugs and holding may be too intrusive at this time, but the child may accept a touch on the back or stroke on the head. Statements like "It looks like you want to be alone because you are sad at having to leave your foster family" can help the child identify the emotions he is focusing on or avoiding through withdrawal.

Often the person in withdrawal wants to be part of the group but does not want to talk about his loss and grief. A good way to facilitate this is by establishing cue words the grieving child can use to indicate when he feels encroached upon. The cue word tells those around him that the current topic of conversation is too much for him to bear at the moment and should be dropped. The cue can be anything: "jingle bells," "eggs," "baseball." It need not make sense; nor does it have to be related to the issue. But whatever it is, it should be respected both at home and in counseling. Cues allow the grieving child to acknowledge the pain without needing to withdraw completely. Though these emotions should be discussed at some time, it is also possible to overtalk them. A special time of day may be set aside to allow the child to talk about his emotions; but if he chooses not to, that too should be respected.

The cue-word technique also gives the grieving child healthy control over her emotions. One adopted fourteen-year-old girl described her image of a box she kept inside her to contain her emotions about having been abused in the past. She used to shut away the box all the time, with twenty-seven elephants on top to keep it closed. But once she was able to finally tell someone what happened, she found she could occasionally let up the lid a bit and examine the incident and her feelings. Sometimes someone else would say something or an event would trigger a memory and the box would open by itself. If the timing was inopportune, she had to quickly close it again. Use of cue words allowed her to choose a safe time and place to confront these emotions. It also helped her learn to choose when and how to express and act on her emotions.

Cue words, offering your presence and touch, and gentle support are techniques that can be used effectively with adults in withdrawal, too.

Replacement

In our cumulative society, our first inclination is often to attempt to resolve loss through replacement. When a child's pet hamster is dying, even veterinarians—who presumably understand how attached people become to their pets—have been known to say, "You can always get a new one for $3.50. The cost of saving this hamster isn't worth it." When the family dog dies, it is the adults in the family who rush to buy a new one in hopes of alleviating the children's pain—and their own.

Adults find it very painful and frustrating to watch children grieve. Seeing a child in pain cuts deep into our emotions and memories, recalling for us what it was like to hurt as a child. When we cannot retrieve what was lost, we feel even more uncomfortable because we don't like to appear powerless before our children. But when we tell children, "Don't cry; we'll go to the pet store and buy a new dog tomorrow," we are telling them, first, that they should not express their grief, and second, that the solution to grief is replacement (James 1986, 37–45).

Lessons of childhood carry into adulthood, and it's no surprise that parents are often inclined to quickly replace a child who has died, was stillborn, or miscarried, either by becoming pregnant again or by adopting. Bowlby writes:

> There are reasons for doubting the wisdom of these very early replacements, since there is danger that mourning for the lost child may not be completed and that the new baby is seen not only as the replacement he is but as a return of the one who has died. This can lead to a distorted and pathogenic relationship between parent and new baby. . . . A better plan is for parents to wait a year or more before starting afresh to enable them to reorganize their image of the lost child and so retain it as a living memory distinct from that of any new child they may have. (1980, 122)

Completing the grief process and achieving integration is crucial to future relationships, especially ones of the same type as the lost relationship. The need to resolve a lost relationship before moving on to another is well recognized when an intimate adult relationship ends, as in divorce. Even most lay people know that on-the-rebound relationships are usually fraught with problems.

The issue of replacement, however, becomes more complex when the circumstances involve providing new parents for a child. The child is expected not only to accept the adoptive parents as his own, but in many cases even to call them by the same names—Mama, Dad—he used for his birth or foster parents. Seldom in adult relationships does a new mate have the same name as the former. It's no wonder that children who are adopted when older sometimes project onto the adoptive parents anger for things their birth parents did.

While adults are able to take the time they need to grieve before moving into a new relationship, it is very difficult, if not impossible, to provide similar time for children because they still need adults to care for them. Prolonging the period between removal from birth home and placement in the adoptive home may at first seem like a good solution, but it is hardly practical and could possibly cause more harm than good. But when circumstance or the law necessitates an intermediate placement, that time should be used to help the child work through his grief for his birth family. Professional counseling, support from a caring adult with whom the child feels safe, and a secure environment can help the child to better understand and experience his emotions and begin the work of grief. Neither children nor adults should be left to grieve alone. (This does not mean they should not be allowed private time while they grieve.)

How We Learn to Grieve

Children learn from their parents to label and express their emotions. Yet the tendency is to shelter children from adults' grief, whether it is over a death or a lost job. When a family member dies, children are sometimes shipped to relatives or friends to protect them from seeing their parents' pain or the "horrors" of the funeral. But according to Rando, children need to see the adults around them grieve in order to learn about their own feelings and appropriate ways of expressing them:

> It is frightening for the child to see adults upset, but this must not be hidden since it is a natural reaction. Children need to know that it is permissible and normal to express grief. Of course its expression should be somewhat tempered in order not to overwhelm them. Jackson (1965) points out that sadness is quite different from despair and that reasonable expression is different from complete collapse. He advocates that children be spared extreme expressions of adult breakdown, which might overtax them emotionally. However, children can contend with much stronger reactions than adults believe and, in general, it is better to err in the direction of sharing the feeling than concealing it from the children. The most important thing is that the child receive an explanation of the adults' feelings as normal responses to grief. (1984, 167)

At the same time, care should be taken to ensure a secure environment for the child. And grieving parents need to reassure their children that their love for them remains constant even though they are very upset.

Losses in Your Life

Before we can teach our children to recognize and express their grief we must first understand how we as individuals deal with our own losses. James in *The Grief Recovery Handbook* (1986) has developed an excellent exercise for doing just that. We suggest you try the portion of James's exercise described below to help you recognize your own losses and how you dealt with them—or are still dealing with them.

Begin by drawing a time line on a large sheet of paper. At the left end put the year you were born and at the right put the current year. (If it's easier for you to think of your life in terms of your age rather than calendar years, label the time line using age instead.) As you reflect on your losses, enter on the time line the dates (ages) they occurred. The only points on the time line are years that mark losses. Remember that a loss does not have to be a death. Your list will probably grow the more you think about it.

As you recall each loss, take notes about what you were influenced to believe. Were you told it wasn't important, that you would get over it or find something to replace it? Did you search for an intellectual reason for what happened? If you couldn't find one, did you blame God or someone else? Did you feel guilty? What emotions did you suppress when you first felt them? Did you think you should not feel certain ways about the loss? Which losses did other people seem to think were unimportant? When were you told you were overreacting?

James recommends that you work on your graph alone, but that you have a partner who is also doing the exercise. When you have both completed your graphs, discuss them with each other, with first one person explaining his entire graph and then the next person doing the same with hers.

By the end of the exercise you should have a better understanding of what you were taught about loss, both correct and incorrect. You will also have an idea of which losses still cause you pain. Some of these unresolved losses may hinder your ability to help your child grieve. If you would like to work further on resolving these losses, we recommend you read *The Grief Recovery Handbook* (see reading list below).

For Further Reading

• *Attachment: Attachment and Loss; Separation: Anxiety and Anger;* and *Loss: Sadness and Depression* by John Bowlby. New York: Basic Books 1969, 1973, and 1980, respectively.

Bowlby's trilogy on attachment and loss in children provides a wealth of clinical material for practitioners.

• *The Grief Recovery Handbook* by John W. James. Beverly Hills, CA: Grief Recovery Institute, 1986.

In this educational workbook designed to help adults heal after their losses, James also teaches the reader a great deal about grief. We strongly recommend that all professionals working with prospective adoptive parents and older-child placements review this handbook as a source for insight and clinical techniques. The book is available through the Grief Recovery Institute, 8306 Wilshire Blvd., Suite 21-A, Beverly Hills, CA 90211, phone (213) 852–0375.

• *Helping Children Cope with Separation and Loss* by Claudia Jewett. Harvard Massachusetts: The Harvard Common Press, 1982.

Helping Children Deal with Separation and Loss is essential reading for *all* people—lay and professional—living or working with children who are facing loss. Jewett gives recognizable descriptions of behavioral reactions to loss and practical, doable techniques for assisting children in their struggle to integrate loss.

• *On Death and Dying* by Elisabeth Kübler-Ross. New York: Macmillan, 1969.

Though Kübler-Ross's book focuses primarily on loss brought on by death, it is an empathetic challenge to the living to understand the processes of dying and grief. A superb resource for practitioners, it is also written in language that lay people will understand. This book is especially pertinent for those who work or live with children facing an impending separation or loss, such as a move.

• *Recovery from Bereavement* by Colin Murray Parkes and Robert S. Weiss. New York: Basic Books, 1983.

Through their examination of bereavement in widows and widowers, Parkes and Weiss offer insight into why some people recover easily from loss while others do not. Parkes and Weiss incorporate research and theory in their effort to isolate factors that contribute to healthy recovery and integration of loss in adults. This knowledge is critical in addressing the question of children's healthy recovery from loss.

• *Grief, Dying, and Death: Clinical Interventions for Caregivers* by Therese A. Rando. Champaign, IL: Research Press, 1984.

An excellent, comprehensive review of the clinical work, studies, and theories on grief. Rando summarizes, compares, and contrasts the major theories on the grief process, enhancing our understanding of the complex "cycle." We strongly recommend this book for all professionals and paraprofessionals working with grieving people. Lay people will find this work easy to follow and an excellent primer on grief.

4

❦

Identity and the
Adopted Child

*T*he primary goal of healthy parenting is to equip the child with an overall positive self-image, an identity separate from that of his or her parents, and a general sense of capability. Adoptive parents may become frustrated if, despite all their efforts to build the child up, the child continues to display low self-esteem through his or her behavior. Children's interpretations of why they were placed for adoption, who they are genetically, and what their lives were prior to placement—among many other possible factors—all may compete with the parents' messages about the child for a primary defining role in the child's identity. That is why it is important for adoptive parents and professionals working with adoptive families to have a basic understanding of how identities are formed, including the role shame can play in the process and how individuals come to accept either positive or negative images of themselves.

Two Types of Shame

The emotion of shame plays an important role in healthy identity formation. In its healthiest forms, shame teaches the child that he is human, with limitations and fallibility. Taken to an extreme, however, shame can lead a child to feel flawed as a human being, even to the point of being somehow less than human.

In his book *Healing the Shame That Binds You,* John Bradshaw distinguishes between these two types of shame as healthy or nourishing shame and toxic/life-destroying shame. According to Bradshaw, "Healthy shame is the basic metaphysical boundary for human beings. It is the emotional energy which signals us that we are not God—that we have made and will make mistakes, that we need help. Healthy shame gives us permission to be human" (1988, 4). It is healthy for a child—or anyone else for that matter—to feel ashamed of transgressions. A child who *never* feels ashamed about hurting others or for breaking the basic rules of society may have serious psychological problems.

Toxic shame, on the other hand, is a debilitating form of this emotion in which the individual feels much more than the normal guilt, regret, and embarrassment over a particular thought, word, or deed. Toxic shame develops when the healthy emotion of shame is "transformed into shame as a state of being," Bradshaw explains. Instead of feeling shame or guilt over a particular event or even a series of events, a person experiencing toxic shame feels ashamed about his very existence. Bradshaw writes, "To have shame as an identity is to believe that one's being is flawed, that one is defective as a human being. Once shame is transformed into an identity, it becomes toxic and dehumanizing" (1988, vii).

Risk Factors for Shame-based Identity

Discussions of identity formation and the adopted child usually focus on issues of ethnic and genetic identity. While these are undoubtedly crucial elements of a healthy identity, even children who are adopted by families within their culture and who have all the information they need about their ancestry and genetic makeup are vulnerable to struggles with identity formation. Even in the best of homes and with the best of parents, adopted children may be at risk for developing a shame-based identity. We know that it is not unusual for children, adolescents, and even adults to blame themselves at least in part when their parents divorce. Likewise, adults in dysfunctional families often search themselves for the root cause of the dysfunction. People in abusive relationships often believe they somehow provoke the abuse and even that the abuser is justified in "punishing" them. It's not surprising then that at one time or another most adopted children entertain the possibility that something they did or something about themselves caused their birth parents to choose not to raise them.

Adoptive parents work hard to counter this by explaining to their children that adoption is a very special way of forming a family. They tell their children over and over, "You were chosen and are very special." But to be a "chosen child," someone first had to choose not to parent the child, and for most children, this dichotomous aspect of the chosen-child message does not go unrecognized for long.

Abandonment, whether real or perceived, is one of the primary risk factors for developing a shame-based identity. Adopted children are at risk for believing and feeling they were abandoned, regardless of their current home life or the amount of painstaking—even loving—care their birth parents may have taken in their decision. As a normal part of the grief process, the child will ask, "Why did this happen to me? Why didn't my birth parents raise me? Who caused this to happen?" If the child blames herself and is unable to resolve these feelings, accepting the thought as fact and incorporating the resulting implications into her identity, she is likely to develop a shame-based identity.

By recognizing and validating your child's feelings, you can reduce the chance that your child will incorporate this shame into his identity. Validating your child's feelings means letting him know it is OK to feel as he does. This is not the same as telling your child that the beliefs behind the feelings are correct (for example, telling him directly or indirectly that he *did* cause his birth parents to "reject" him). If a child is told directly or indirectly that he should not feel as he does about having been placed for adoption, he may feel not only that he was not valuable enough to warrant the love of his birth parents, but also that, despite the number of times you tell him he is valuable, his feelings (i.e., his very being) are not acceptable.

Other Conflicting Messages

Dichotomous messages that may place a child at risk for developing a shame-based identity may also come from the cultures in which the children find themselves. It is helpful here to consider culture at two different levels: the microculture, or the "culture" of the family unit; and the macroculture, or the culture of the larger community in which the child lives now or used to live. The issue of conflicting cultures is pertinent in varying degrees for all adoptive children. Even when the child's adoptive family and birth family are from the same macroculture—they live in the same or similar communities, have basically the same economic status, and are of the same ethnic heritage—there will usually be some degree of difference between the microcultures, the cultures within each family unit.

The older the child is at time of placement, the more poignant the cultural contradictions are likely to be for him. For example, a child who spends the first six years of life with his birth family or in foster homes may have been taught that an acceptable measure of success is finishing high school— or not finishing high school—and finding a job. If he achieves this he will be a success. His adoptive family, however, may have quite different expectations. Perhaps "everyone" in their family earns advanced degrees and becomes a professional of one sort or another. Their definition of success may be nothing short of becoming a doctor or lawyer. If the child is comfortable with and accepts the first definition of success—maybe he even becomes a highly skilled and successful carpenter or cabinetmaker—he may have problems within his adoptive family. If from his early years and what he knows of his genetic heritage he believes he is inherently incapable of achieving the second definition of success—or simply has no desire to pursue such goals—he may become frustrated trying to live up to the expectations of his adoptive family or simply feel he does not belong. If the issue of achievement becomes an explosive, ongoing family battle, the adopted child may be at risk for low self-esteem, and possibly for developing a shame-based identity.

Children adopted during infancy and those raised within their genetic families may face similar issues if their genetic endowment leads them to paths different from those of the rest of the family. Even if parents give verbal acceptance of their children's different goals and interests, some children will find it difficult or impossible to feel they are ever really accepted unless the parents themselves demonstrate through friendships and associations that they are not merely making an exception for their own children. For example, one parent we know became frustrated when her son refused to accept that the family, all of whom were college educated or college bound, didn't care that he was not interested in continuing his education beyond high school. Even when he eventually decided to pursue vocational training, he believed his family considered this an embarrassment. It was not until his mother, a single parent, began dating a man who had not gone on to college that the son finally was able to believe what the other family members, especially the mother, had been telling him all along: that as long as he was content with himself, he was a success in their eyes.

Macrocultures, too, may convey opposing expectations to adoptive children. For example, in many countries and cultures a child becomes an adult somewhere between the ages of thirteen and fifteen. In the United States and other industrialized nations, one is not an adult until about the age of eighteen; and even this may be delayed well into the person's twenties through the moratorium of higher education (Hogan writing on Erikson, 1976, 172). A child who is raised in another culture before being placed with an American family may have a conscious or unconscious alarm clock set to awaken her into adulthood at age thirteen. Yet when she reaches that age, society and economics prohibit her from functioning as the adult she feels herself to be. She may quickly become frustrated at being treated like a child (even more so than the average American teenager). If she expresses her frustration in a manner unacceptable to her adoptive family or the macroculture in which she finds herself—for instance by running away, becoming sexually active, refusing to go to school, smoking, or using drugs or alcohol—she may also be at risk for a shame-based identity: I *do* bad things, therefore I *am* bad.

Identity Formation

To understand why adopted children may be at risk for developing shame-based identities despite the many positive messages their parents give them, it helps first to understand identity. At the simplest level identity is who the individual believes himself to be. This, however, changes throughout life. At age thirty, most people would probably say they are not the same person they were when they were twenty, or ten. At age fifty, many would say they are no longer the same person they were at thirty. Identity is at once a process and a point-in-time definition of who we are as individuals. Our identities grow and change with each life change and may even be "periodically lost and regained" (Hogan, 172). Identity is changeable because it is in part formed in response to one's roles, environment, and significant others, all of which can vary throughout life.

Identity formation is a complex equation of inputs and outputs where neither side of the equation alone provides a complete explanation for the individual's chosen identity. Rather, what the person takes in from others and what he puts out in response combine to determine who that individual is. Factors influencing identity include the following:

Inputs:

- what happens to or around the person, including that person's interpretation or fantasies about the micro- or macroculture in which he is raised or to which he feels he belongs;
- how others react to the person (what they tell the person regarding himself and how they act in response to him) and the expectations they convey;
- role models, family members, and other people the individual identifies with (by looking to others for examples, the individual determines what his or her chances are of achieving a particular identity);
- societal definitions of beauty and how one's personal body image fits those definitions;

Outputs:

- what the person "does" in the sense of work or industry, her various roles in society and family, and what she believes she is capable of doing, whether realistically or not;
- the person's emotional responses to each of the inputs above; and

- the person's behavioral responses to his emotions, including choosing not to respond.

Identity Formation Versus Identity Crisis

Erikson identifies one of his eight stages of psychosocial development as a crisis of identity. Though he states that this phase occurs as a culmination of the first four stages in childhood, he does not see identity as something that is completely forestalled until the late teen years or, once defined in early adulthood, as being set for life. Erikson writes: "While the end of adolescence . . . is the stage of an overt identity *crisis*, identity *formation* neither begins nor ends with adolescence: it is a lifelong development largely unconscious to the individual and to his society" (1980, 122).

Identity crises are often described as a "search for self." The person experiments to find her talents and capabilities, enters a variety of social contexts to see where she belongs, and basically searches for a comfortable setting and role. Successful completion of the search depends in part on feedback from other people and an assessment of the reliability of those providing the feedback. The seeker also examines her perception of her past and projects herself into potential futures.

We learn about ourselves in much the same way as we learn about characters in works of fiction. We learn about fictional characters by the following:

- what they say, do, and think;
- what other characters say or think about them and how they respond to them;
- how the narrator interprets the character's actions, circumstances, relationships; and finally,
- what we know of the character's social and cultural setting, both from the narrator and from our own knowledge or beliefs about similar settings in real life.

Notice the similarity between this list and the list of inputs and outputs to identity. At the same time that we are "living" our lives, there is also an unconscious part of each of us who *watches* and *interprets* all that happens in our lives. This latter aspect of the individual—the spectator and interpreter—is the core identity, that sense of "being" which we all have.

To derive our identity, then, we look not only at what we do, feel, and think, but also at how others respond to us. The others to whom we listen are narrators, each telling *our* story as they see it. They provide us a reflection of ourselves. We choose whether or not to accept that reflection as accurate; if we believe it to be accurate, we incorporate it into our self-definition. We reject the telling if it does not mesh with what others tell us or with what we already believe about ourselves, or if we believe the narrator is for some reason unreliable.

Balance Theory and Cognitive Dissonance in Identity Formation

Almost any explanation of identity formation—even ours—will be a gross oversimplification. There are simply too many factors impacting each person's identity to be able to comprehensively explain them all. Because of this, we rely on theories to provide generalized explanations of how identity is formed. An important aspect of identity theory is how we reconcile our own conflicting thoughts, actions, beliefs, and attitudes.

Since 1946, when Heider first presented his balance theory of attitudes, many others have built on this concept and the entire arena of cognitive dissonance theory. We are about to add another twist to these theories: that is, how adopted children resolve conflicting beliefs and messages about themselves and how that resolution can affect behavior.

The basic theory states that each person consciously or unconsciously organizes his or her attitudes about *related* subjects, individuals, or events to bring them into consistency with each other. For example, many parents who have adopted interracially have experienced opposition from grandparents or other relatives. In time, however, many of these grandparents and relatives come to accept their new grandchildren. We can use Heider's model to illustrate such a grandparent's attitudes about interracial adoption, people of the child's racial group, and the grandchild as an individual.

To begin with, a grandmother is prejudiced against people of the child's race and because of this is opposed to interracial adoption. Yet she also loves her son who intends to adopt a child of another race, and feels she should support him in his choice to parent. Before learning of her son's plans to adopt this child, the grandmother's racial attitudes were totally unrelated to her feelings about her son and her potential grandchildren. But now that the two have been brought into juxtaposition, the grandmother must find some way to resolve the uncomfortable inconsistency she is experiencing.

A triangle is often used to illustrate the balance theory. In the case of the grandmother this triangle would look like Figure 4.1. The lines connecting the points of the triangle represent the positive or negative attitudes the people at each of the points have about the persons, events or beliefs at the other points. Cognitive consonance—the state of comfortable agreement among attitudes—is achieved when the product (through multiplication) of

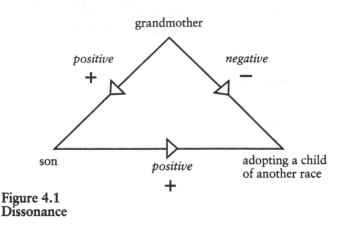

Figure 4.1
Dissonance

all the signs is positive; that is, when either all three signs are positive or two of the signs are negative.

To achieve consonance, the grandmother has basically three choices:

- *Change the attitudes or actions of the other person involved.* This is often the first course of action because it is often more comfortable and perhaps less threatening to oneself to try to change another person than it is to change oneself. In this case, the grandmother could try to dissuade her son from adopting the child, thereby eliminating the issue altogether. If she is able to achieve this, the new balanced triangle would look like Figure 4.2.
- *Change her relationship or attitude toward the other person involved.* Another alternative would be for the grandmother to change her attitude about her son, perhaps choosing to have no further contact with him because of his choice to adopt a child of another race. While this certainly has been done in some families, it is often very difficult to maintain such a dissolution forever. The new triangle in this case would look like Figure 4.3.
- *Change her attitude toward the event or concept.* The final option for the grandmother would be to change her attitudes about people of the child's race and about interracial adoption, or at least to make an exception for her new grandchild. This may be a difficult option because changing an attitude or belief may mean admitting we were wrong. That's why it would not be unusual if the grandmother decided that her racial beliefs were still correct, but that her new grandchild

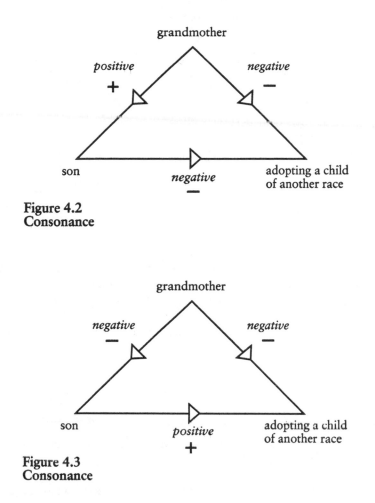

Figure 4.2
Consonance

Figure 4.3
Consonance

was somehow unlike others of her race. This would allow her to accept her grandchild, continue her relationship with her son, and still maintain her racial beliefs. The new triangle would look like Figure 4.4.

Balance theory has been used primarily to explain how people resolve conflicting beliefs and attitudes. We believe, however, that it can also be used to explain how people form self-images or identity. It works because

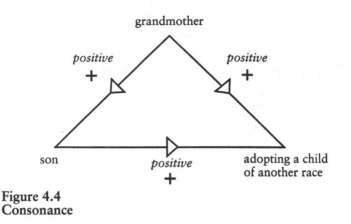

Figure 4.4
Consonance

self-identity is largely attitudinal: it is who you "believe" yourself to be. This adaptation of balance theory can be used to explain adopted children's efforts to balance the conflicting messages, inferred or real, of "I am adopted and therefore chosen by my adoptive parents" and "I am adopted and therefore rejected by my birth parents." How the child resolves this dissonance, as well as other dissonant beliefs and feelings, will have an impact on the child's self-definition, and subsequently on his or her behavior.

Applying Balance Theory to Identity Formation

To apply balance theory to identity formation, we must consider the individual in two parts:

- The core identity, who acts as a spectator, interpreting what the individual does, believes, and feels, as well as other people's reactions to the individual; and
- The self-image (or self-identity), which is based on the core identity's interpretations of who the individual is. The third point in the triangle represents other "narrators" or important events in the individual's life, such as the adoptive parent, the birth parent, the adoption, the separation from the birth family, a report card from school, and so on.

To illustrate that we are looking outward from the perspective of the core identity toward the self-image and other events or people, the triangle

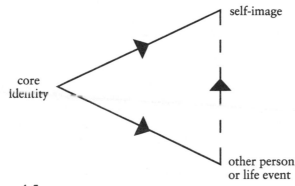

core
identity

self-image

other person
or life event

Figure 4.5

is turned sideways, as shown in Figure 4.5. Furthermore, since identity is rarely, if ever, based on a single event or the opinions of, or messages from, a single narrator in a person's life, we can build on this triangle to reflect the impact that a multitude of events and narrations in that person's life has on her self-image (see Figure 4.6). At various times, a particular event or person may take precedence over the others; or the impact of a once-important event or person may in time dwindle to insignificance. But balance must be achieved within each triangle of core identity, self-image, and event, person or belief. In one area, the individual may have a negative self-image ("I am a poor athlete"), while in another the self-image is positive ("I am a likable person").

Each of the inputs to the individual's identity will carry a weighted value, with some having a greater impact on the individual's overall self-image than others. Trust is an important factor in our choices of which narrations to accept and which to reject. What those closest to us—our parents, lovers, intimate friends, mentors, role models—tell us about ourselves usually carries more weight than the responses of strangers or people for whom we hold no respect. Whether a person's overall identity will be positive or negative will be determined by which factors are most important to the person at the time.

Balancing a Negative Self-Image and Positive Messages
Most adoptive parents try hard to raise their children to feel good about themselves. Despite their attempts, some parents find their children persisting in negative, even self-destructive, beliefs and behavior. How can this

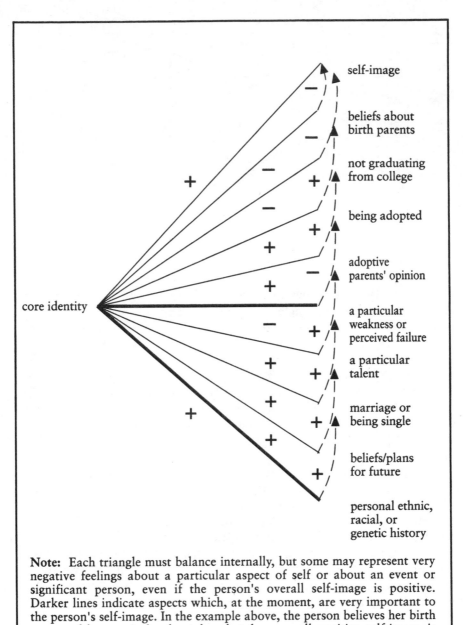

core identity

self-image

beliefs about
birth parents

not graduating
from college

being adopted

adoptive
parents' opinion

a particular
weakness or
perceived failure

a particular
talent

marriage or
being single

beliefs/plans
for future

personal ethnic,
racial, or
genetic history

Note: Each triangle must balance internally, but some may represent very negative feelings about a particular aspect of self or about an event or significant person, even if the person's overall self-image is positive. Darker lines indicate aspects which, at the moment, are very important to the person's self-image. In the example above, the person believes her birth parents felt negatively about her, but her overall positive self-image is maintained because she is currently angry with them for the decisions they made (negative x negative x negative = positive = consonance).

Figure 4.6

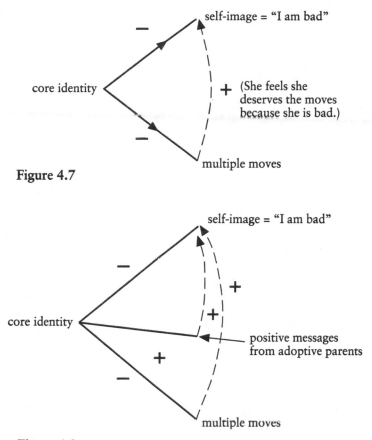

self-image = "I am bad"

core identity

+ (She feels she
deserves the moves
because she is bad.)

multiple moves

Figure 4.7

self-image = "I am bad"

core identity

positive messages
from adoptive parents

multiple moves

Figure 4.8

be? Take as an example a child who was adopted sometime after age three, and moved from birth family through three foster homes before finally being placed with her adoptive family. With each move she believed, consciously or subconsciously, that she had done something to cause herself to be removed from the home. Her feelings of inadequacy or of being a "bad" child were reinforced with each subsequent move, even though none of the caregivers ever told her she was to blame. It was not long before the girl began to believe she was somehow inherently flawed and unworthy of a permanent home and to incorporate this into her self-identity, despite each of the caregivers' efforts to convince her that she was a good, lovable child. Her "triangle" looks like Figure 4.7. The dotted line between the points

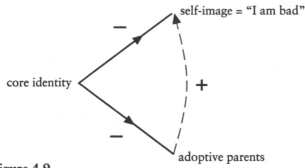

Figure 4.9

representing the multiple moves and the child's self-image is positive because it is in agreement with the child's interpretation that she "deserved"
to be moved because she was bad.

Rather than accept her adoptive parents' consistently positive messages
about her capabilities and who she is, the child may reject those messages,
and instead, continue to base her self-image on her interpretation of her
role in causing the moves, as in Figure 4.8.

Again, each triangle must balance on its own. In this case, however, the
child is out of balance (negative x positive x positive = negative = dissonance) because she feels positively about her adoptive parents, negatively
about herself, and her adoptive parents are giving her positive messages
about herself. It is often easier for an individual to regain cognitive balance
by adjusting her beliefs and feelings about the narrator, rather than
changing the self-definition she has already established. One easy way for
the child to regain balance is to discredit the positive messages by changing
her opinion of the messenger (her parents), as shown in Figure 4.9. First,
she will unconsciously see that the adoptive parent's compliments are incon-
gruent with what she has grown to believe about herself and with her
interpretation of the other events in her life and other narrators' accounts
of who she is. Second, she will assess her adoptive parents in light of these
other two elements and possibly conclude that either her parents know
nothing about her, they have been duped, or they are simply fools.

Of course, the child may also bring about balance by changing her self-
image from negative to positive, bringing it in line with what her parents
are telling her. She may do this superficially; but if she does, there may
come a time when she can no longer pretend to feel good about herself,
leaving her to find another way to bring about balance. Or she may fully
accept that she is a good person, leaving her to rebalance her attitudes
about her role in the multiple moves. If she accepts the positive self-image

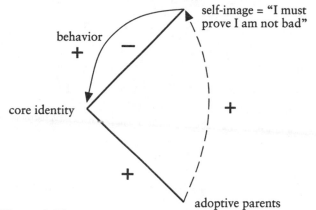

Figure 4.10

only superficially, she may try to convince herself—and others—that the positive image is correct through her behaviors and achievements (see Figure 4.10). It is difficult for anyone to achieve beyond their true self-image forever, and eventually problems will arise. To truly change one's self-image, the wounds that caused the original or underlying negative image must first be addressed and healed.

Another option for the child is for her to try to change her parents' messages from positive to negative, as in Figure 4.11. Children often do this by acting out to evoke the negative response they feel they deserve. This enables the child to continue to respect and feel positively toward her parents because they are only responding to her in the way she deserves.

Balancing Positive Self-Esteem and Negative Messages

The example in Figure 4.11 can be a scary scenario for parents who are trying their best to build their child's self-esteem; but let's consider the flip side. A child who has a predominantly positive self-image will be equipped to endure negative messages about herself with little or no scarring to her identity. She is also likely to consider the message's source—the narrator—and decide that the narrator drawing the negative character image either knows nothing about her, has been misled, or is someone not worth listening to anyway. She may also go out of her way to prove her worth to the other person through her behavior. But she is not likely to change her attitude about herself unless the other person is very significant in her life.

What Parents Can Do

We probably all agree that children need positive reinforcement about who they are and what their capabilities are. When a child is unable to accept

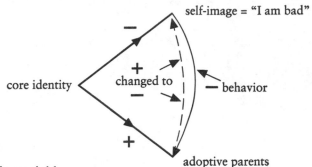

Figure 4.11

such positive messages, professional counseling may be needed to help the child sort out why he feels badly about himself and possibly to put the underlying cause into a new perspective that will enable a better self-image to emerge. As a parent, you can also help your child in the following ways:

- Accept your child's feelings, whether or not you agree with them or understand them. For example, if your child is angry at his birth mother for a specific reason, and you think that reason is not valid, don't say, "You don't really feel that way," or, "You shouldn't feel that way." Instead, ask why she feels as she does. You can then correct facts or offer other perspectives on the situation, but don't "correct" the feelings.
- Teach your child healthy ways of "filtering" or interpreting inputs, particularly negative inputs, from other people. For example, teach him to ask, "Does this person really know me well enough to make that judgment of me?"
- Help your child learn to accept positive inputs, particularly compliments, even if she disagrees with them. Teach her to feel good that someone else likes her, likes something about her or something she has done. For example, if someone compliments a picture she has drawn or her hairstyle, she can feel glad that they liked it, that someone else found pleasure in something about her, even if she is displeased with the object of the compliment.
- Teach your child to control his "outputs" by teaching him appropriate and acceptable ways of expressing his feelings, especially anger.
- Be honest and genuine in praising your child.
- Accept your child's abilities and goals, even if they do not match those of the rest of the family.

- Develop an understanding of your child's interpretation of his personal, genetic, and cultural history, especially if it is not the same as yours.
- Help your child reframe past traumas by talking about what happened, why, and what power he did and did not have over the situation.
- Validate and then gently challenge your child's feelings and misperceptions about her past.
- Help your child to see his strengths and to identify ways to make the most of his weaknesses.

5

⚘

Pregnancy Without a Due Date: Preplacement and Postplacement Stress

A ny good book on child care includes a discussion of pregnancy. Though adoptive parents do not experience the child in utero, they without doubt have a time of "pregnancy" in the sense of expectation and waiting, which begins at the time they first receive the referral and continues until the placement is made and the adoption finalized.

This time, while joyous, can also be highly stressful. Legal proceedings, agency approval processes, birth parents, foreign governments, or whoever else might be involved, and the general fear that something might go wrong are just some of the stresses prospective parents may experience. Unfortunately, such stresses don't always disappear when the child finally arrives; they can carry over into the early months of parenting, primarily by affecting your expectations of the child and your emotional reaction if he or she doesn't quite meet those expectations. By recognizing those things that create stress for you and your partner, understanding how each of you responds to such stress, and finding healthy ways to cope, you can help prevent preplacement stresses from affecting your parenting or your new relationship with your child.

Stress and Powerlessness in Adoption

While both adoptive parents and biological parents face some of the same prearrival jitters, the preplacement wait in adoption poses several unique issues and stresses. In particular, adoption presents a greater sense of powerlessness and unpredictability for the expectant parent than does pregnancy. A pregnant woman can do many things to help ensure everything goes well with the pregnancy, including taking care of her health through diet, rest, exercise, and regular doctor visits. Both she and her partner can experience the reality and inevitability of the baby-to-be every time it kicks, makes her nauseous, or causes her body to change. Expectant adoptive parents, however, often feel at the whim of agencies, courts, governments, and birth parents, not only for information and reassurances that all is moving along well, but also for ultimate "permission" to have a child.

Parenthood is one of the most "adult" roles we have in our society. Yet those who choose adoption generally find themselves at the direction of other adults, at least until the adoption is finalized. This outside involvement in the normally intimate decision to parent can be particularly poignant for infertile couples. These couples often have already undergone the unpredictability and invasiveness of medical treatments aimed at enabling conception. They have also faced the many ramifications of infertility, including what it means about their sexuality and how it affects their sense of mortality and immortality ("What will I leave behind when I am gone?"). If the grief and loss surrounding the infertility have not already been addressed and resolved, the stresses posed by adoption can compound existing issues surrounding the infertility, often without the couple's even knowing it.

The array of options pertaining to the type of child you wish to have and the method of adoption you wish to pursue, while offering a regained sense of control, can also be a source of confusion and stress. Biological parents don't have all these choices. Biological parents indirectly choose their children's potential genetic endowment when they choose a mate. A pregnant woman and her partner might also opt for certain prenatal biotechnological tests (amniocentesis or maternal serum alphafetoprotein testing) as potential safeguards against giving birth to a child with severe abnormalities. But when it comes down to it, biological parents are not asked to choose a child or to decide—or have others decide for them—in advance whether they are appropriately suited to raise a particular child.

Another potential stressor is the relative uncertainty of the period between selection of a child and placement and finalization. The countdown in adoption is far more variable than the nine months of gestation. Once parent and child are paired for adoption, the process can take two months, two years, or sometimes even longer to complete, depending on the type of adoption and any special circumstances that might be involved. Though each type of adoption (international, domestic, open, agency-facilitated, private, adoption involving involuntary termination of parental rights) has its own average time frame, each also has its own potential complications which can prolong the wait. For example, each year in October courts in India close for six weeks. This can be very disconcerting for Americans—for whom patience is not a national attribute anyway—waiting to finalize adoptions of Indian children. Even more disconcerting, however, is that when the day finally arrives for the courts to reopen, the judge may simply decide to extend his vacation.

Coping While You Wait

The word *cope* is interesting in itself. Often it carries the connotation of "subsisting" or "putting up with." Yet according to *Webster's New World Dictionary*, the word *cope* actually means "to fight or contend (with) successfully." In order to cope in a healthy way with feelings of frustration, powerlessness, anger, or sadness that may arise during the adoption process, you need to be aware of your feelings and to actively seek ways to address your emotions and their cause.

Too often, parents look to their child's arrival as the climax of all the difficulties and intense emotions they've endured during the wait. When parents fail to recognize their emotions or fail to find ways to deal with them at the time, their expectations of the day of placement—and even of their child—may be heightened unrealistically. One day cannot wipe away all the pain and frustration of previous weeks and months. And one child (or two, or even more) cannot heal the pain, anger, and frustration you may have gone through to get him.

But there are ways to heal these hurts and to keep them from interfering with your relationship with your child:

Know the process. Parents need to know in advance how long the adoption process will take, what steps are involved, and the potential complications that may arise. By keeping informed of how things are progressing and by doing whatever you can to help the adoption move along, you may be able to counter some of the powerlessness you may be feeling.

Ask from the start about the entire procedure so you know what steps to expect. Then follow up periodically to make sure things are progressing as they should. For those times during the process when there is nothing to do but wait, ask the agency or other facilitator how they will keep you informed of the proceedings. Can you meet with someone in the office every six weeks for an in-person update? Or will they write you when each phase is completed? Just knowing you did your best to help move things along can help reduce your anxiety during the wait.

Find support. At times, circumstances may arise that are beyond your control. When complications come up, it helps to vent your frustrations and anxieties. Many agencies sponsor support groups or mentoring programs (called Buddy Families) for this purpose. If you are adopting privately, find someone who has been through it already to talk to when things get rough.

Take control of what you can and let go of the rest. Manage your frustration by taking whatever action is practical, but don't berate yourself (or your partner) for failing to do more than you are realistically capable of. Such guilt only adds to the stress.

Pay attention to your feelings about the process. While you might not be able to change your feelings, awareness of them may help you avoid taking your emotions out on other people, including your child, your spouse, or other family members. Remember, too, if the process has been difficult for you, it has probably been difficult for your partner. To reduce tension among yourselves, you each need to be aware of how the other responds to anxiety and frustration.

Caring for the Rest of the Family

While the wait itself may be more difficult for those adopting a first child, those who already have children must balance the preparations and anxieties for the new child with ongoing family activities and responsibilities. Children already in the family may need extra attention as they try to understand why it is taking so long for their new brother- or sister-to-be to arrive. Time moves differently for children than for adults; a "long time" for an adult can be "forever" for a young child.

Furthermore, no matter how carefully you explain what is happening— particularly when there are complications—your child's understanding of the situation may be far different from what you have told her. For example, when their first child was about two and a half years old, Holly and her husband began proceedings to adopt Joey, a three-year-old boy from India who had no arms. They showed their son, Colin, pictures of children who had no arms and talked about Joey's coming to join their family and be his big brother. After much work—and eventual success—to find a way to finance the expenses of the medical care and prostheses he would need, the adoption agency in India pulled him, saying first that the process was becoming too complex and later that they could not place Joey with Holly and her family because they were not of the same religion as the agency. Six months after the proceedings to adopt Joey fell through, Holly and her husband adopted an infant girl, Deena. A year and a half later, when Colin was four years old, they adopted another boy, Chad, who was eight and from South America. Despite his parents' attempts to explain that Chad was not Joey, Colin remained for some time impressed that his big brother had grown new arms.

When complications arise, you will not only need to find ways to explain what is happening to your children, you will also need to help them find ways to cope with the tension they will sense coming from you. Sometimes it can be difficult explaining the reasons behind delays, but it is better to give your children whatever information they can understand and handle, than to leave them in the dark to develop their own theories. It is also important to let your children know how you are feeling and why so they don't blame themselves for your moods. If you can't predict how and when the problem will be resolved, tell them so.

Getting Ready

Whether your child takes two weeks or two years to arrive in your home, as an expectant parent you need some sort of "nesting" time to prepare your home and yourself for a new family member. Some people are inclined to prepare a nursery or bedroom, or begin collecting clothes and toys as soon as they are matched with a child. But too much preparation too soon can lead to heartache if the adoption falls through. Disassembling a nursery that has never been used or deciding what to do with clothes and toys purchased for a child who will never be yours can be very painful.

Other people, however, find themselves waiting until the very last minute—either because they prefer to wait or are given short notice—to make any preparation, thereby compounding the stress of placement of the child.

Choosing the right time to begin preparations and how much to do in part depends on you (and your partner's) personality. Some people want to focus on physically preparing their home for the new child, or on buying clothes, toys, furnishings, or whatever else they feel the child will need. While these may be important, one of the best ways to use the waiting period is in preparing yourself to care for your child. If you are adopting internationally, interracially, or interculturally, begin to familiarize yourself with the child's ethnic heritage. If your child has a chronic illness, disability, or congenital problem, learn all you can about the condition and how you can best care for your child's special needs.

Whether or not your child has a special need, it's always wise to use the time simply to prepare yourself to parent. Books or parenting classes on child development, play and nurture, discipline, or spirituality may be helpful. Just talking with other parents about their experiences can be very helpful, too.

This is also a good time to begin looking for baby sitters to allow you time out, either alone or with your partner, after the child arrives. You may even want to arrange for a friend or relative to help out during the first several weeks after your child arrives. Such visits are commonplace when a child is born into the family, and they do more than just allow for physical recuperation following birth. Outside help can free new parents to focus on the new family unit and the many adjustments in daily routines that need to take place. If you become so emotionally or physically exhausted trying to do it all alone, you won't have energy for your child or anyone else. If you do choose to have someone help out, make sure it is a person both you and your partner enjoy being with. The last thing you need at this time is someone in your home with whom you are uncomfortable.

If you are the type who likes everything in order as soon as possible, buy one or two things—say a stuffed animal—and put them away for later.

If your child will have his or her own bedroom or sleeping area, save decorating until the adoption proceedings are almost finished and the placement is more certain. If you are adopting an older child, it is better to wait for the child's input on room decor, clothes, and toys. In the meantime, budget for the inevitable expenses. Even toddlers have likes and dislikes to which you need to be sensitive. Of course, this does not mean you should "consult" your seventeen-month-old on how to decorate your home. But by waiting until after your child arrives and you've had a chance to get to know her, you will have a better idea of what will make her feel most "at home." Are there certain textures, such as the pilling or satin edging on a blanket that he likes? If you are decorating with a theme, are there certain cartoon characters, animals, or toys that your child is particularly fond of? Your new son may prefer stuffed animals to baseball; or your new daughter may have more fun with trucks than Barbies.

Finally, in all your preparations, *begin as you mean to go on*. When your child arrives, don't back off from disciplining for behavior you do not intend to tolerate later, and don't establish a standard of living for the child beyond what you know you are willing and able to maintain in the future.

Arrival: Emotional Issues for Parents

The day of arrival and the first few weeks can be a time of exceptional joy for parents. It represents the successful culmination of what is often a long struggle to have a child. Even though joyful, the first few months of parenting a new child are also a time of stress as you and your child get to know each other and as you adjust to the added demands of parenting a (or another) child.

The first few months of parenting a new child can present a myriad of emotions, affecting each parent individually and their relationship with each other. The emotions and stresses are much the same for parents who have adopted and those who have given birth. Any area in which genetically related parents normally feel depressed, unsure, or worn out may pose a more intense problem for adoptive parents because of the heightened concerns about their feelings for the child ("Can I really love this child?"), claiming, bonding and attachment, whether or not the child will love them in return, and fears that somehow the child might be taken from them. While there are no easy answers for making these uncomfortable feelings disappear, it certainly helps to know that they are normal and common. Recognizing the roots of the emotions, too, can help you deal with them, even if you are unable to change them.

Here are some common emotional issues new parents face:

Feelings for Your Child

After the initial excitement of having a new child wears off, parents sometimes become concerned if they do not "feel" love for the child. You may find yourself fearing that if the child were suddenly gone you would not miss him—that your life would simply revert back to what it was before he arrived. Or you might wonder if your frustration over adjusting to lost autonomy, the demands of caring for the child, and even lack of sleep is in fact a sign that you don't really love the child. You may miss some of the things you enjoyed doing before but for which you no longer have the time or energy. At the same time you may be totally absorbed in parenting and watching your child grow.

Parents who have given birth to their children experience these same emotions. In fact, it is normal for the primary caretaker (usually the mother) to take from two to six months to form strong love feelings for her child, and it can take even longer for the other parent. It simply takes time for the initial infatuation parents feel for their children to grow into a deeper love. And once the realities of parenting hit and the infatuation subsides, you may feel a bit ambiguous while your love for your child is under construction.

Issues Affecting Parents Individually

Parenthood brings with it a change in lifestyle for mothers and fathers alike, especially with the arrival of the first child. It represents a change in identity and new roles and responsibilities. And as any seasoned parent can tell you, the changes continue well into your child's early adult years. But, as with marriage, the first year with a new child is often the hardest—and then the second year is spent getting used to each other! It sounds like an exaggeration, but whether they are aware of it or not, it often takes parents two years to fully adjust to the new demands.

As we discussed in Chapter 3, any change is a loss. Perhaps that is why many parents experience some degree of disintegration in the first few months of parenting. As you concentrate on developing competency in your new role of parent, or of parenting another child, you may find that your competency in other areas of your life, such as work, hobbies, or your role as a spouse, may disintegrate temporarily. If you continue to work during this time, you may suddenly find yourself making mistakes while doing the most rudimentary tasks of your job. One mother we know tells about how she unwittingly erased from her computer system an entire book she had just spent fifteen hours copyediting. When the publisher sent the computer disk back to her for further changes, she was horrified to see what she had done, as she pulled up chapter after chapter of blank computer documents. Eagan (1985) refers to this parental disintegration as living in a fog. Even if you dedicate yourself to the work of caring for your child and your home, you may still find yourself having difficulty completing routine tasks or making ridiculously simple mistakes—but at least you won't risk being fired for them. If you find yourself struggling with the fog, the best we can tell you is this: Be reassured—it won't last forever. Before long you will return to your usual capable self. As your competency in your new parenting role and your relationship with your child grow, you will begin to regain and integrate your former skills with your new ones.

The sense of disintegration may be intensified for the primary caretaker if he or she must return to work before feeling emotionally ready to do so. Gender often plays a role in this, with women usually being affected more strongly than men. Men grow up with the expectation that they will work outside the home and will not be providing primary care for their children. Though women's roles in society have changed dramatically in the last forty years, most are still faced with the question of whether or not they should work outside the home and what their decision means about them as parents. In addition, they often grow up believing that they will have the option to remain at home to care for their children—an option that is no longer economically available to many women today. Mothers of infants who must return to work before their children are four months old often find it difficult to concentrate on their jobs, especially if they did not feel emotionally ready to give up the round-the-clock care of their children.

In addition to disintegration, in a "traditional" family (father works, mother provides primary care for the children, even if she also works) fathers are often faced with feelings of loneliness, a sense that they have "lost" their spouse to the new child, and grief, envy, and resentment that they have less time available than the mother to build a relationship with their child. The mother usually does not face these issues because her interaction with the child encompasses much of her attention, fulfills her need for physical contact and closeness (though not sexual), and provides her greater opportunities to feel that the child is reciprocating her attentions (as in the bonding cycle).

Issues Affecting the Marriage

This last point leads us to how the marital relationship can be affected by the arrival of a new child. Any good counselor, or even your grandmother, will tell you that having a child is no way to save a shaky marriage. Even the most stable relationship will likely experience rough waters during the first year or so after the addition of a new child to the family, particularly with the first child. The emotional roller coaster each parent finds himself or herself in, individually, may affect the marital relationship, especially if either or both of the partners are having difficulty dealing with or understanding their feelings. The book *How to Stay Two When Baby Makes Three* does an excellent job of explaining how the arrival of a new child can affect a marriage. In it, Dorman and Klein write:

> The birth of a child changes the single, paired relationship—the so-called dyad between husband and wife. When a baby comes into a couple's life, the dyad changes into a triad. The baby makes possible alliances and splits in the family. Where there had previously been one dynamic interaction,

Husband◄——►Wife

> there is now potential for at least six:

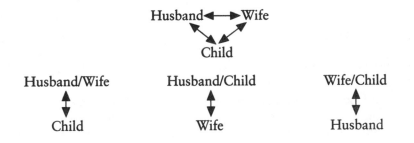

> If we substitute father and mother for husband and wife in these diagrams, we acknowledge another dimension of dynamic interaction. So when husband and wife turn into mother and father, and baby makes three, the amount of psychic energy in the family will have to be redistributed (1984, 12).

Dorman and Klein later go on to explain:

> It seems to us that when one part of the triad gets stuck difficulties occur. If the mother-child dyad fulfills all of each other's needs, the father may experience loss and dissatisfaction. If the father focuses all his love and attention on the baby, the mother will feel a sense of loss. And in some cases, the marital pair may not make enough space in their relationship for the child. The baby will then experience frustration when wanting his needs satisfied. Without a working balance, the new family will feel stress and disruption more than joy and exhilaration. (1984, 70)

Likewise, if either parent is receiving the preponderance of "negative" reactions from the child (inconsolable crying, temper tantrums, lack of cooperation, etc.), he or she may begin to resent or envy the other parent, creating potential friction in the marital relationship.

The new role of parents may also make simple communication difficult. New parents may find themselves temporarily unable to maintain an intelligent conversation among themselves—and often with anyone else—about anything but their child and parenting. This is particularly poignant if one parent is staying home to care for an infant or very young child, while the other continues to be employed outside the home. The at-home parent may crave news from the "outside world," yet because her day has revolved so totally around meeting the child's needs, she may feel at a loss for anything to contribute to the conversation or even to get it going in the first place. The employed parent may return home from work either wanting to hear all about what the child did that day or wanting to discuss other things. Conversation about other topics, however, may be difficult because his partner, though craving adult conversation about other matters, can think and talk of nothing but the child. At the same time, she may be tired of talking about the child. Each partner needs to realize that the other wants to hear about and discuss topics related to both the home and the outside world. And each needs to express interest in and take time to listen to what the other has to say about his or her day.

A good technique to help facilitate such sharing is the "timer technique." When the working parent returns home, he or she is allowed twenty minutes' quiet time to relax from the day's work and make the transition to spouse and parent. Then each parent is given ten minutes, or whatever amount of time they agree upon, to talk uninterrupted about their day. Once their time is up, they must drop the subject, especially if the subject is the problems they are having with the child. Of course, holding an uninterrupted conversation can be difficult with children around. One way to work around this is to have a healthy snack available for the entire family, either before the working parent comes home or after his or her quiet time, to tide everyone over until dinner is ready a little later in the evening. Model this time after an English afternoon tea. Snacks such as cheese and crackers, yogurt, or half sandwiches are high in protein and will hold off hunger, especially for the children. The "teatime" also allows the children time to greet the working parent. Then they can return to play while the parents finish preparing the evening meal and take their time to talk with each other about their day. Later in the evening, the home-based parent should be allowed twenty minutes alone to relax and unwind, just as the parent working outside the home received earlier. If both parents work, use teatime as a time to make the transition from work to home; then put the children to bed at least an hour before your own bed time to allow each of you a chance for time alone.

Parents who are having difficulties with their child because of his behavior are also particularly prone to discussing nothing but the child and the problems he is creating. For such families we recommend expanding the timer technique by charging a fun "penalty" every time either spouse mentions the subject outside their daily ten minutes. One couple used a kiss as the penalty; by the end of the first week, the husband said he had kissed his wife so many times he felt as if they were dating again. Another family began by charging a quarter for each mention of the child's behavior and eventually upped that to a dollar. In time they saved enough money in penalties to take the entire family—minus the child who was creating the disruption—to the Bahamas. While it may sound cruel to leave the child behind, the trip afforded the rest of the family a much-needed break from the excessive disruptions he had been creating.

Issues for Single Parents
Like their married counterparts, single parents are likely to find their new role creating issues in their relationships with other people, as the amount of time they have to devote to those relationships is lessened. Likewise, their focus on their new child—which is only natural—may leave significant others (family, friends, or lovers) feeling left out. And just as it is often difficult for couples to maintain a sense of intimacy for a while after the arrival of a new child, establishing a new romantic relationship at this time is likely to prove difficult for the single parent.

To deal with the stresses of parenting, it is important that single parents allow themselves time out to relax. One way working single parents can do this is by taking an extra fifteen or twenty minutes between leaving work and picking up the child from day care. During this time, read a book, sit in the car, find a coffee shop, go home and enjoy the empty house, go to a park—in essence, find your own space to be alone and relax. Parents who have tried this say it is well worth the extra expense in day care fees, even when money is tight. If you can't afford to do this every day, try it at least once a week. Then, perhaps when you eventually get a raise, you can use the additional money to buy yourself more time.

Another way to ease the transition from work to home is to prepare meals the night before, after you have already eaten dinner. Then when you and your child get home, all you have to do is heat it and eat. After you and your child's stomachs are satisfied and you've had a chance to relax, you can prepare dinner for the next night.

Feeling "Entitled" to Parent Your Child

One type of emotional stress that is unique to adoptive parents is that created by the issue of "entitlement." The term *entitlement* is commonly used in adoption to refer to the adoptive parents' "right" to parent their adopted children. Usually it is used in the context of reinforcing parents: You do have the right to have your child and to care for, discipline, and love your child. The issue of adoptive parents' rights to parent their children may seem moot on the surface, but parents often feel challenged in many ways. People will ask, "Don't you want children of *your own?*" or, in the case of interracial, intercultural, or international adoption, "Are you being fair to the child by taking him away from his people?" Adoptive parents are often as vulnerable as their children when such comments are made. Both know that children *can* be separated from parents and parents *can* be separated from children.

Furthermore, in a society in which we no longer feel obligated or allowed to discipline or correct other people's children, it may take adoptive parents a while to feel comfortable disciplining their children. This is particularly an issue when the child is already past infancy at time of placement. Older children may even challenge their new parents in time of conflict, saying, "You aren't my real parents. I don't have to listen to you."

Formal rituals have long been used to sanctify relationships and to mark the passage from one role or stage in life to another. One might expect that the finalization proceedings in court would serve this purpose in adoption, but in most cases, by the time the judge is ready to sign the final documents, the proceeding is a cursory formality. Likewise, there is usually no ceremony surrounding the placement. A name-giving and dedication ceremony, such as a christening or baptism, may help; still these types of ceremonies don't meet the exact needs we are speaking of here. Parents need something that in essence formally and publicly transfers to them the right to parent their child. If you are adopting an infant or very young child, you may want to ask your pastor, priest, rabbi, a justice of the peace, or even your placement social worker to help design and officiate over an "ordination into parenthood." If your child is already in your home, but the adoption has not yet been finalized, have the ceremony before the finalization to help validate your rights to parent. Take pictures of the event and plan a reception afterward, inviting your friends and family. As your child grows older, you can show her the pictures as other parents would show hospital birth pictures.

If your child is older, a marriage-like ceremony in which the parents and siblings take the new child into their family and the adopted child takes the parents and siblings to be his family might be an option. If neither of these suggestions seems right or viable for you, at the very least plan a reception following the finalization.

When You Feel Overwhelmed

Your child's pediatrician may prove a good resource should you begin to feel overwhelmed with stress or concerned about the emotions you are experiencing. Since you are likely to visit the pediatrician anyway for checkups, immunizations, and common illnesses, take the opportunity to draw on his or her expertise. A good pediatrician should be familiar with the trials of new parenthood as well as healthy ways of coping with them. He or she can also provide feedback on your child's social and emotional development, evaluate your bonding and attachment with your child, and provide reassurance and direction for you in your parenting skills. If you are having more serious problems, your pediatrician can probably refer you to other professionals, such as therapists, psychologists, or psychiatrists, for additional help.

Activity: Creating a Family Storybook

Claiming and belonging are important pieces in the attachment puzzle. Adoptive children need to know that their life stories, including their lives before placement, are an integral part of their family's story. Such knowledge can help anchor the child to the adoptive family and serves as one more enhancer for attachment.

Family storybooks are a way of recording how a particular family came into being and of honoring each member. The family storybook traces the life of the family, from each parent's childhood to courtship, marriage, decision to become parents, to how each child joined the family, and who each child is. Each child has a chapter in the book with his personal history, including whatever might be known of the birth family and his life before placement.

Writing a family storybook takes time, but is well worth the effort. The writing process itself opens the door to many of the complicated issues parents must face sooner or later. It allows them a chance to safely explore ways to address delicate issues, such as infertility, birth parents, previous abuse, and other topics that may be uncomfortable. The finished product models for children the "OKness" of ambivalent feelings around sensitive issues and ties family members together. By thinking these issues through early on, you will be better prepared to help your children and may even be able to ward off a few crises in the process.

A good time to start writing the family storybook is while you are waiting for your child, but it can also be done anytime after placement. The book should be written at a level your child will be able to understand. If your children vary greatly in age, you may want to write the entire book so that the youngest member can understand, or vary the style and complexity of each child's chapter according to his level of comprehension. Later, as your child or children grow, older you may want to rewrite the family storybook, adding information you may not have been comfortable including the first time around and also writing at a more sophisticated level.

How to Write a Family Storybook

Family storybooks can be very simple or extraordinarily elaborate. The topics suggested below are the minimum requirements for tracing the growth of a family. You may add on as you wish. Each section described can be completed in as little as two or three sentences. Write as much for each section as you feel is needed.

The family storybook should record thoughts and feelings as well as events. In this way, each person in the book becomes a three-dimensional character: a real human being, instead of just a name. For example, when writing the "mischievous story" from your childhood, tell not only *what* you did but *how you felt* during and after the event. Emotions are shown through feeling words (sad, angry, happy, confused) and related actions (they cried, he laughed).

Older children can participate in the writing especially of their own chapters. If desired, books can be illustrated with photos, pictures by talented adults or enthusiastic kids, stickers, cutouts, and so on. Old-fashioned scrapbooks are wonderful for "publishing" family storybooks. Write a first draft of the book on scratch paper. When the manuscript is ready for publishing, use an indelible fine-line marker to print the story on scrapbook pages. An easy way to lay out the book is to use the left-hand pages for illustrations and right-hand pages for copy; but get as creative as you like.

What to Include

Here's an outline for the types of information to include in your family storybook. You may not have access to all the information requested, and not all items will necessarily apply to you and your family. Just write about what you know.

"In the beginning, Mom and Dad were kids, too!" Start with the older parent, or flip a coin to decide who goes first. For each parent, record the following information:

- Date and time of birth; place; names of parents (your child's grandparents), their ages at the time, if known, and maybe something brief about them, for instance what they did for a living.
- Brothers and sisters by name and age at the time the main character (Mom or Dad) was born. Tell how old the main character was when each of his or her younger brothers or sisters was born or adopted.
- A funny baby story. For example: "Jane (Mom) was nearly three and still in diapers. Grandma (Jane's mother) was frustrated with changing diapers and kept saying, 'It'll be a miracle if you ever learn to use the potty.' One evening when guests were over for dinner, Jane ran into the dining room yelling, 'Mommy, it's a miracle! It's a miracle!'"
- Brief details of childhood, including information such as likes and dislikes, favorite toy, or activities.
- One brief "proud" story, to be contributed, if possible, by the main character's parents. This is a good way to involve grandparents in the preparations for the new child and can help them to "claim" him as their grandchild.
- One brief mischievous story. Again, grandparents can help here. Kids enjoy hearing that their parents made mistakes when they were children. Parents laughing at their own mistakes, in a kind way, models that no one is perfect and that it is OK not to take yourself too seriously.
- Education and career choices. Before concluding the chapters on the parents' childhoods, each parent should write about his or her education and career choices.

Courtship and marriage. Marriage, like adoption, is a legal blending of two distinct genetic lines into one family. Here is the information you will need for this portion of the book:

- The story, in brief, of how Mom and Dad met. Again, be sure to give parents feelings through words and actions.
- Tell briefly about the wedding day and perhaps about the proposal and engagement. Tell about both parents' feelings on that day. Possibly include a humorous wedding story.

- If yours is a blended family, tell briefly about the previous marriage(s) and divorce(s). Tell how you felt about your divorce. Show that it took a while for you to get over those feelings. This can help demonstrate for your children that you, too, have experienced losses.

For single parents. If they desire, single parents can write briefly about their decision to remain single or about their courtship experiences. For example: "Dad dated many nice women, but never found one he wanted to marry." Or: "Mom was engaged once but she and her fiance decided not to get married. Mom was sad for a while. She missed . . . , and she was afraid she would never marry and would never have children. Sometimes she cried. But after a while she decided it was OK if she didn't marry. She learned about adoption and knew she could have children without a husband to be the Daddy. This made her happy again."

Decision to adopt. For the storybook's purposes, the decision to adopt is essentially twofold. First, there is wanting to have a child; and second, there is choosing adoption as the way to have one.

- **Wanting a child.** Begin this section by telling about your desire to have a family. If infertility was an issue, this is the time to introduce the subject. For example, you might write: "After Mommy and Daddy had been married for a while they decided they wanted a baby. They were married . . . years, but no baby grew in Mommy's tummy (for older children, 'Mommy didn't get pregnant'). Mommy and Daddy were very sad. They cried."

  If you are single and did not write about your courtship experiences or did not tell about your desire for children in that section, write about it now.

  If you are building your family both through procreation and adoption, simply write a few sentences about wanting a family.
- **Choosing adoption.** Describe how you learned about adoption. Demonstrate joy at the prospect of adoption through your feelings and actions.

  Describing why you chose adoption when you can or already have given birth is quite simple. For example: "Mamma and Dad enjoyed being parents. They wanted more children. Mamma and Dad heard there were children all over the world without parents. They decided their next child was already alive and waiting for them. 'What does she look like?' Mamma wondered."

Becoming a family. Each child is given his or her own chapter, in the order in which they joined the family (not necessarily in order of age). For example, if Sam is twelve and Sandra is two, but Sandra was born into the family before Sam was adopted, Sandra's chapter would come before Sam's. The idea is to construct the book chronologically, mirroring the family's growth.

For each child, describe the pregnancy or adoption process, showing how you felt and what you did in preparation for the child. Tell about the feelings you had (fear, frustration, love, excitement) as the adoption process or pregnancy progressed—or at times didn't progress.

Next, describe your child as you first met her. Did you meet her at the airport or the agency? Did you spend time together before placement? What did you do during these shared times? What were you told about her before you met? Or for a birth child, describe the birth: How loudly did he cry when he was born? What did he look like? Was he born later or earlier than expected?

If you are writing about your adopted child, this is the place to tell what you know about her birth, her birth parents, and their relationship. If you know first names, include them. Tell why they chose not to parent her, if you know the reasons, or use "maybe" statements ("Maybe they were too young and couldn't take care of a baby"). Describe any arrangements for openness between you and the birth parents. The objective here is to give facts clearly and honestly and to demonstrate the feelings the birth parents might have had, creating a realistic picture of "real" people.

As you describe the day of arrival or birth, tell who was there. Include one or two first-day tales. Finally, describe your child as he is today. Record his weight, age, and height. List his favorite colors, toys, things to do; who his best friends are; what school he attends; and so on. Try to include at least one "great moment" story: something he did that made everyone proud.

If your child is older and has had several foster families or other temporary placements, discuss this, too. For example: "Billy moved lots of times in his life. He had four foster moms and dads, and lived in two group homes by the time he was nine. Like lots of kids who have lost their birth parents, Billy just wanted to go home to Mama. He didn't understand why Mama couldn't take care of him; he would help. Billy was confused and angry and often didn't understand his feelings. Maybe, like lots of kids, Billy thought it was his fault because he was a bad boy. But it wasn't, and Billy was not bad. Billy needed help to understand what had happened to him in his life and why. The social worker told Billy he would be adopted."

In the family storybook, you may choose to elaborate on each life change, or you may make a separate life storybook for each child and refer to those books in the family storybook.

Family traditions. After completing each child's section, close the book with a chapter on the family. Tell about family traditions, holidays, or vacations. Include your family's address, names of pets, and any other pertinent information. This chapter binds together all the preceding chapters about individual family members. Include a funny family story, one that does not poke fun, but sees humor in family struggles.

For Further Reading

• *How to Stay Two When Baby Makes Three* by Marsha Dorman and Diane Klein. Buffalo, NY: Prometheus Books, 1984.

Though written for biological parents, Dorman and Klein's book is packed with wonderful explanations of what new parents go through, and ways to protect your marriage from permanent damage while you adjust to your new roles. With chapters on family, parenting, parents who bottle-feed, expectations of parents-to-be, problematic ways of coping (such as extramarital affairs and workaholism), as well as techniques for renewing your relationship, we're sure you will find this book helpful. It is written in a clear and easy-to-read style that won't take you long to get through. You may, however, wish to skip the chapters on the "nursing couple," as well as the exercises for postpartum women. Even if you have had your child for a few years, this book may bring new insight into your marriage.

• *The Newborn Mother: Stages of Her Growth* by Andrea Broff Eagan. New York: Henry Holt & Co., 1985.

While the entire book is excellent, the first chapter "The Fog" validates for all prospective parents that even birth parents don't instantaneously love their new babies at first sight.

• *Be-good-to-yourself Therapy* by Cherry Hartman. Meinrad, IN: Abbey Press, 1987.

This is a wonderful little booklet, filled with brief encouraging reminders for taking care of yourself and staying happy.

6

🌸

On Moving Children

*J*ust as parents need time to prepare for a new child, children need adequate preparation to ease their transition to a new home and family. Unfortunately, a variety of circumstances and beliefs stand in the way of such preparation, and children are sometimes simply moved and expected to adjust. Adoptive parents, foster parents, agencies, and placement workers, however, can do a variety of things to make the transition smoother and less traumatic for the child.

Age as a Factor

The child's age, both chronological and developmental, is an important factor in how the child understands, feels about, and interprets the move from one home and family to another. In the past, it was believed that infant adoptions were virtually trouble free and that the older the child the more difficult the move became. All other factors being equal, this principal generally holds true. But in addition to age, the child's life experiences, healthy attachments, and past traumas also play a role. For example, a five-year-old who has been well cared for, never abused or neglected, and who has had a healthy attachment with a previous caretaker will probably make the transition to permanent placement with her adoptive family much more smoothly, and will be emotionally and psychologically healthier in the end, than will an infant moved at four weeks of age who has been severely neglected during the first month of her life.

Other factors that affect how a particular child reacts at the time of the move include the following:

• the child's personality and sensitivity to specific life events;

- the parent-child fit in the new adoptive family and in the child's past relationships with other caretakers;
- the child's life history, both what has actually occurred and how he perceives past events;
- how well the child is prepared in advance for the move; and
- follow-up the child receives to help her work through and express her feelings in healthy ways.

Common Reactions to Moves

In her book, *Helping Children When They Must Move*, Vera Fahlberg, M.D., (1979, 10) describes three basic reactions children commonly have when they are moved from one home—be it the birth parents' or a foster home—to a permanent home with an adoptive family. According to Fahlberg, children tend to believe either that they were taken away or kidnapped without their parents' consent, that they were given away, or that they did something bad to cause the move. In addition to these, children who are adopted from other countries, in particular, sometimes believe they were lost. The child's age, the events surrounding the move, and the child's awareness of such events may each contribute to these perceptions.

Taken away or kidnapped. During middle childhood (five and a half to ten years of age), children are particularly prone to believing they were kidnapped from their birth parents. While this is also a common passing fantasy among adopted children who are placed at earlier ages and who know their adoption story, children placed during middle childhood may hold on to this fantasy as part of the denial phase of the grief process. Eventually, the fantasy may become reality in the child's mind. When this happens, it can create for the child on overriding sense of anger or lack of belonging in the adoptive family, and may also inhibit healthy attachment to the adoptive parents (whom the child may believe to be the kidnappers). The child may also become stuck in yearning, pining, and searching for the previous caretakers. Ironically, though being kidnapped would logically create a sense of powerlessness, children who believe they were kidnapped may simultaneously feel responsible for their situation.

Given away because the birth parents didn't like them. Children who are placed or learn about their adoption while preschoolers often believe they were given away, usually because there was something wrong with them or because they weren't good enough in behavior, appearance, or some other quality. At particular risk for this belief are children who have physical, mental, or emotional disabilities. Children who believe they were given away may become stuck in intense anger and sadness at the birth parents for abandoning them or at themselves for not being "better" children. Unfortunately, for some children there may be a bit of truth behind this belief. Some children *are* abandoned by their birth parents, and some birth parents choose not to parent children because they are unable to cope with their disabilities or provide the care required as a result of the disabilities. In such cases, adoptive parents need to let their children know that the birth parents' choice says more about the birth parents than it does about the children. You can tell your child, "We would not have made the same choice; that was their disability. Their decision hurt you, but it was not about who you are." If your child expresses her anger by saying something like, "I hate my birth mother; she was stupid," you can respond by saying, "Her decision was stupid and you are angry, I agree." At times you should also point out that your child's birth mother also probably had good points, but it is all right for your child to occasionally simply be angry without looking at her birth mother as a complete person with both good and bad aspects.

Child caused the move. Children who are placed as adolescents or during the preschool years, or who learn about their adoption while preschoolers, sometimes believe they were neither given away nor taken away, but that they somehow *caused* the move. While it's obvious that a very young child or infant is not responsible for his birth parents' decision not to parent him, for some adolescents this belief may be based in truth. Some adolescents in foster care, adoptive homes, or even birth families will push limits or have severe behavioral problems that contribute to the parents' decision to relinquish their parental rights. In some cases, this may even be the young person's conscious goal. Most often, however, such teens are stuck in uncontrolled anger and distancing behaviors stemming from unresolved grief, lack of a sense of belonging, or negative self-image or self-hate, which in turn reinforce the belief that they caused the move because of the reactions they get from those around them. But whether the child believes he intentionally or inadvertently caused the move, this belief—unlike the others—creates a very frightening sense of power for the child. Children need help to reframe their understanding of what happened, to see where they did and did not have control or power, and then to learn, in the future, to control the things they can and accept that they are not responsible for all situations.

Child was lost. Children may also believe they were accidentally separated from their birth parents. This belief is not unusual among children who are adopted internationally. Unfortunately again, in some situations it is based in truth, particularly for children in countries experiencing mass migrations or wars, or where the incidence of homeless children with no families (street children) is high. Often such countries lack the means to reunite children with their families; thus, children who become separated from their parents may suddenly find themselves in orphanages.

An example of such a situation is the case of Amy.* Amy's birth family had just moved from a rural area in India to a large city in that country. She still has fairly clear memories of the day she got lost. She was about five years old at the time and had gone to the store with a cousin close to her own age. On the way back, Amy decided she wanted to take a different street home, but her cousin insisted they return the way they came. After arguing, Amy went down the other street and her cousin returned down the street they had come. Amy never saw her birth family again.

Children who believe they were lost from their birth families may become stuck in the yearning, pining, and searching phase of grief. They may feel bewildered at how this turn of events came about, or blame themselves if they feel they caused the separation, perhaps by not following their birth parents' directions or rules. They may also feel angry at the birth parents for not taking better precautions to prevent them from getting lost or for not searching hard enough for them. Often this anger is internalized and turns to depression and hopelessness.

Children placed as infants. Children who experience the "trauma" of being moved from one caretaker to another, but who have no verbal memories to explain what was happening at the time, may react inexplicably to things that remind them of the move experience. For example, if the infant's adoptive parents or the caseworker wore glasses at the time, but none of her previous caretakers did, she may for some time be scared of glasses.

Preparing Children for the Move

While no one can change a child's age, life history, or personality, parents can work to ensure that children are prepared in advance for the move. Since appropriate preparation varies with the child's age, we will give more specific tips on what you can do to help your child in later chapters when we discuss the various stages of child development. But the basic rule is to take great care when moving children. It is important that your child have a good idea of where she is about to go and with whom she will become family. Here are some tips for helping your child before and after the move.

---

*Name has been changed.

Visit your child. The most obvious reason for visiting a child prior to adoption is to let both you and your child get to know each other. If you are adopting domestically, it is a good idea to visit your child in the foster home, if possible. Try to meet the foster parents and learn about the family: how many children there are, pets, and so on. At least in this way, when your child talks about the foster family you will be better equipped to carry on a conversation. But even more important than this, visiting your child in the foster home provides a familiar and comfortable setting in which your child can become accustomed to you and provides an opportunity for the current caretaker to transfer parental authority to you, and to discuss the child's habits, likes, dislikes, daily routine, and so on.

When adopting internationally, visiting the child in her homeland will allow you to see her country firsthand. If your child is very young at the time of placement, you will be able to tell her about it when she is older; or if your child is already older, such a visit will help you talk with your child about her homeland. A visit will also give you a clearer perspective of the culture from which your child comes. Even if the laws of that country do not allow you to actually visit your child, you will benefit from seeing the country and experiencing the culture. If traveling to a foreign country is out of your financial means, go to the library and learn as much as you can about where your child comes from before your child arrives.

Send pictures. If your child is a toddler or older, assemble a photo album with pictures of yourself, other children in the family, pets, your home—inside and out—and places you and your child will go regularly, such as the school, church or synagogue, parks, or the neighborhood in general. Shooting a roll or two of film is preferable to a single studio portrait (although this is fine, too) because the former gives a clearer image of the life your child is moving to. Try not to make major changes in your appearance between the time you take the pictures and your child's arrival, especially if you have not been able to visit with your child prior to placement. Don't shave off or grow a beard or mustache, switch from contact lenses to glasses, or make a major change in your hairstyle. For that first meeting, it may even help to wear the same clothes you wore in the pictures. The purpose of photographs is to help your child recognize you and become a little familiar with both you and your home. Major changes will defeat this purpose, especially since children often latch on to single details in photographs.

Let your child say his goodbyes. It is essential that children be allowed to say goodbye to the people who are important to them: their friends, caretakers, siblings, pets, the home, or favorite toys they may be leaving behind.

If your child is already in your home and didn't have an opportunity to say goodbye, you can help him achieve the closure he needs by letting him write goodbye letters or draw goodbye cards. Actually mail them if possible; if not, the process of writing or drawing should still help. If your child left his previous home as an infant, ask the previous caretakers to write a goodbye letter, talking about what their lives were like with your child and what their future relationship will be (such as "Even though we probably won't see you again, we will be thinking of you and hoping your life will be good").

Don't expect a blank slate. If possible, maintain some sort of "contact" between your child and the previous caretakers or birth parents. This may mean open adoption with direct or indirect contact, but it can also be achieved to some degree in a closed adoption. You can maintain "contact" of sorts by talking about the previous caretakers or the birth parents, just as you would do to enable a child to "know" deceased grandparents. By talking about these important people in your child's life you will help maintain a sense of continuity for your child, which will help prevent him from moving deeply into fantasies about who these people were and why he is no longer with them. Let your child know that the previous caretakers are still concerned about him and still care. If your child has pictures of the previous caretakers or if you can obtain them for your child, allow him to keep copies. Since children, out of grief, anger, or accident, sometimes destroy such pictures, you should keep an original set locked away out of the child's reach, perhaps even in a safe deposit box. He will appreciate this later in life.

If older (past the age of infancy), trying to erase the chalkboard of your child's memory and start with a clean slate is unrealistic. Your child did have a life before joining your family, and this life will remain an important part of who your child is. Again, by talking with the child about her early life you will help preserve her sense of continuity with her past. In other words, you will reinforce that her life before coming to you is as much a part of who she is as her life since joining your family.

Allow the child to keep transitional objects. If your child has a favorite blanket, doll, stuffed animal, or other transitional object he uses to comfort himself, let him keep it, even if you think it is the most ragged or filthy thing you've ever seen. Wait until your child chooses to give it up; and even then, save it for him as a memento for later in life. Do the same even if the child discards the toy or object. While mementos of early childhood are important to most people, they can be particularly meaningful for adopted children because they are often the only tangible remnants of their lives prior to placement, especially if they have no contact with previous care-takers or their birth family.

Give your child choices. If your child is a preschooler or older, try to give her some choices during the move. This may simply be a matter of asking her whether she would like to put her toys in the closet or in the toy box, or if she would like to unpack her clothes herself or would like you to do it. By allowing the child to make decisions during the move, you will ac-tively involve her in the process and reduce any feelings of powerlessness she may have.

You may not be able to do all of these things. Perhaps you can't afford to travel to your child's homeland, or the agency or child welfare system through which you are working prohibits visits in the foster home. Just do your best! Find a compromise wherever you can to derive the greatest possible benefit for your child.

Counseling During the Move

The move from one home to another can be emotionally difficult for a child. The adults in the child's life need to acknowledge the child's feelings and help her express them in acceptable, nondestructive ways. Some agen-cies provide preplacement counseling or "classes" for children; others do not. If you are working through one that does, do your best to ensure that your child is allowed access to this resource. If you are adopting privately, you may or may not be able to arrange for such counseling prior to placement.

Whether or not you seek the help of a professional counselor or therapist at this time, it is important that you find some way to help your child understand and express his feelings. In their book *Crisis Counseling with Children and Adolescents*, Van Ornum and Mordock write:

> Knowing how children feel is essential. Also essential is under-standing cognitive ability: knowing the way they think. Children of different ages think differently, and their thoughts color their perceptions of a crisis. . . . We believe that knowing how children *feel* and *think* and helping them to clarify their own thinking will enable crises to be resolved constructively, not traumatically. We believe that a child's misperceptions can influence behavior many years later. (1987, 16)

When talking about the move your child is about to make or has just made, you need to recognize where your child is at cognitively and emotionally, rather than simply "lecturing" on the points you feel are important at the time. For example, you may be concerned that your child misses his foster parents, while at the moment he is most distraught over whether someone at the foster home will continue to feed and care for the dog he found and brought home while he was there (not to say that he isn't missing the human family members as well). If the dog is currently at the top of his emotional concerns, that's the issue you need to help him deal with. Throughout your discussions about the move, be honest about what has happened and why and what will happen in the future.

If possible, find out from the previous caretaker how your child expressed strong feelings such as anger or grief, and also what manners of expression were acceptable in the home. If these modes of expression do not fit with your values (i.e., the child was allowed to throw objects when he was angry as long as he wasn't aiming at someone or breaking things, but you disapprove of throwing altogether), realize that you may have to work gradually to change the behavior and that you will need to offer acceptable alternatives for your child rather than simply condemning the behavior you find unacceptable. It is difficult for children to deal with strong feelings, but it's even harder if they must deal with an adult's negative response to their expressions without any direction as to what is acceptable. One way to address this issue would be to tell your child, "I know you are (angry) and I know that in your (foster home/birth mom's home) it was OK to (throw things), but it isn't OK here. You can (punch a pillow) or (go to your room to be by yourself) if you need to, but you cannot (throw things)." Your child may not drop the old mode of expression immediately. But unless the behavior is absolutely intolerable (such as hitting a sibling, hurting your house pets, or breaking your possessions), hold off on punishing your child for the behavior, at least at first. If the behavior persists and continues to be problematic, consequences may be needed.

Whether "counseling" is provided by the child's caretakers or by professionals, the goals are threefold (Van Ornum and Mordock, 1987, 11–12):

- *Improving the child's relationships.* This involves not only working to improve specific past or current relationships, but also helping the child to build relationship skills.
- *Affirming relationships with important caretakers,* even if your child no longer has contact with those caretakers. You can do this by letting your child know that the caretaker is still thinking about her and still cares even though they are no longer together.
- *Look for mature coping efforts.* Lower your child's anxiety level by pointing out to him ways in which he has coped well with difficult situations in the past, and what things he is doing well now to help

himself cope. In this way you will affirm your child's ability to handle the situation and enhance his self-esteem. Such affirmation, however, is more than saying, "You're a big boy now. You can handle this." It is acknowledging your child's feelings, while showing him from his own personal history that he is capable of coping; it is not *ordering* him to cope.

What's in a Name?

Changing an adopted child's first name has long been an accepted—and even encouraged—practice because it allowed parents to increase their claiming of the child. We, however, advise against it. First-name changes interfere with the continuity of the child's life. For older children, it can also interfere with their sense of self, possibly even conveying the message that they are somehow not acceptable as they are. In the child's mind, the old name may even come to represent the "bad" child who was not worthy enough for her birth parents to keep.

Before we send you into a panic, if you have already changed your child's name, don't chastise yourself for causing *irreparable* harm to your child—you probably haven't. But if you are currently in the process of adopting, consider keeping your child's first name the same or somehow melding parts of your child's former name into a new name. Some ways to do this include:

- maintaining the former first name as it is and adding a new middle name, which you might use as a "nickname"; or
- using the former first name or last name as a middle name.

Of course, some children may *want* a new name (particularly if they are coming from another country and have been told they will get an "American" name when they get here). If this is the case, still try to incorporate parts of their former name into their new name. Sometimes when children are adopted internationally, their original names may be difficult to pronounce for people who do not speak that language. Even so, it is a good idea to incorporate the other-language name into the new name—though probably not as a first name.

Whether your child's first name remains the same or changes after adoption, it is important to let the child know what her birth parents or other caretakers called her. You can offer this information as another fact of your child's life story; you needn't wait until she asks.

Gathering Medical and Family History

Information related to your child's medical and family history will prove important throughout your child's life. If you are currently in the process of adopting, now is the ideal time to gather this information, since it may be difficult to track down later. In addition to information pertinent to your child's health care, you should also try to collect information about the birth family that will help your child know about *who* he is, as well as the genetic history of his body. Be sure to collect a complete history of previous placements (foster homes or orphanages), including why and how the child was moved, ages at the time of each move, information about the household, important people in the child's life, and how the child reacted to the moves. Figure 6.1 is a work sheet you can use as a guideline for gathering medical and other information about the birth family. Wherever names are requested, try to provide at least a first name.

For Further Reading

• *Crisis Counseling with Children and Adolescents: A Guide for Non-Professional Counselors* by William Van Ornum and John B. Mordock. New York: Crossroad/ Continuum, 1987.

A must for all professionals, paraprofessionals, and parents working with children who are struggling to cope with and understand losses, moves, and other traumas. Van Ornum and Mordock present a sensitive and clearly outlined approach for treating and supporting children through crises, past and present.

• *Helping Children When They Must Move: Putting the Pieces Together* by Vera Fahlberg, M.D. Evergreen, CO: Michigan Department of Social Services, 1979.

Widely recognized by professionals in the adoption and foster-care fields, this book, as well as others in this series, is loaded with helpful information parents can also use.

• *Adopting the Older Child* by Claudia Jewett. Boston: Harvard Common Press, 1978.

A sensitive, caring, and insightful look at children aged five and older who join new families through adoption. Jewett provides a detailed look at adjustment problems and behaviors that commonly occur when these children and families merge.

Figure 6.1

Medical and Family History Work Sheet

Medical History

	Birth Mother/ Maternal Side of Family	Birth Father/ Paternal Side of Family
Name		
Age at time of child's birth		
Any previous pregnancies (for birth mother only)		
Any miscarriages, stillbirths, or elective abortions (for birth mother only)		
Name of grandmother		
Was she living at time of child's birth?		
If yes, how old was she?		
If no, at what age did she die and what was the cause?		
Name of grandfather		
Was he living at time of child's birth?		
If yes, how old was he? If no, at what age did he die and what was the cause?		
Names and ages of siblings at time of child's birth (if half-brothers or half-sisters, indicate which parent the children have in common)		
Names, ages, dates, and causes of death of any siblings who may have died prior to the time of the child's birth		
How long was the mother in labor? Where was she when it began?		
Were there any complications during pregnancy or delivery?		

Figure 6.1
(continued)

Medical History

	Birth Mother/ Maternal Side of Family	Birth Father/ Paternal Side of Family
Did anyone in the family have a history of any of the following conditions (indicate relationship):		
Heart disease (indicate age at diagnosis)		
Anemia		
Arthritis (give type if known)		
Asthma		
Cancer (give type if known)		
Depression		
Diabetes (give type if known)		
High blood pressure		
Kidney disease		
Mental illness		
Alcoholism or other chemical dependency		
Sickle-cell disease or trait, Tay-Sach's disease, thalassemia, or other genetic blood disorders		
HIV, AIDS or other sexually tranomitted disease		
Congenital anomalies or conditions		
Stomach ulcers		
Other chronic illnesses or conditions		

Figure 6.1
(continued)

Family History

	Birth Mother	Birth Father	Maternal Grand-mother	Maternal Grand-father	Paternal Grand-mother	Paternal Grand-father
Name						
Height						
Weight						
Eye color						
Hair color						
Ethnic or racial background						
Last year of school completed						
Favorite subject in grade school						
Least favorite subject in grade school						
School-age hobbies						
School-age sports						
School-age clubs						
Adult hobbies						
Other talents						
Habits (nail biting, etc.)						
Personality characteristics (shy, outgoing, jovial, talkative, introverted, etc.)						
Religion (formal affiliations and actual practice)						
Occupation(s)						
Other interesting facts						

Figure 6.1
(continued)

Family History

Is any of the above information available on other siblings or aunts and uncles?

To whom did the mother turn for support during the pregnancy and birth?

What was the relationship between the birth mother and birth father before, during, and after the pregnancy? Was he aware of the pregnancy and part of the decision making?

Why did the birth parents choose to place the child for adoption?

Did the birth parents leave a letter for the adoptive parents or the child?

Would either birth parent like to have contact with the child? If so, what type of contact do they prefer (limited contact, contact only when the child is an adult, never in person, written or phone contact, etc.)?

Section II

7

Growing Up Adopted: The Developing Child

The more a mother knows about the behaviors which commonly characterize each different age level, the better job she can do in dealing with her child. If she knows that despite her best efforts all will not be smooth sailing, she can be better prepared to meet and recognize the different problems she will inevitably face as the child grows older.

The mother-child relationship cannot, no matter how skillful and gifted and kindly a mother may be, always go smoothly. But fortunately the problems she will meet are not all unpredictable. Despite individual differences, there are many similarities in the development of different children.

—Ilg and Ames,
Child Behavior from Birth to Ten

Though about birth mothers, the above passage holds true for all parents—mothers and fathers, through adoption or birth. Child development theory is as useful a tool for parents as it is for professional therapists. With a sound understanding of the basics, parents are better equipped to effectively handle—or cope—with behavior that might otherwise be interpreted as misbehavior, conscious attempts on the part of the child to irritate the parents, or signs that the child is somehow failing to develop normally or to internalize the parents' values.

In addition to basic child development theory, adoptive parents and professionals working with adoptive families also need to understand how children at each developmental stage commonly interpret, feel about, and react to the facts of their adoption. Just as most children follow a basic sequence in their physical, motor, cognitive, emotional, social, and sexual development, most adopted children follow a general pattern—which is tied to development in these other areas—in the way they come to understand their adoption and incorporate it into their identity. And, just as children can be tripped up at other points in their development if they are not given or are unable to receive the appropriate support, adopted children have times in their development when they are more vulnerable to becoming fixated in unhealthy beliefs about their own role or the roles of their birth parents or adoptive parents in their adoptions.

Adopted children are first and foremost *children*. To understand the development of the adopted child, the first thing we need to look at is basic child development. The next step is to add the layer of adoption with no special issues: a same-race adoption with placement immediately after birth. The focus here is the effect adoption normally has on the child at each age.

The third step is to look at how children at each developmental stage interpret and react to their adoption if it takes place at a later age. This third step is important not only because it helps parents understand and predict how their child will respond upon arrival in their home, but also because it is the most likely place for the child to become stuck. For instance, an eight-year-old may at first fantasize that his adoptive parents and the agencies or other people involved in the adoption process conspired to kidnap him from his birth family, who are now desperately searching for him. Such a fantasy is part of the child's normal cognitive development and may help him temporarily cope with the loss of his birth family. But if the fantasy persists overly long and he convinces himself that it is reality, it will inhibit him from trusting and attaching to his new parents and experiencing healthy grief for his birth parents. By the time he reaches thirteen, he may be running away from home to reunite with his birth family, or he may turn his rage for the loss of his birth parents on himself or his adoptive family.

Another factor to consider is how cross-cultural placements affect the child and what parents may do to help their child work through these issues. Issues related to the family life cycle are also relevant because of the impact they can have on parenting and the family as a whole. Finally, each developmental stage bears a potential impact on the child's overall development. If a child is experiencing emotional, behavioral, or developmental problems, parents and clinicians can look for specific symptoms to help them identify which stages may not have gone well. Often in adoption, we do not have complete and accurate information about our children's lives before placement. By knowing what signs to look for, parents and professionals will be better equipped to identify the source of emotional, behavioral, or developmental problems when they occur and to find remedies for them.

Rhythms of Development

Keep in mind throughout this section of the book that child development theory provides only a general guide to the order and ages at which children achieve new skills. Most children will be late developing some skills, "on time" with others, and early with yet others. As Ilg and colleagues point out, "it is more important for you as a parent to recognize the rhythms of growth, the alternations between expansive and inwardized ages or between harmonious and inharmonious periods, and to recognize that calm is very often followed by storm and vice versa, than to expect your own child to fit exactly into any given timetable or pattern" (1981, 15-16). Children do not develop in a smooth progression. As they struggle with each new skill, frustration or insecurity can bring regression, causing them to temporarily lose the mastery they recently achieved in another area.

Personality, too, has its part in how a child develops. Some children are by nature more daring or inquisitive, willing to try new things sooner, even before they are fully equipped for the task. Others forgo the early experimentation, waiting until they can do it "right" the first time. For example, some children will insist on trying to ride a bicycle at age three, before they can even reach the ground with their feet while sitting on the seat. They are not put off by repeated falls. Others are content to wait until they fit the bike and are better able to catch themselves before they fall.

Finally, always remember that each child is unique and may not develop or think and feel about adoption exactly according to the theories. Still, the information presented here can help you as a parent to anticipate your child's next developmental phase and to understand, cope with, or correct her current behavior. We strongly suggest you read through this section from beginning to end at least once. Even if your child is older, understanding what has gone before can help you better understand what he is now or will soon be going through. It can also help you identify unresolved pieces of the puzzle that may still need addressing.

Because our focus is primarily the adopted child, we haven't space enough to cover everything parents need to know about growing children. Therefore, we recommend that you supplement our descriptions of basic child development with one or more of the many books devoted entirely to this subject. At the end of the chapter we list several books we believe are particularly good.

Cyclical Nature of Childhood

Throughout childhood, children alternate between times of equilibrium and disequilibrium (Ilg, Ames, and Baker, 1981, 12–13). Equilibrium is perhaps best described as those periods when the child's "drives and efforts [are] happily well balanced by his abilities" (Ilg, Ames, and Baker, 1981, 18). Disequilibrium is characterized by those periods when the child is struggling to expand his abilities and boundaries, but does not yet have the skills required for the new endeavors. The second year of life (twelve to twenty-four months of age) provides the classic example of disequilibrium as the child explores the world around him and stretches almost daily to master new skills.

In earlier chapters, we described how adopted children rehash old issues with each new cognitive stage. The alternations between equilibrium and disequilibrium provide another cycle. Again, by recognizing the patterns, parents will have a better sense of whether their child is "doing OK" or whether there may be a problem with which the child is struggling.

Ilg and colleagues delineate this cycle nicely in their book *Child Behavior.* Table 7.1 is an adaptation of one originally published in that book. Between ages two and seven, children tend to alternate between seasons of equilibrium and disequilibrium about every six months. From age seven through adolescence these seasons change about once a year.

Table 7.1 also reflects the larger cycles of cognitive development we discussed earlier. Essentially the same cycle of developmental tasks and approaches to those tasks which a child goes through between ages two and five are repeated on a new level from ages five to ten and again between ages ten and sixteen. Within these three larger cycles are times when the child's focus is primarily on his inner self and relationships with others, times when the focus is on exploring the outer world and his limitations and roles within that world, and times when he works on a combination of these two.

As we've already mentioned, each child will follow this course uniquely, in her own time and with her own ways of exhibiting what she is going through. Some children sail relatively smoothly through childhood—even during times of disequilibrium. At the other extreme are those children who seem to be perpetually in a state of disequilibrium. This can be particularly difficult for parents to cope with. When there is a preponderance of negative markers in what should be positive stages, parents never get a break. Over time, this can create stress and distance between parents and their children; such children are often diagnosed as "unbonded" or "unattached." Bonding and attachment, however, are not always the issues. Grief, identity issues, or the lack of a sense of belonging in the adoptive family—all of which are inhibitors to the growth of healthy attachment—can lead a bonded child to act out even during the times that are supposed to be characterized by equilibrium.

Table 7.1.
Cycles of Equilibrium
and Disequilibrium in Childhood

Preschool Years	School Age	Adolescence	Equilibrium/ Disequilibrium	Characteristics
2	5	10	Strong E	Cheerful, independent, participatory.
2½	5½–6	11	D	Sassy; "I hate you" is often a favorite saying at these ages.
3	6½	12	E	Cooperative, more give and take; "yes" replaces "no," particularly for 3-year-olds.
3½	7	13	D	Often moody, sensitive, touchy, morose; withdrawn from others as they work on their "inner self"; an often pessimistic attitude toward life.
4	8	14	E	Outgoing socially; trying new things beyond their abilities; challenging limits; experimentation, both good and bad; common ages for frequent nightmares.
4½	9	15	D	Looking both inward and outward at the same time; easily "wounded"; trying new things, but with less assuredness than in the previous stage.
5	10	16	E	Smooth, consolidated.

Source: Based on chart in Francis L. Ilg, M. D.; Louise Bates Ames, Ph.D.; and Sidney M. Baker, M. D., *Child Behavior*, rev. ed. (New York: Harper & Row, 1981) 14.

Again, personality—both the child's and the family's—plays a strong role in how the child responds to the various stages of development. When personalities of parents and children clash, both periods of equilibrium and disequilibrium will be that much more difficult for all concerned. That's not to say we just throw up our hands and resign ourselves to irreconcilable differences. Family counseling can often help parents adjust their expectations of their children and help children find ways they can please their parents.

The last point we need to make about these cycles is that times of disequilibrium are not all bad. Parents and children usually find plenty of enjoyable times even during the height of disequilibrium. Likewise, the times of equilibrium will not be without their rough moments.

For Further Reading

• *Child Behavior: Specific Advice on Problems of Child Behavior* by Francis L. Ilg, M.D., Louise Bates Ames, Ph.D., and Sidney M. Baker, M.D., of the Gesell Institute of Human Development. New York: Harper & Row, 1981.

Ilg and colleagues present child development with a humorous flair that parents find easy to understand. We recommend not only this book, but the entire series, beginning with *Your One Year Old* and proceeding through adolescence.

• Systematic Training for Effective Parenting (STEP) three-volume series: *Parenting Young Children* (1981), *The Parents' Handbook* (1989), and *Parenting Teenagers* (1990) by Don Dinkmeyer, Sr., Gary D. McKay, and James S. Dinkmeyer. Circle Pines, MN: American Guidance Service.

The STEP series is a very good primer for parents on responsible and effective parenting techniques.

• *Parenting with Love and Logic* by Foster W. Cline. Colorado Springs, CO: Piñon Press, 1990.

Foster Cline has worked extensively with foster and adopted children. His approach and techniques are especially effective with children healing from loss or trauma.

• *Different and Wonderful,* by Darlene Hopson, Ph.D., and Derek S. Hopson, Ph.D. New York: Simon & Schuster, 1990.

Written primarily for African-American parents raising genetically related children in today's society, this book is a wonderful exploration of the challenges of promoting positive self-esteem in a prejudiced society. We highly recommend this book for all parents of children of color—African-American or otherwise.

• *Worker's Assessment Guide for Families Adopting Cross-racially/Cross-culturally,* a project of the U.S. Department of Human Services and the Minnesota Department of Human Services. Available through Adoption/Guardianship Section, Minnesota Department of Human Services, 444 Lafayette Road, St. Paul, MN 55155–3831, phone (612) 297-4880.

For adoptive parents and those contemplating cross-cultural adoption, this handbook provides a thought-provoking look at issues they may face.

Books for Children
• *Being Adopted* by Maxine Rosenberg. New York: Lothrop, Lee & Shepard Books, 1984.
• *Growing Up Adopted* by Maxine Rosenberg. New York: Bradbury Press, 1989.

Resources for Books and Other Materials
• Adoptive Families of America, 3333 North Highway 100, Minneapolis, MN 55422, phone (612) 535-4829. (Publishers of *OURS Magazine,* a bimonthly magazine on adoption and adoptive parenting.)
• Afro-Am Distributing Company, 819 South Wabash Avenue, Chicago, IL 60605, phone (312) 922-1147.
• The Heritage Key, Inc., 6102 East Mescal, Scottsdale, AZ 85254, phone (602) 483-3313.
• People of Every Stripe!, P.O. Box 12505, Portland, OR 97212, phone (503) 282-0612.

8

❦

Early Infancy—
The First Six Months

The First Month of Life

*I*t's been said that being born is the most traumatic experience of life. Whether this is true or not, the newborn certainly has many adjustments to make once she leaves the safe, warm confines of the womb for the vastness of the outer world. It is believed that, for the first month of life, the newborn is unable to differentiate between internal and external bodily sensations, between herself and her mother, and between physical and emotional needs. For the newborn, feelings of hunger, pain, or comfort are whole-body experiences, rather than a rumbling in the stomach, a prick to the heel, or a pat on the back. Newborns seem unaware that they are separate from their surroundings or from other people; the blanket in which the infant is swaddled may as well be the baby's own skin. Eagan (1985) uses the term *fog* to describe the mother's engulfment in her child during the first month of her child's life. We feel the term is also descriptive of the newborn's experiences during the first month, which has also been called the *autism stage*. While the newborn is in this state of autism or fog, the lines between herself and the world are blurred (Edwards, Ruskin, and Turrini, 1981, 4). The newborn's concept of self might be summed up as "I am the universe; the universe is me." Throughout this first month, however, the newborn gradually grows in her awareness of the world, until by the beginning of the second month, she sees herself as one with her mother, forming a dyad that is separate from other people and the surrounding world.

The newborn's developmental task during the first month of life is to establish physiologic homeostasis or equilibrium. As a physical need arises, the unconscious goal is to meet the need and return to relaxation or equilibrium.

The first month is an important time for establishing the cycle of meeting needs to fulfill the bonding cycle. In the beginning, the infant may not calm until after the need has been fully met. For example, a baby who is crying because he is wet may not stop crying until both the wet diaper is removed and the dry diaper is in place. But as the infant's physical needs are repeatedly met, he will begin to associate the act of meeting the need with being soothed, rather than continue crying until that need is fulfilled. For example, instead of continuing to cry throughout the diaper change, the baby may quiet once the mother begins to remove the soiled diaper.

From the infant's perspective, the primary caretaker—usually the mother—meets the infant's physical needs with her smell, touch, movements, voice, and face (particularly the eyes and forehead). But at this point, the association between the mother and soothing is not yet fully ingrained in the infant. This is why, in the first four to six weeks of life, newborns are comforted relatively easily by people other than the mother; the satisfaction of meeting the physical need suffices to comfort the baby. By sometime in the second month of life, however, the baby finds comfort in the particular way in which the mother meets the needs, and begins to desire her mother's presence, smell, touch, movements, voice, and face as much as she wants the food, a dry diaper, or a nap.

At this age, the baby has not yet developed an identity, but she does begin to establish the precursors to her first human relationships and self-love, and a very rudimentary ability to delay gratification.

Family Life Cycle
For both the infant and parents, the first month of a baby's life is a time of adjustment: the infant adjusts to life outside the womb, and the parents adjust to new responsibilities and new schedules. While this is a time of physical recuperation for birth mothers, adoptive mothers are also recovering during this period. For the adoptive mother, the recovery is a psychological one, as she recuperates from the stress of pregnancy without a due date. The adjustment to lack of adequate sleep for birth parents and adoptive parents is essentially the same. Likewise, issues of decreased sexual drive, particularly for the mother (see Chapter 5), are the same for both adoptive and birth parents, even though an adoptive mother does not have the same physical restrictions to having sexual intercourse as does a woman who has just given birth. At the same time, mothers in particular may feel a slight degree of sexual arousal while caring for their infants. Though this is relatively common for women who are breast-feeding, it can also occur during bottle-feeding or in the course of cuddling the baby. Sexual arousal

is a normal reaction to close human touch. While such reactions are obviously not something to act on, parents shouldn't be overly concerned by them either. As new parents become more comfortable with the physical closeness, the "sexual" sensations will subside.

(We refer to the primary caretaker of infants as "mother" because there is a difference between mothering and fathering. The classic role of the "mother" is to give the child his first human interactions and relationship, and enable the child to move from having no sense of self to a sense of self as one with the mother, and finally into a sense of self as an individual. The "father" serves to draw the infant into the outside world, to other relationships and experiences apart from the mother/child dyad. Mothering and fathering roles, however, are not dependent on the gender of the person fulfilling either [Mahler 1968, 1972]. Thus, a man may serve in the mothering role or a woman in the fathering role. At least through the early years of life, we use the terms "mother" and "father" to refer to the parents fulfilling these respective roles, apart from their gender. By age two, however, children do need clear role models of men and women.)

According to Eagan (1985), mothers are in a state of fog for the first month after a child is born—or joins the family. To onlookers (including the father), the mother's focus on the child seems total, but her real focus is on adjusting to her new role as parent of this baby. In fact, mothers usually do not feel a deep "love" for their babies until the second month of life. Eagan writes:

> At some time during the second month most mothers do begin to love their babies. While it is a rare woman who will admit that she did not love her baby at first but has recently begun to do so, the fact is that in the first month women do not act as if they love their babies, and in the second month most of them do. (1985, 43)

As evidence of this is the fact that parents usually refer to newborns as "the baby," rather than by the child's name, for much of the first month. While both birth mothers and adoptive mothers have a similar experience in this regard, it may be more upsetting to adoptive mothers, as it reinforces their fear that they will not be able to love a child they did not give birth to. For fathers, the sense of love for their babies usually does not set in until sometime after the fifth month. We must add, however, that even though parents usually do not "fall in love" with their babies immediately, this is not to say that they may not have a deep sense of caring and concern, even infatuation, for them.

If Moved During the First Month
When children are moved during the first month of life, the transition is relatively easy. Because infants at this age have not yet begun to associate

the mother or other primary caretaker with comfort, another adult can usually step in with few problems, so long as a routine to fulfill the bonding cycle is established.

Following placement of a newborn in your home, your most important goals as parent are to keep the baby's schedule as routine as possible, and to build a sense of comfort for the baby. Fulfilling the bonding cycle is relatively easy at this stage, but by keeping to a basic schedule, you will be able to make up for the repetitions of the bonding cycle you missed before the child came to you. This does not mean that if you must be late with a feeding or delay a diaper change, you will throw the entire cycle off kilter and thus fail to bond with your child. Just keep things as routine as possible. It is the preponderance of comfortable times, as opposed to a few painful or uncomfortable moments, that is important for your baby.

To further enhance bonding at this time, you can carry your baby in your arms rather than in an infant seat, use a front Gerry®-type carrying pack, and rock the baby more often. All these things will help your baby begin to associate your smell, appearance, sounds, and touch—both tactile (as in textures) and kinesthetic (as in feeling rhythms and the position in which the baby is held)—with comfort and relief.

Watch to see if your baby responds more to any one of these sensations than to others—for instance to touch more than to sound—and then employ that sensation in your quiet, relaxed times with your baby, or when you are trying to calm her. For example, if the baby quiets down better when you sing than when you rock her, sing to her while you are feeding her, even if you really enjoy rocking better.

One tool that may help parents identify their newborn's "likes and dislikes" is the neonatal behavioral assessment scale (NBAS), developed in 1973 and revised in 1984 by T. Berry Brazelton, M.D. The NBAS is designed to interactively assess newborns' innate characteristics and behavioral responses. According to Brazelton, Nugent, and Lester, "The revised NBAS assesses the newborn's behavioral repertoire on 28 behavioral items. . . . The scale measures the coping capacities and the adaptive strategies of the infant that emerge as he recovers from the stresses of labor and delivery and adjusts to the demands of the extrauterine environment" (1987, 783). Brazelton recommends that at least two, but preferably three or more examinations be performed: one each at two to three days after birth, seven to ten days, and again at fourteen days to one month. After the assessments are completed, the findings are explained to the parents to help them interact with their child in ways that will draw out the infant's innate interest in the world, while being sensitive to how much stimuli the infant can tolerate. For example, some infants will fall asleep to shut out certain types of stimuli they find uncomfortable or excessive, while others will simply enjoy and take in those same stimuli.

We encourage adoptive parents whose children are placed during the first month of life to seek an NBAS from a person certified in this interactive assessment tool. Local children's hospitals or perinatal centers may have staff trained to perform NBAS; if not, they should be able to refer you to someone who is. When children are born into a family, their parents often have extended family who can help interpret and offer suggestions for addressing the newborns' behaviors, based on experience with other babies in the family who responded to the world around them in much the same way. Because an adopted child's genetic endowment may lead him to respond to stimuli differently than genetically related children in the adoptive family, adoption agencies should be encouraged to have someone trained in NBAS on staff or available for referrals.

Other points to keep in mind during your child's first month of life are the following:

- While a shared experience of pregnancy or a biological tie can enhance bonding with a newborn, the absence of such an experience is not an inhibitor to bonding.
- To our knowledge, there is no evidence that babies who are breast-fed bond better than those who are bottle-fed. For the infant, the primary advantages of breast-feeding are physiological—such as the transmission of antibodies from the mother to the infant—not psychological. While some adoptive mothers have successfully breast-fed their adopted babies, often the effort it takes a woman who has not recently given birth to produce an adequate supply of milk can create added stress and use up valuable time she could otherwise spend focusing on her baby, other family members, or even herself. If you wish to try, however, go for it; you may find it works just fine for you. If it doesn't work or if you do not care to try, the important thing to remember when bottle-feeding a newborn is simply to cradle the baby at about breast level, facing you, to allow eye contact with the infant.

If the First Month Does Not Go Well
Though children almost always do well when moved during the first month (autism), if this stage of development does not go well somewhere with someone, the child is likely to have continued difficulty throughout childhood. A child who has not had a healthy autism stage will have difficulty differentiating between his internal body and his external body, as well as between different sensations. He will lack the ability to self-sooth, have difficulty delaying gratification, and have poor self-esteem. The grief process, too, will be more difficult for such children because they do not know how to experience relief from frustration and pain. As a child is returned

to a state of relaxation during the bonding cycle, he learns such relief as well as pleasure and security. If his needs were not adequately met, he may have poor self-esteem because of his inability to experience pleasure (and positive self-esteem is pleasure with oneself).

Factors that can inhibit a healthy autism stage include the child's physical condition, especially if she has an illness or congenital problem that prevents her from completing the bonding cycle and returning to a state of relaxation; stresses in the primary caretaker's life that prevent him or her from providing adequate care; a poor parent/child fit in which the parent is unable to identify the child's needs, even if he or she has been able to do so with a previous child; and abuse or neglect.

Some of the symptoms in older children that autism may not have gone well include the following:

Inability to recognize when they are injured, or reacting out of proportion to the injury (for instance screaming when they are gently bumped).

Apparent lack of personal hygiene. Because these children have not developed the ability to differentiate among sensations or between their internal and external body, they may be inclined to have bowel- and bladder-control problems several years or more past the age children normally gain control, and then fail to recognize that they are wet or soiled when they have an accident. Adolescent girls may not recognize when their menstrual period is beginning or may not change their pads frequently enough.

Strong aggressive drives or excessive passiveness. It is normal for children at various stages of development to have an unrealistic sense of omnipotence, while at the same time being dependent on adults. But children who have had an unhealthy first month of life, during which their physical needs were not adequately met, often feel utterly powerless. As a result of this sense of powerlessness, aggressive drives such as anger and frustration may predominate among the child's emotions, because from the child's experience, they must first reach a point of extreme frustration and pain before their needs will be met.

On the other hand, children who had a poor autism stage may also be excessively passive, neglecting to even ask for what they need. During autism, such children learned that aggressiveness doesn't bring comfort, so why bother. Whether one eats or has other needs met is seemingly a whim of nature for these children, and they often are left feeling very insecure.

Fortunately, for the vast majority of children the first month of life goes well. The normal adult response to a newborn is to meet the child's needs.

That is why most people are so appalled when they hear of a newborn being abused or neglected.

Symbiosis: Two to Five Months of Age

Symbiosis is the stage during which infants begin to interact socially with other people, particularly the mother. At about two months of age, the baby's first smiles appear. At this point, the baby smiles at people, but does not restrict the smiles to just one person. By the end of symbiosis the baby will smile more frequently at the mothering figure than at other people, but will also smile at the father. This marks the beginning of the baby's first real relationships.

The infant's first relationship with her parents comes out of having her physical needs met. But by about four and a half months, a real social relationship is apparent between mother and child. Greenspan and Greenspan (1985) refer to this interaction as *wooing*. It begins with the parent wooing the child with smiles, coos, touch, rocking, and a great deal of eye contact to elicit a smile from the child. Gradually, the baby begins to initiate the wooing by making sounds or smiling to gain the mother's attention. Such wooing is an integral part of the positive interaction cycle, reinforcing the parent's claiming and the child's sense of belonging. By the end of symbiosis, the primary sign of healthy attachment between parent and child is that the child not only responds to the parent's wooing, but will also initiate interaction by wooing the parent. Greenspan and Greenspan write:

> Over time, your baby should be showing an increasing capacity to maintain a loving exchange. The interchange that lasted for a minute or two should grow to five or even ten minutes. When the wooing is interrupted by a loud noise or a jostle, a baby whose attachment is stable will quickly be able to return to a state of involvement with you. This stability reflects, in part, the baby's capacity to cope with stress and maintain his or her developmental accomplishments.
>
> With a baby whose attachment is less stable, you may have to spend more time, first wooing baby, then letting the baby woo you. Pay special attention to what helps your baby recover after stress—for instance, a calming smile, soothing voice, gentle massaging, or rhythmic motion. (1985, 45)

A healthy symbiosis stage is based on a healthy autism stage. If the child's physical needs were met most of the time during autism, the child is free to turn toward more social relationships. Much of the social relationship during symbiosis, however, is still focused on meeting the child's physical needs. But as those needs are repeatedly met, the baby begins to take comfort in the mother's presence, voice, touch, or smell as assurance that the physical need is about to be met. This is the root of the ability to delay gratification and the very early beginnings of logical thinking ("I'm hungry. I cry. Mom comes. I will be fed soon. I can stop crying").

The term symbiosis refers to the child's perception that he is one with the mother. The infant's self-concept changes during symbiosis from "I am the universe" during the fog stage to "We are the universe," with the "we" referring to the infant and the mother. Because the infant perceives herself as one with the mother, the mother's comforting presence is also experienced as self-comforting. This contributes to the baby's sense of omnipotence during this stage. Furthermore, if the mother and child dyad is the child's universe, and all is safe within that relationship, then the world is a safe and comforting place. This sense of safety and trust protects the infant against the fear of being destroyed during the first year of life. Without this protection the infant feels incredibly vulnerable. Healthy symbiosis also offers a very early precursor to positive self-image and identity.

Family Life Cycle

The sense of oneness the infant experiences during symbiosis is also experienced by the mother figure. This is the time during which the mother "falls in love" with her baby. As the positive interaction cycle moves into full swing, with the baby responding socially to the mother and even initiating interactions, the mother's focus naturally turns increasingly to the child. This focus is often more intense with first children because the mother is not only concentrating on the baby, but also on mastering her role as parent. Mothers who return to work during this stage of their baby's life often report feeling focused on the baby even when at work. They may also feel a sense of guilt or regret for not being with their babies.

As the mother's focus on the baby intensifies, the father's feelings of loneliness and of being left out heighten. Sensing Mom's absorption with the baby, other siblings in the family may also feel left out or become jealous of the baby. Often the mother's needs for physical contact are still being met through the baby, leaving her less likely to turn to her husband for physical or sexual contact. Furthermore, the continued demands of meeting the baby's physical needs may leave the mother exhausted most of the time.

Couples can do several things to help relieve some of the tensions of this period. For example, fathers might share in the night feedings or bring the baby to the mother to feed in bed. This not only provides closeness and inclusiveness for the father, but also decreases the mother's level of exhaustion, leaving her more likely to have energy for an intimate emotional and sexual relationship with her husband.

While the mother is engrossed in the baby, the father often finds his relationships with other children in the family growing closer as he helps fill the gaps in meeting the needs previously met by the mother. Families, however, might also plan time for the father to care for the baby while the mother spends time with the other children. And perhaps most important, both parents need to regularly plan time to spend alone with each other.

If Moved During Symbiosis

Babies who are placed in adoptive homes between the ages of two and five months usually adjust well. But such a move still creates what we would call a "benign trauma" for the child. Adoptive parents need to take extra measures to ensure that the trust the child has begun to develop in the previous caretaker is transferred to them.

Even at such a young age, transfer of authority is important. It is helpful to visit the infant prior to placement, with the previous caretaker present. Transfer of authority is achieved in gradual steps. You might begin by offering the child a toy while she is sitting on her foster parent's lap. When she is comfortable accepting a toy or responding in other types of play, you might take over a feeding or spend time holding her. Eventually, the goal is to take over all care of the child (diaper changes, feeding, comforting, and playing) in the caretaker's presence and then alone. This may take several visits, and even after your baby clearly feels safe with you, she may still seem "distressed" and show signs of an infantile form of grief for a short time after placement.

With separation from the previous mothering figure, the infant begins to lose the sense of safety and comfort she provided. You may notice that your child is easily startled, much the same as a one-month-old (in the fog stage) would be. To help your child begin to associate you with comfort (or to transfer the bond), it helps to increase the moments of physical closeness between you and your child. Instead of carrying your baby in an infant seat, hold him in your arms, bringing the seat along if you will be needing it. You might also carry your baby in a Gerry®-type front carrier as you work or move around the house, to further help him become accustomed to your rhythms, smell, voice, and touch.

In essence, you will be making up for the time you missed with your baby before he came to you and doing many things you might normally do with a newborn. While this "regression" is important, be sure to keep in mind your baby's chronological age and what tasks infants normally are working on at that age. For example, while you will want to increase moments of eye contact and cuddling with your baby, you will also need to provide times when she is turned away from you to see the world around her, and plenty of "floor time" (time when she is lying on her back or stomach on the floor with toys close by to explore and play with) to ensure continued development of gross- and fine-motor skills.

This basic advice holds true for children of all ages; while your child may regress following a move or need your help or encouragement to regress to make up for an uncompleted developmental stage, you also need to encourage your child to continue with any age-appropriate developmental tasks he may be working on.

Wooing and comforting your baby may be easier if you know what she has responded well to in the past. If you are unable to discuss this with the previous caretaker, ask the placement worker to gather this information for you. For example, does a certain lullaby or rhythmic movement help her calm down? Are there certain "games" she takes pleasure in? Do certain sounds, sensations, or objects startle her more than others? Bear in mind, however, that what worked for someone else might not work for you—but at least you will have more information to begin with.

Whether your child has just arrived in your home or has been with you since birth, you can help smooth "negative" reactions to specific things by placing them in proximity to things your baby does enjoy. Begin by listing which sounds, types of touch, rhythms or movements, positions, and sights your baby seems to like and which ones he dislikes. For example, babies and young children are sometimes startled or frightened by men with facial hair. If the baby's adoptive father has a beard and doesn't particularly wish to shave it off, he might approach the baby singing a song the baby usually finds soothing, or rock the baby in a rhythm she normally finds comforting. If you find it difficult to identify which sensations help your baby return to a calm state and which seem to make matters worse, ask a friend, counselor, or your pediatrician to observe you with the baby to help identify these things.

A word about day care. It is common for children to begin day care at about six to eight weeks of age. While it is clear that many families today must have two incomes to make ends meet—and, of course, for single parents, taking an extended leave of absence is likely out of the question— if at all possible, adoptive parents should try to delay placing an adopted child in day care for *at least* three to five months following placement— the longer the better. Parental or maternity leave serves more than just to allow a birth mother to recuperate following delivery. It also provides time to establish healthy bonding and attachment. For parents who have just adopted a child between the ages of two and five months, this also allows them time needed with the child to substitute the new mother for the previous mother as the child's source of comfort and safety. While some employers provide parental leave for adoptive parents as well as birth parents, others do not, and you may have to advocate for the same leave privileges your employer offers to birth parents. To maximize the time you have to spend at home with your new child, consider reserving your vacation time for your child's arrival. You may also find it necessary to explore other options to enable you to have this time with your child—possibly even quitting work, at least temporarily.

If Symbiosis Does Not Go Well
One of the primary advantages of the foster care system over orphanages is that children are cared for by just one or two adults. Such one-on-one care is particularly important during infancy and early childhood.

As with the first month, symbiosis goes well for the vast majority of children. For children in institutionalized settings, such as orphanages, where care is provided by numerous adults, or in cases of neglect, symbiosis may not go well. Infants who have not had a healthy symbiotic stage are usually unresponsive to social interaction and other stimuli (including discomfort), and may be fretful, scream incessantly, or both. Whether utterly unresponsive or constantly crying, such children are unable to return to the state of relaxation necessary to complete the bonding cycle. Without successful completion of the bonding cycle, the child does not develop trust in the world around him. If symbiosis and fog do not go well, the frustration and fear the infant feels may continue into later years, eventually turning to an ongoing state of rage, which is a combination of hopelessness, helplessness, and anger. Likewise, the infant's ideation of omnipotence remains stuck at this stage of development. A child who does not have a comforting mother figure (male or female) feels omnipotent in causing bad things to happen, which leads eventually to low self-esteem and a negative identity.

An unhealthy symbiotic stage can also lead to behavior problems, and learning and developmental delays throughout childhood as the child remains focused on meeting his primary needs and surviving. Without healthy bonding and attachment to a parent, the child is not free to focus his attention on things other than survival. Furthermore, if a child fails to learn to soothe herself or accept comfort and to delay gratification, she may have problems with hyperactivity.

Another scenario that sometimes occurs when symbiosis does not go well is that the child will self-soothe, but not accept comfort from others. As we discussed in the chapter on bonding and attachment, if the child and parent are unable to experience a cycle of positive interactions, the child will not form a healthy attachment, thus affecting her ability to form healthy self-esteem and positive relationships. A classic example of this type of self-soothing is children who rock themselves (we aren't talking about in a rocking chair).

There are, however, ways to help a child who exclusively self-soothes to accept and associate comfort with the parent. While the child is rocking or doing whatever it is she does to comfort herself, offer another form of comfort in tandem with that activity. In other words, if the child is rocking, you might rub her back or sing a song to add to her sense of comfort. At other times, when the baby is not upset, you can swaddle him loosely in a blanket and hold him in the breast-feeding position, as you would a newborn. (This latter technique, however, should be reserved for very young children, unless it is done under professional guidance. For older children, "holding" therapy can be enraging and cause more problems than it cures if not done carefully under professional supervision.) Watch to see what sensations your child is most responsive to. Eventually your child will turn to you for comfort instead of turning immediately to himself, enabling both of you to complete the bonding and positive interaction cycles in a healthy way. Once a healthy attachment is established, if your child turns to the same self-soothing techniques as before, you should not be concerned. It is normal and healthy for children to comfort themselves, so long as they also have trust in and can accept comfort from others.

For Further Reading

• *First Feelings: Milestones in the Emotional Development of Your Baby and Child* by Stanley Greenspan, M.D., and Nancy Thorndike Greenspan. New York: Penguin, 1985.

An excellent book for all parents of infants. The Greenspans trace children's emotional growth from birth to age five, teaching parents ways to promote healthy emotional development and attachment. Photographs round out the text by illustrating parent/child interactions the authors discuss.

9

The Older Infant—
Separation and
Individuation:
Six to Thirty-Six Months

*A*fter working hard during the first four and one-half to five months
to establish the mother/child bond and entity, the child's next developmental task is to separate from the mother figure and begin to establish an identity of her own—a process which then continues throughout life. Given a secure relationship with their parents, by three years of age most children have developed a separate identity. The security established throughout these early years enables the three-year-old to feel confident and safe when away from the parent for short periods of time, such as when left for several hours with a baby sitter or while at day care. By three, a well-attached child is able to transfer this sense of security from parent to other adults, such as a day care provider.

The separation-individuation phase of development is generally divided into four overlapping stages: differentiation (five to ten months), practicing (nine to eighteen months), rapprochement (fifteen to twenty-two months), and consolidation of individuation (twenty-one to thirty-six months). We will look at the dynamics of each of these stages separately.

Differentiation: Five to Ten Months

The primary theme of differentiation is the baby's increasing awareness of himself as separate and different from his mother. The child's growing social, motor, and language skills help facilitate this awareness as the child is more and more able to interact with other people and explore his environment. The first sign that differentiation has begun is when the infant begins to prefer facing away from the parent when held. This is also the age when infants typically begin to sit unassisted, crawl, and sometimes even walk, allowing for greater mobility and independence in exploring their surroundings. The infant's interaction with others is further enhanced as the child begins to babble in syllables. The process of differentiation is aided not only by the baby's exploration of the world around him and interaction with other people, but also through his exploration of his mother's features through touching and grabbing at her face, ears, hair, and teeth.

This age can be an exciting time for other family members as the baby begins to show more interest in them. Babies at this age also find strangers fascinating and will normally stare and visually explore strangers' faces. Most babies, however, will not use their hands to explore a stranger's features. If the parent is present, a five-month-old baby who is being held by a stranger will look back, both to compare the stranger's features with those of the parent and to reassure herself that Mom or Dad is still there. An early sign that there may have been difficulty during autism and symbiosis is if the baby does not do this "flirting" with strangers.

By six or seven months, however, stranger anxiety usually begins. While a well-attached baby may still react positively to strangers if her mother is close by or holding her, it is common for babies of this age to be fearful when an unfamiliar person approaches, and cry or refuse to look at the stranger. Unlike during the earlier developmental stages, the baby may no longer be comfortable going to unfamiliar people.

Stranger anxiety is closely followed by separation anxiety. As the infant's awareness of the separateness of himself from his mother grows, so also does his fear of being separated from her. Separation anxiety usually begins at about seven to ten months and often continues until twenty-four months or even later. In fact, the older the infant gets, the more she may experience separation anxiety. Some children cry and physically cling to the mother when she is about to leave and continue crying for a while after she is gone. Other children become withdrawn, taking little interest in the person or people in whose care they have been left or in their surroundings; but when the parent returns, they brighten up again. Infants who are doing well in day care will usually be responsive and accept cuddling from the care providers, but their responsiveness often increases when either parent returns to pick them up. If the parent has been away for a long period (an eight-hour day or longer), some children will hug once and then turn away or withdraw for a half hour or so before warming up to the parent; others may turn away first, waiting a while before hugging or otherwise acknowledging the parent's presence.

Around five to seven months, babies also enjoy playing peekaboo, eventually initiating the game themselves. The baby's interest in and ability to play peekaboo games is a very important developmental marker, as it shows that the child is beginning to learn object constancy: that an object or person (such as Dad) still exists even when out of baby's sight.

Family Life Cycle

For fathers, this stage of development works much like symbiosis for mothers in attaching with the baby. With the baby more responsive to him, the father begins to feel love for his baby. He is also less likely than he was during the earlier months to feel left out or lonely. This is in part because the baby is now responding to him to a greater degree and in part because his partner—the mother—is also "hatching" (Eagan 1985, 102) from her intense focus on the baby.

Just as the baby begins to separate from the mother, the mother separates from the baby. She begins to focus on who she is as an adult woman and on regaining the sense of self she had before she became a mother. If she has not returned to work, she may find herself wanting to go back now. If she is already working, she may feel less preoccupied with the baby during her work day. Women who are not employed outside the home, and have no plans to be, often pick up other interests at about this time, or simply feel more able to leave the house with the baby.

For many women, this is also about the time when their sense of sexuality begins to return, thereby relieving some of the tension that may have developed in the marital relationship. This regained sexual and emotional relationship between the parents, together with the father's new relationship with the baby finally brings balance to the family triad; no longer does the mother/child dyad outweigh the intensity of the other relationships in the family. The mother's regained sense of sexuality stems from more than a physical recovery from childbirth. Adoptive mothers and mothers who have given birth alike must undergo a psychological adjustment of meshing the roles of mother (who is often seen as a nonsexual being) and those of lover, wife, and adult sexual woman. Possible barriers to this integration of roles and return of sexual desire include interruptions from the baby, fear of being interrupted or of waking the baby, change in spontaneity, or simply no longer having the option to be spontaneous. Men, too, may have difficulty integrating their images of the mother their partner has now become with the lover and wife she used to be. In either case, both husband and wife may become frustrated at about this time if the other—or themselves—

remains uninterested in their sexual relationship, thereby leading to increased marital tension.

While it would seem that the mother's reemergence as an individual would be an exciting and relieving time, it isn't always experienced so positively by all women. "When this change begins," writes Eagan (1985, 104), "women often feel confused, disoriented and frustrated." As mother and baby begin to separate, the mother may experience the change as a loss. The child may not want to be cuddled as often, sometimes even pulling away from the mother or crying. For some mothers, the grief over the baby's "growing up" may be particularly acute, especially if the baby is less passive during feedings or wants to hold his own bottle, or simply as the "nursing" experiences (whether by bottle- or breast-feeding) become less frequent with the introduction of solid foods. Furthermore, as the child's stranger and separation anxieties increase, the mother—or the father—may feel guilty when leaving the child even for a few hours. This guilt in turn may heighten the mother's feelings of confusion and frustration as she tries to reestablish her other adult roles. Separation anxiety usually intensifies before it gets better. The closer an infant gets to one year of age, the greater the anxiety usually becomes. This can be particularly difficult for adoptive parents, who are more inclined to hesitate at leaving their child for fear that their child will feel insecure or that the separation will somehow interfere with bonding and attachment. By not leaving, however, the parents validate the child's fears that he is not safe without them. Children learn security when parents leave and then return. Never leaving the child does not enhance attachment; and in fact, your child's anxiety at your leaving is a sign that healthy attachment is occurring. Furthermore, to be a healthy adult, every parent needs some time away from the children to refuel. While it is not healthy to leave a child all the time, both parent and child benefit from occasional brief absences from one another.

If Moved During Differentiation

The infant's reaction to a move during the differentiation stage of development depends on whether or not the child has moved into separation anxiety. But in either case, the goal is to transfer the trust or bond your child had with her previous caretaker to you as the new parent.

Children moved during the early part of differentiation may experience a temporary delay in their exploration of the world outside the mother/child relationship. Such children may also show signs of premature or heightened stranger anxiety as a result of the move experience. Whether the child actually regresses to symbiosis with the new parents or is simply delaying the exploration that is a natural part of differentiation, parents can help their child by following the advice in Chapter 8 for helping a baby in symbiosis adjust to the move.

Children who have already begun to experience separation anxiety often have more difficulty attaching to new parents than do children at earlier ages. Not only has their fear of losing their mother been realized, but babies at this age have a more intense grief reaction to the loss than do younger infants. Often, however, these difficulties go unrecognized because the babies find ways to cope with the change without attaching to the new parents. Fortunately, babies in differentiation can be helped to transfer their attachment to new parents. Here are some things you can do:

Transfer authority. Prior to placement, visit your child in the presence of the previous caretaker, gradually taking over feeding and other caretaking while your child is in a familiar setting with familiar people. As your baby grows more comfortable with you, begin to initiate play, perhaps by first handing the baby toys or playing peekaboo or other games the baby enjoys.

Maintain your baby's routine. Now is not a good time to dramatically change your baby's schedule. Find out what your baby's daily schedule was like in his previous home and try to establish a similar one once he is in your home. For instance, if he has been napping in the afternoon, don't try to change his nap time to morning. Likewise, feeding times are best kept at about the same times as before. As your child grows more accustomed to you, showing signs of attaching and of progressing developmentally, you can begin to gradually alter the daily routine. Keep in mind that babies sometimes change the routine themselves—for instance, by no longer taking a morning nap. If this happens, go with the flow. Don't try to force your baby to continue in a routine that no longer meets his needs.

Play games with your baby and initiate positive interaction. Find out what games your baby enjoyed with her previous caretaker, both immediately prior to the move and at earlier ages. Use these games to initiate positive interactions, beginning with those your child has most recently learned and liked. If your baby does not respond or does not seem to be enjoying the game (has a "flat affect"), try some of the games she liked to play at an earlier age. Sometimes a particular game may trigger your baby's grief for her previous caretaker. If your baby is unresponsive to a game you have been told she has always enjoyed, simply set it aside, perhaps to try again in a few weeks.

Allow your baby to grieve. Adoptive parents who have been through this before will tell you that the cry of a grieving baby is different from any other cry. As with grieving adults, there may be times when your baby will not accept consolation. You need to help your child through the grief by allowing her to cry, without abandoning her to it. Try holding your baby. If she continues to cry for more than about ten minutes, let her lie down, with you sitting near her and touching her until she is able to relax. You might also try singing a soothing lullaby. Such cries can be very painful—even grating—for parents to listen to because of their pitch, continuousness, or mournful sound. If you are finding it difficult to endure the sound, try earplugs or a Walkman with a soothing tape. This will help you stay in the room with your baby to offer the comfort and presence she needs, while preventing you from becoming overly frustrated or feeling that the crying is a personal thing against you. When your baby finally begins to wind down, pick her up. She may cry harder at first, but that's OK. By offering your comfort at this time, you will help your baby begin to associate you with the comfort, even though she has probably generated it herself. You might try rocking her to sleep, swaddling her loosely in a blanket, or simply holding her close.

Seek a balance between regression and age-appropriate interactions. As we've mentioned earlier in this chapter, children often need to repeat parts of a previously completed developmental stage to help make up for lost time with the new parent and to bring the new relationship up to par. For example, babies at this age like to spend much of their time upright and looking outward. But for at least a few minutes a day, try to hold your baby in a nursing position, perhaps even loosely swaddled. Your baby may resist at first, but try to find a time of day when he is most responsive to being held in this way—perhaps while having a bottle before bedtime or a nap. The goal is to facilitate the eye contact and relaxation achieved during the nurturing of the earlier months. At the same time, allow plenty of opportunities throughout the rest of the day for age-appropriate interactions.

Other reactions children may have at this age are to move prematurely into the next stage of development, or to "self-parent." If your child seems unusually precocious, especially within the first few months after placement, be particularly certain to watch for signs that she is still attaching. Parents and professionals may become so encouraged and excited about a child's rapid development—for instance, walking or crawling at such an early age—that they miss the signals that the child is not attaching. Again, one sign to look for at this age is whether your child looks back at you for security when strangers are present or when she is exploring a new environment.

Children who have lived in orphanages prior to placement or who had poor attachment with their previous caretakers may also show signs of self-parenting or self-soothing. Rocking—sideways, or back and forth—is one way infants self-soothe. As discussed in Chapter 8's section on symbiosis, if your child is self-soothing, he may not be associating you with comfort and relaxation. Without such association, attachment is inhibited because the positive interaction cycle cannot be completed. By gradually participating with your child while he is comforting himself, you will help him grow to associate you with relief. If your child is self-rocking, put him in a larger bed and rock alongside him. If he is banging his head, place a pillow or your hand on the surface where he is banging. Gently massaging the back of your child's neck while he is banging his head may also loosen his neck muscles and stop the banging.

If Differentiation Does Not Go Well

Failure to differentiate is extremely rare. A more common problem, however, occurs when an infant differentiates too soon, before she has been able to fully experience the closeness of symbiosis. This may happen if an infant is moved in the middle of symbiosis or early on in differentiation, when severe medical conditions inhibit the infant's ability to experience the parents' comfort, or if the parents are overprotective (sometimes because of medical conditions) to the point that the infant feels smothered and reacts by pulling away before she is developmentally ready.

Premature differentiation leads the infant to develop compensatory techniques to mitigate anxiety and provide comfort. Two common self-comforting techniques are self-rocking and fast-and-frantic sucking. The child using these techniques will eventually fall asleep from exhaustion and the repetitive rhythm, without truly achieving comfort. Head banging is the most common way infants try to mitigate anxiety alone. Some will continue to the point of bruising, and still keep going. A child who is rocking or head banging for self-comfort will usually have an intense expression on her face and a far-off, often glazed, look in her eyes. Children with normal development will sometimes rock or bang their heads on a soft surface for the pleasure of the rhythm; the key difference is that these children are calm, laughing or having a good time, while a child in premature differentiation is not.

Some children will also take to self-feeding. A child who is simply very independent may do this, too, but will still accept the parents' help sometimes, perhaps before bed or a nap. A child who is differentiating too early will not accept spoon feeding or having the parent hold a bottle or cup for him, even occasionally.

Premature differentiation can lead to three types of problems:

Premature ego development. Even at a very young age, these children act as if they can handle any crisis. Unfortunately, they also tend to live in a crisis mode, either creating their own crises, or perpetually anticipating one around every corner. Thus, such children do not feel safe to explore the world or to comfortably develop a sense of curiosity. A child with premature ego development will have a false sense of confidence, with no real mastery, making even the smallest of life's changes into traumatic events.

False sense of self. If differentiation begins too early, instead of differentiating himself from other people, the child may become like a chameleon, taking on the characteristics of whomever he happens to be with at the moment, with no thread of personal core identity.

Grandiose ideation. Instead of developing a real sense of his own abilities, as the child gets older—even into adulthood—he will place more value on creating and believing fantasies about his abilities and stature in life. Those who have a realistic vision of their attainments, but grandiose ideation of their abilities, will become frustrated with their reality, feeling they are being unfairly deprived their just desserts.

Practicing: Nine to Eighteen Months

The term practicing refers to the infant's "practicing" at being a separate, independent individual using his newly attained motor skills. The stage is generally divided into early and late practicing: Early practicing coincides with active creeping and crawling, while late practicing is considered to be when the child is able to walk.

During practicing, the child has a "love affair with the world" (Greenacre 1957, as quoted by Edward, Ruskin, and Turrini 1981, 20). Not only is the child excited about discovering the world around her, but parents and other adults also take joy in watching the child grow and achieve new skills. Such joy and encouragement is important because it builds the child's self-esteem and enhances her joy at her own accomplishments. The child's focus during practicing is on inanimate objects and the other-than-mother world. At about eight months, visual memory develops, allowing the child to hold the image of the mother in her mind. This provides a secure base from which the child may begin to venture out.

Other characteristics of this age include the following:

Growing father-child relationship. The interest the child began to take in other family members during differentiation is continued in practicing, leading to stronger relationships between the child and her father and siblings. Though the father also provides nurturing, one of his most important roles is to help the child explore the other-than-mother world. In single-parent families, there is almost always someone who fulfills this fathering role, stimulating the child to explore. Though the mother shows interest and joy in her child's accomplishments, it is helpful for the child to have another person available with whom she can explore. Again, the roles of mother figure and father figure are not gender dependent. When the sole parent is the child's father, though male, he is probably fulfilling the role of the mother figure; thus, single fathers may need another person to help fulfill the child's need for a father figure who will help her explore.

Despite the growing relationship between father and child, children usually turn to their mothers when tired, ill, or in need of comfort. In fact, this is a sign of healthy attachment at this age. Children in this developmental stage who are not attaching well will not turn to, or will have difficulty accepting comfort from, the mothering person, whether a birth parent or an adoptive parent.

Growing interest in toys. At earlier ages, the child was fascinated by human faces. Now, however, there is growing interest in toys and other inanimate objects. Initially the infant explores primarily those toys that are handed to him, but eventually he finds objects on his own which he wants to explore. If you haven't already child-proofed your home, now is the time to do it!

Enjoyment of chasing games. Children at this age love to be chased and caught, but once caught they also like to be let go. Children use games to build skills. In this case, the chase is a physical enactment of the child's balancing between separateness from and oneness with the parent. It is the next step up from peekaboo.

Growing ability to delay gratification and use transitional objects. During practicing, the child's ability to delay gratification expands from several minutes to segments of hours. Often this is facilitated by a transitional object, such as a blanket, stuffed toy, or even a thumb, which the child also uses to help him self-soothe and handle anxiety. The transitional object reminds the child of the mother and the comfort and safety she provides. The smell and texture of the object are vital components of its comforting qualities, which is why it is often better not to wash the object, even though it is filthy. Once washed, it may take awhile before the object regains its ability to soothe the child. Not all children, however, have or need transitional objects. If your child does have one, you may find that it makes your life a little easier.

The child's growing ability to delay gratification and the presence of a transitional object both show that the child is beginning to internalize the mother's image and the sense of security she provides. They also demonstrate that the child is beginning to learn to self-soothe.

Checking back and refueling. As the child ventures out to explore the world around him, he will also repeatedly check back visually or physically with the mother for reassurance that she is still there and that it is safe for him to continue. When he has gone as far as he desires, he will return to the parent, either joyfully, in need of comfort, or simply to check in. Once refueled with a hug, comfort, or a smile and an encouraging word, most children wriggle off mom's lap and return to their exploration.

Joy versus temper tantrums. Practicing is characterized by both stages of equilibrium and disequilibrium. Early practicing is usually a time of joy in accomplishments; but once the child has begun to master walking in late practicing, fear and frustration often set in as he begins to want to do more than he is capable of. Language development also plays a role in this frustration as the child begins to use words and phrases, but is still unable to fully communicate all of his wants and needs. The "terrible twos" often set in during late practicing. The temper tantrums of fifteen- to eighteen-month-olds, however, stem from fear, powerlessness, frustration, and humiliation as the child's desires exceed his capabilities. At this age, tantrums serve to discharge the child's frustration; rarely are they used at this point in development for self-assertion or to coerce others into allowing the child to have his own way. In the early months of the second year of life, tantrums are usually characterized by crying, kicking, and screaming, rather than aggression toward others (Fahlberg, *Child Development*, 1982, 22).

Learning outlines of own body. At the same time the child is learning to crawl and walk, she is also learning her physical dimensions. The combination of less-than-masterful coordination skills and lack of full awareness of spatial relationships, particularly of the child's own body, leads to many bumps and bruises at this age. Children in this stage of development also begin to learn gender identification. Boys, in particular, notice and take interest and pleasure in their genitals at this age. This is natural and nothing to be concerned about.

Separation anxiety. The separation anxiety that began during the differentiation phase of development continues into the practicing stage, often peaking at about twelve months and then subsiding gradually. It is not unusual, however, for children to continue to experience separation anxiety throughout this phase.

Family Life Cycle

As the father and other family members begin to develop stronger relationships with the baby, the mother's relationship with the baby takes on a new form. For the first time, the mother finds herself often taking a back seat to other people as far as her child's interest and attention are concerned. She remains, however, an essential source of refueling and an anchor of safety for her child, even though she increasingly sees the child turn away from her and toward other people. For some mothers this can be very difficult, especially if they perceive this normal and healthy turn of events as rejection or if they feel they are losing their baby. To achieve balance in her life, the mother must begin to integrate her other functions in life with her role as mother. In a healthy relationship, the separation from the baby that began during the child's differentiation stage should be continuing now so that the mother no longer needs the extreme closeness with her baby that she had when the baby was younger. While this can be a difficult time for some mothers, others are relieved to find that their child no longer requires their constant mothering presence and focus and that they now have more freedom to pursue other interests or simply to take a little more time for themselves.

Most first-time mothers also experience a change in their relationship with their own mothers at about the time their baby is nine or ten months old (Eagan 1985, 190). The mother turns to her mother for approval of her parenting. If she receives the approval, her sense of having successfully taken on the role model her mother provided for her is reinforced. If she does not receive approval, however, she is faced with additional stress and conflict as she must then work harder to assert that her parenting techniques and her parenting of this child, in particular, are good. Such conflicts between the generations can have an inhibiting effect on the parents' claiming of the child, as their attention turns to some degree from the child as a person to the methods they are using to raise or "manage" the child. Fathers face similar problems when grandparents disapprove of their parenting style or of their children, but they usually are not affected to the degree that mothers are because men traditionally vest less of their self-esteem in their role as parent. Adoptive parents may be particularly sensitive to such disapproval, especially if the grandparents have rejected the adoption or the child. But no matter what the specifics of the situation are, criticism from either side of the family can create stress and difficulty for the parents, especially if the extended family live close by or if there is frequent contact.

If Moved During Practicing

A child who is moved during practicing will need help transferring the trust he has developed with previous caretakers to the adoptive parents in order to feel safe to continue his exploration of the world around him. Though the child is older, the same basic techniques described for helping younger infants transfer trust also apply to the toddler.

Knowing where the child is developmentally and in terms of attachment is important because it tells the adoptive parents what to expect in their own relationship with their child. Age and mobility (crawling or walking) are not the best indicators for determining whether a child has begun practicing. A better way to tell is by observing the child with the current caregiver. If the child is moving away from the caregiver to play and explore, and coming back to "refuel" and reassure himself that the caregiver is still available, he is in the practicing stage and is showing signs of healthy attachment. If the child moves away but does not check back with the caregiver, he may be in practicing, but probably has not attached. If the child is not moving away from the primary caregiver, but is exploring her face while sitting on her lap, then he is probably still working on differentiation and not yet up to the outward exploration of practicing.

Regardless of the child's chronological age, he will not begin the new relationship with his adoptive parents at a developmental stage he has not yet reached under the care of his previous caregivers. A twelve-month-old child who is still in differentiation might be expected to begin building a relationship with the new adoptive parents with behaviors typical of the child in differentiation, even though he is already past the normal age range for this stage. And even these behaviors will probably not begin to appear until the child has had time to become comfortable in the new home (usually about one month after placement). Some children will begin by exploring the mother's face; others must first regress to symbiosis before moving again to differentiation and then on to age-appropriate practicing behaviors, such as moving away and checking back, among others. The cuddling, cooing, and nurturing of symbiosis is an important part of building attachment. Regression back to symbiosis gives the child a needed sense of safety for exploring the world around him, and a feeling of being valued in the new family.

Again, children at this age check back with their parents frequently while playing and exploring to reassure themselves of the parents' presence and approval, both of which reinforce the child's sense of safety. If the child is moving away, but not checking back on his own, parents can artificially instill the checking-back behavior. This can be done by placing a selection of favorite toys (though not *all* of your child's toys) out of your child's reach. Tell your child he may play with those toys if he asks. To reinforce checking back with both parents, Mom can tell the child to check with Dad, and Dad can tell him to ask Mom. So long as the child asks first, he should be allowed to play with those toys. This technique may also be used in other circumstances. For example, when visiting another family, tell your child he must first check with you before going off to play with the other children and before moving with the children to another area of the home (such as from the family room to a child's bedroom or outdoors). Eventually, your child will check back naturally—a sign that he has begun to internalize that you are the source of his safety.

If Practicing Does Not Go Well
The goal of practicing is for the child to experience enough pleasure and self-confidence in exploring the world in her parents' presence that, as she moves into separation and individuation (the next developmental stage), the joy of exploration overcomes her fear of losing her parents. Extreme overprotection can lead the child to frustration and fear rather than joy and self-confidence. At the other end of the spectrum, if the primary parent is not there when the child checks back or if that parent regularly disapproves of the child's exploration or accomplishments, the same negative results may occur. Poor parent/child fit is one possible factor preventing parents from expressing joy at what their child sees as an accomplishment. When a child cannot secure positive attention, he is likely to seek negative attention. Other possible complications of an unhealthy practicing stage include the following:

Inability to overcome separation anxiety. Instead of the normal waning of separation anxiety, these fears may persist, eventually interfering with completion of future developmental tasks.

Withdrawal, with limited ability to experience joy. Practicing builds on the shared joy established between parent and child in healthy symbiosis. The child learns to take joy in his own accomplishments and personhood, as well as from interactions with his parents. If the child is unable to accept or the parents are unable to express joy in the child's accomplishments, he will not experience joy in just being himself—a primary foundation for positive self-esteem. When there is little or no joy or sense of accomplishment between the inevitable toddler temper tantrums, the child may become withdrawn or develop a frustrated sense of hopelessness, which often appears similar to depression. The child may also continue to feel helpless and bewildered into later years.

Low tolerance of frustration. Joy in accomplishments counterbalances the frustration toddlers often feel because of their inability to exert their will on people and objects around them. Without this counterbalance, the child will have difficulty learning to mitigate frustration and control aggressiveness. Instead of biting other people when frustrated, then learning that this is not acceptable and finding another means to express or control frustration—as most children do—the child will build an increasingly large repertoire of aggressive behaviors and continue to use the full arsenal beyond the normal ages for such behaviors. For example, at age ten the child will still be biting others when angry, just as a toddler would.

Emotional hypersensitivity, paranoia, worry, and aggressiveness are all traits that may be inherited (Bouchard 1984, 57; Wellborn 1987, 62). For the child who has any of these traits in his genetic endowment, poor practicing can make them more intense, while healthy practicing may lessen their severity.

Reparenting techniques described later in this chapter may help the child who is struggling through practicing now or showing symptoms of unhealthy practicing in the past.

Rapprochement: Fifteen to Twenty-Two Months

Mahler (1972) refers to much of the second year of life as *rapprochement*, which means "establishing friendly relations." Other people call this time the "terrible twos." Because of the many developmental milestones children are working on at this age, they tend to alternate between courting their parents' love, attention, and closeness, and trying their limits.

For the first time since the child was born, the overriding word in the household becomes "no." The child hears it often from the parents, and to their chagrin, the parents hear it all too frequently from the child. The child's increasing abilities put him at higher risk for hurting himself and others, and for damaging things around him, making it necessary for parents to set limits, reinforce positive behavior, and correct negative behavior.

Following a successful practicing stage, the young toddler is much more aware of her physical and emotional separateness from her mother. This awareness, combined with a growing desire to do more than she is capable of and to communicate beyond the limits of her language development, make this a time of disequilibrium. Many children have temper tantrums at this age, but unlike those seen later at about two and a half years, tantrums tend to be a discharge of frustration, as opposed to aggression against someone else. Young toddlers will often kick, cry, and scream during a tantrum, but don't usually lash out at others (Fahlberg, *Child Development*, 1982, 22).

In addition, though young toddlers see themselves as individuals, they don't always perceive other children or adults as human beings with feelings. This egocentric nature often leads toddlers to such behaviors as hitting and kicking when others try to control them; but again, this behavior is not "vindictive." Toddlers also tend to be rough with animals and other children.

Other characteristics and behaviors common to this age include the following:

Wooing and coercion. Increasing awareness of her separateness leads the toddler to actively woo the mother, particularly when Mom's attention is elsewhere. At first, this behavior is usually welcomed by the mother, but as the child's demands for attention increase, many mothers eventually find it annoying. Wooing eventually turns to coercion, with the child physically pulling at the mother or doing other things—including throwing temper tantrums—to gain back her attention. Mahler (1972) refers to this coercion as *rapprochement crisis*. The toddler's goal is to return to a oneness with the mother that excludes not only other people, but also other interests the mother may have beyond the child.

Though irritating, wooing, coercion, and temper tantrums are all normal for this age, but this doesn't mean that as a parent you should simply give in to your child's every desire. Toddlers need firm limits during this time to maintain their sense of safety. They also need times of one-on-one attention. But at this age, it is often impractical—and unhealthy—to give your child the constant attention he would like. Bedtime rituals, story times, and meals all provide good opportunities for you to give your child the full attention he needs. When your toddler attempts to woo your attention at other times—such as when you are trying to talk on the phone, complete a task, or just take half an hour for yourself—it is important to give your child a few seconds or minutes attention and then firmly redirect him to do his own thing. If you consistently give in to your child's wooing or coercion, you give the message that he is indeed not OK without you. Fortunately for parents, since children at this age are still fairly easily distracted, their attention can usually be turned to other activities.

Separation anxiety. The toddler's growing awareness of his individuality at this stage often leads to a return to separation anxiety and shyness or fear of strangers. For times when you must leave your child to go to work or out for the evening, developing some kind of ritual for leave-takings can help reduce subsequent crying or tantrums.

While separation anxiety can be painful for children, it is a natural and necessary part of their development. Often adoptive parents, after learning about the effects of loss on adopted children and the importance of bonding and attachment, are afraid they will cause irreparable damage to their child by leaving her, particularly if the child is crying and begging them not to go. But children need temporary separations from their parents if they are to learn that parents do return and that their parents provide for their safety and care for them even when they are absent. These lessons are what eventually enable the child to experience temporary separations from their parents without trauma.

In addition to more obvious forms of separation anxiety, toddlers also experience an increasing awareness of the marital relationship, the mother's relationships with other people, and the mother/father/child triad. Some children become jealous of their mothers' relationships with others, including the father (what Freud referred to as the *pre-Oedipal stage*). At this age, toddler's relationships are usually much smoother with the father than they are with the mother, simply because the dynamics between father and child are different.

It's important for parents—and adoptive parents, in particular—to understand that all of these behaviors are normal. A child who has recently joined the family may react in a similar manner, experiencing more conflict with the mother than with the father. This, however, is not a rejection of the mother. Like Dr. Dolittle's two-headed llama, toddlers experience a "Pushmi–Pullyu" syndrome; on the one hand they want independence, on the other they want to be immersed in the mother. This obviously leads to frustration, not only for the child, but also for the mother as she deals with the subsequent behavior.

Shadowing and darting. Another behavior commonly seen at this age is shadowing and darting. The child may return to a seemingly constant concern about where Mom is. Often toddlers will follow their parents around (shadowing) or dart away to briefly play or explore and then quickly come back. A good example of darting is the way toddlers play at the park. Simply having the parent within visual and hearing range isn't enough; young children will run back to their parents, say essentially, "See what I did," and run off to do it again. Having learned through the bonding cycle that their security comes from their parents, shadowing and darting in toddlers is a sign of healthy attachment. Shadowing and darting reassure the toddler that his dependent needs will be met while he works on building greater independence.

Language development. During this phase, language development can be both a source of frustration and a means to better self-control for the child. In the early months, frustration may result when he can't express his increasingly complex needs and desires. This is a good time for parents to begin helping the child interpret his feelings and experiences. Such observations as "I know you're angry, but it's not OK to hit" offer validation of the child's feelings, as well as help him to identify what they are. At this age you can also begin to offer the child alternative behaviors for ones you find unacceptable, for instance, stamping your feet instead of hitting another child.

As mentioned previously, "no" becomes a favorite word at this age, especially beginning at about eighteen months. Toddlers use "no" not only out of frustration and to assert their independence, but also as a way of associating with the person in authority. As the sense of omnipotence that carried the child through the first year of life gradually diminishes, the child is more aware than ever before of his own helplessness and powerlessness. By saying "no" the child feels more like those in power—presumably his parents—who at this point are probably saying the word more frequently than even they would like.

Conscience development. The roots of conscience also begin to appear in the second year of life. As you see your child reaching for something she shouldn't, you tell her not to touch it. She touches it anyway, but imitates you by saying "no." As she learns that she isn't supposed to touch that object, she will touch it, tell herself "no" or look back at you for the usual reaction, and then pull her hand back. At this point your child is beginning to learn your standards and values, while associating or imitating you as the person in authority.

Play. Toddlers play more by themselves or alongside other children (parallel play) than *with* other children. As they are still learning ownership, it is often difficult for them to share toys, and fights can arise quickly when more than one toddler wants a particular toy. But play is very important to both the child's social and physical development. It enables the child to master large- and small-motor skills, provides an opportunity to express wishes and fears through symbolic play, acts as a tension reducer, and teaches ways to work out conflicts.

Discovery of gender. Boys and girls alike begin to notice gender differences at about this age. While boys discover their penises for the first time at a much younger age, there is often more discovery now, particularly as attempts at toilet training begin. Growing awareness of adults as individuals leads toddlers to be more aware of the shapes of adults' bodies. As language develops, particularly past the age of twenty-four months, so do questions and comments about gender differences—sometimes without end.

Family Life Cycle

As children become more independent and begin to exert their will with greater intensity, parents often react in ways reminiscent of their own childhoods. Often this leads children to have difficulties in the same areas as their parents. For example, if a parent finds separations difficult, she may overreact to her toddler's separation anxiety, because deep down she feels much the same as he does. Her reaction, however, tells the child that he really does have cause to fear the separation. In this way the parent's difficulty is passed on to the child. Similarly, a child's refusal to cooperate with the parent's wishes can trigger the parent's own issues of powerlessness and drives for autonomy.

If certain areas of your child's behavior are particularly frustrating or irritating, look first to see if they are normal given your child's age. If they are not, they may be a clue to other problems or unmet needs your child may have. In addition to looking for the cause of the behavior, parents also need to examine themselves to determine if they perhaps are "overreacting." Control is an issue at one time or another in most relationships, but especially when a child is working to establish autonomy. Is the child's behavior frustrating to you because you cannot control it? Check to see if the real issue is lack of control or if the behavior is truly detrimental to the child or others. One way to check this out is to ask yourself if you have felt similarly in other situations. Make a list of those other times and think about what was happening then. You may find that your child's behavior is reminding you of past situations, either when you were your child's age or in working with another child at that age.

If Moved During Rapprochement

Rapprochement is a difficult stage for placing children in either a foster family or with a permanent adoptive family. Even if the child has done well developmentally and emotionally until this point, if the child is between about fifteen and twenty-two months of age—or regressed back to or developmentally delayed at this age—he or she will likely have difficulty attaching to new parents. After all, the child's greatest fear—losing the person to whom he is attached, whether birth parent or foster parent—has been realized, and it is difficult for the child to form an attachment with a new person for fear that the same thing might happen again. Often children moved at this age become more aggressive than normal. Others may withdraw or cling to the new parent for fear of losing that person also.

This is not to say that transfer of the bond and development of an attachment are impossible, or even that healthy attachment is unlikely, but that they will require extra care on the part of the adoptive parents and even the previous caretakers. You can do several things both before and after the move to lessen the trauma and help your child work through her feelings:

Activities to transfer trust. If at all possible, visit your child in the presence of the current caregiver before placement. While both you and the current caregiver should talk with your child about the move before it occurs, it also helps to act out the move in play. Because your child's verbal skills will not be developed enough to fully express his feelings, you may need to help him identify emotions such as fear, anger, sadness, mixed emotions, or others, letting him know that his feelings are OK. (See Chapter 6 for more information about transferring trust and preparing children for placement.)

Record the circumstances. It is important for the adults involved in the move to write down details of the placement day, for example, the color of the car, the type of plane, what the airport looked like, what the weather was like, who was there, what the social worker looked like, who the child said good-bye to and where. As your child's verbal skills develop, she will need to rework her emotions of that day; details about the day will help her understand what happened, why, and what it all means about her. Keep in mind that children often fix upon small details, such as the color of a car or something someone important to them was wearing. Write down as many details as you can, even if you never use them all.

Maintain ongoing contact with previous caregivers. Children need reassurance that the people they loved and who cared for them are still out there somewhere. "Postplacement contacts with previous caretakers are important to toddlers," writes Fahlberg (*Child Development*, 1982, 24). "If they do not occur, it is common that children will, at age four or five, think that the previous parental figures are dead."

Because children at this age are still in the process of separating their sense of self from the primary caregiver, loss of that person also means a loss of a part of themselves. This can threaten their sense of security and even make them fearful of personal annihilation.

Maintaining contact, however, may not always be possible. Contact may also be frightening for adoptive parents for a variety of reasons: they may feel threatened by the ongoing love the child has for the previous caretaker; they may fear losing the child back to that person; or they may become worried if the child regresses when around that other person. All these reactions are natural and to be expected. To help ease both your fears and your child's reactions to the contact, there are several things you can do:

- **Visits.** If you are able to have your child visit the previous caregiver, the visits should be spaced far enough apart to allow your child to discharge resurfaced emotions and enable the two of you to work on building your relationship. Visits may be kept short; remember that their purpose is simply to reassure your child that the previous caregiver is still around and still cares for her. While there is no exact formula for how often you should provide such visits, weekly visits are too frequent and not advisable at this age.

  You as the adoptive parent should be present during visits with birth or foster parents. And during visits, the previous caretaker should redirect the child to you for permission to do things, for discipline, or to have needs met, like getting a snack, a diaper changed, or help in the bathroom. This is not a time for the child to be alone with the previous caretaker; such visits only reinforce the child's belief or fear that she will be going back.

  Both adoptive parents, the previous caretakers, and birth parents involved in open adoptions must keep in mind that adoption is not a joint-custody arrangement and neither you nor the previous caretaker or birth parent should be put in a position of potential conflict with the other over issues related to your child. This can be difficult, but if adults can't stay clear about their roles, then the child won't be able to either. During visits, the previous caretakers are no longer disciplinarians or caregivers. They can still give your child a hug, but they also need to convey to her that it's OK and expected that she go with and turn to her new adoptive parents.

  During the first weeks and months of placement, visits are a time to continue the transfer of authority and trust from the previous caretakers to the adoptive parents, not a time to talk about why the adoption took place. Furthermore, each time you visit and leave is an opportunity to address your child's grief.

- **Cards and phone calls.** It is fine to allow your child to speak with the previous caretaker over the phone as soon as a few days after the initial move. In fact, if visits are not possible, cards and phone calls offer a good alternative for maintaining contact. Like visits, mail and telephone contact will trigger your child's old emotions of pain, anger, sadness, and other feelings. And though it would be easier for you not to deal with this, the resurgence of emotions actually helps the toddler clear the way to form new relationships by dealing with and adjusting to the separation from the former caretaker.

As time goes by, the frequency of contact, in whatever form, should gradually lessen. Also, allow your child to call the previous caregiver by the name she used to use, but modify it by adding the caregiver's first name. For example, if she called her birth mother Linda "Mom," have her call her "Mommy Linda." To avoid confusing your child, reserve "Mom" and "Dad," or whatever other parental names you choose, for yourselves.

Get pictures. Pictures are also important, especially if your child is moved at this age and there will be no further contact with the previous caregivers. If pictures are not already available, ask the agency or caseworker to take some. If your child was living in an orphanage, the pictures might be of the staff, the inside and outside of the building, cribs, or of other children playing. If your child lived with a foster family, they might be of the foster parents and siblings. Keep in mind that these particular photos are meant to record your child's life, not his genetic identity.

If photos are not available, ask people at the agency or others involved in placing your child if they would go back and take some, or if they would see a police artist to have a composite drawn. Whatever you do, don't give up too easily when it comes to getting pictures. Even in international adoptions, pictures of the orphanages, staff, and so on should be available. Feel free to make an issue of it if they are not!

If even this gets you nowhere, ask for as much description as you can get for all of the caregivers involved (tall or short; heavy or thin; skin, eye, and hair color; facial hair; hair type and length; glasses; and so on) and draw your own pictures. Write on your drawing "As pictured by . . . ," and talk with your child about how this drawing is what you think his birth parents or other caregivers looked like. As your child grows older, have him create his own drawings. Pictures of any kind not only facilitate discussions about the child's feelings, but also "park" the previous caregiver on a page. A child who has a picture is less apt to get stuck in searching as a preschooler. They also help validate and explain the child's memories.

Validate your child's memories. If your toddler tells you a story about a memory she has of her life before the adoption, just say "Wow" or "Oh," even if you doubt the story is true. While toddlers and preschoolers are notorious for tall tales, many adoptive parents have found, in later years, elements of truth in such stories. It's a good idea to write down these stories about your child's past—fact or fiction—whenever you can. Whether the stories are true or not, they are a part of your child—what he thought and felt and dreamed about his past. You can use these later to share with your child as you would share stories of how he mispronounced words in a funny way or other behaviors he has overcome and grown from. These are the stories he'll use when he talks about "When I was a little boy. . . ." Such stories help the child move on to new roles as "big" boy or girl by giving hope for future growth through validation of the child's ability to grow.

Allow for open discussion about the previous caretakers. From time to time, your child will probably need and want to talk about her previous caretakers and family, Because these people were a very real part of your child's life, you need to create an atmosphere in which your child feels free to talk about them and her life with them. One way to do this is by occasionally bringing up the topic yourself. For example, "I wonder if . . . still takes Spot (the dog) for a walk around the park every day." Furthermore, when your child brings up the topic, lend a listening ear; this is not a time to respond with a cursory "Oooh."

Finally, if a child is placed as a toddler, this is not the time to struggle over toilet training. Even if your child is not progressing in this area, don't sweat it. Be assured, he won't go to kindergarten in diapers.

Issues That May Arise

Children who are moved from one family—or care setting—to another as toddlers frequently have greater trouble balancing dependence and autonomy. Throughout rapprochement, the child tries to balance these two, and by the end of this developmental stage it is the child's awareness and understanding that sometimes he is independent and other times dependent that helps him move away from his fear of losing mother and on to the next stage. Children moved at this age, however, may become stuck in this conflict. At later ages, these children often show incredible intrusiveness, coercion, clinging, or premature independence; have difficulty accepting authority; or withhold affection. Whether the child is clingy or distant, the motivation is the same: "Other people are unreliable, so I must take care of myself, either by checking up on you or by simply doing it myself."

According to Fahlberg, these kinds of reactions to separation and loss can last a long time. "Frequently, if not recognized and remedied, these reactions persist for years," Fahlberg writes. "It is not uncommon to see nine-, ten-, and eleven-year-old children in foster care who are still constantly clinging in spite of numerous attempts to break them of this habit. Other children show the effects of extreme autonomy through the grade-school years and adolescence" (*Child Development*, 1982, 25).

Because this is such a high-risk age for moving children, their progress should be monitored by a professional. Since toddlers are rarely placed through private adoption, resources for such monitoring should be available either through the agency, directly, or by referral. Professionals equipped to monitor toddlers' developmental progress include pediatricians, agency placement workers or psychology staff, and family and child therapists experienced in attachment work with adoptive children—or who are willing to learn. Some children adopted as toddlers will need ongoing counseling, but others may only require occasional check-ins. In addition to assessing the child's development and attachment, these check-ins can be used for providing direction for parents as they continue to work with their child, especially in the areas of trust and expression of emotions surrounding the loss of the previous caregivers.

One symptom parents and professionals can look for as a sign that the child is having difficulty is that the child continues to have the same struggles rather than moving on to new ones. This is probably a better indicator of problems than overt aggression or frustration because some children turn these emotions inward on themselves rather than on other people. A professional should be able to identify if a new attachment is forming, explain your child's reactions (normal or problematic), and help identify problems when things appear to be going smoothly. Again, all families adopting children in this age group should be monitored professionally, even though they may not need ongoing therapy or counseling.

If Rapprochement Does Not Go Well
A common long-term effect of problems during rapprochement is difficulty in school performance. During healthy rapprochement, children begin to build a capacity to tolerate frustration, learn to control impulses, and learn that they cannot control their parents and therefore other authority figures. The ability to check reality—to ask and answer the question "Is what I believe true?"—also has its roots in this developmental stage.

According to Kreisman and Straus, disruption of the "rapprochement cycle often results in a lack of trust, disturbed relationships, emptiness, anxiety, and an uncertain self-image" (1989, 65). If rapprochement does not go well, day-to-day frustrations and failures often arouse unusually intense feelings of anxiety and personal deficit. The intensity of these emotions often leads children who have not completed rapprochement in a healthy way to develop, at a very early age, defense mechanisms to protect themselves from their emotions. Some children become withdrawn; others use frequent and intense levels of activity or aggression to protect themselves from the anxiety of separation from the parents. Still other children vacillate between being withdrawn and being excessively active. Some children also become unwilling or unable to accept authority—at home, at school, and elsewhere.

When rapprochement does not go well, separation anxiety may continue into the preschool and middle childhood years, interfering with the child's ability to concentrate and learn in school. Withdrawal or hyperactive behavior may be further heightened when the teacher expresses disapproval or disciplines the child. By adolescence, frequent negative behavior is common both in the classroom and at home. Throughout childhood, the child who had difficulty during rapprochement will continue wooing and coercing the parent, clinging to her when they part and rejecting her when she is present. Hyperactivity and withdrawal may also result from grief and or genetically inherited attention deficit disorder or attention deficit hyperactive disorder. For this reason, the differential symptom in diagnosing problems stemming from unresolved rapprochement is this continued wooing and coercion.

One technique to help lower the child's anxiety and therefore raise her ability to concentrate at school is to allow the child to phone the parents during the day to reassure her that they are still available. Gradually the child will no longer need this. Parents frequently have difficulty convincing teachers that this is really necessary and not merely coddling the child. If your child is having difficulty in this area, you may need to have the family's therapist or physician speak with school administrators and the teacher. One pediatrician trained in attachment work wrote a prescription saying that his patient needed to call home three times a day. Though the school had argued with the parents before this, once the order was written as a physician's prescription, the argument was dropped. The child was excused from class at appropriate intervals "to take her medicine," which was calling home to talk briefly with her mother. These phone calls are not long conversations, but brief check-ins to ask how the child's day is going and for the parents to say "I love you."

To help school staff understand why your child needs this, you can explain that because of the adoption or previous events in your child's life, your child has a developmental delay. Like a preschooler, being away from home and family causes her to become anxious, which leads to the behaviors that are disrupting the classroom and her concentration. Phoning home will prevent the anxiety and subsequent behaviors from getting out of hand. For most children the need to call home usually subsides within several months, though some children require longer.

In some cases, children placed at older ages (two years or older) who previously completed rapprochement in a healthy way, may face much the same difficulties as a child who has not, beginning sometime after trust has been transferred and attachment begun. This mirrors the way children build attachments during infancy. Likewise, children whose parents are in the midst of divorce often need to check in with their parents throughout the day for reassurance that they are still loved.

Consolidation of Individuation: Twenty-One to Thirty-Six Months

The final phase of separation and individuation marks the end of infancy and the emergence of the child's self-awareness. Between the time a child is born and her third birthday, she moves from a sense of oneness with mother to a point where she is truly an individual and experiences herself as such. In his book *The Second Year: The Emergence of Self-Awareness*, Jerome Kagan, psychology professor at Harvard University, asserts, "By 27 months the child has offered enough evidence to conclude that he is aware of his behavior, intentions, and psychological states and of his ability to monitor and implement them. In a more traditional idiom, he has self-consciousness, which seems to be composed, in part, of standards and an awareness of whether he can meet them" (1981, 135). Mahler (cited by Edward, Ruskin, and Turrini 1981, 28) refers to the developmental achievements of this age as *consolidation of individuation*. Essentially, all the work of the earlier phases of separation and individuation are "consolidated," or brought to the target destination of a child who is now no longer a baby, but, as White puts it, "a relatively complete junior human being" (1990, 197). Though the task of separating our identities from those of our parents is essentially a lifelong process, the first real achievement of separateness appears during consolidation of individuation, which begins sometime around the second birthday and continues until about the third birthday.

According to Mahler's theory (cited by Edward, Ruskin, and Turrini 1981, 28–29), the two primary psychological developmental tasks during this period are to establish self-constancy and object constancy. The term object constancy describes the child's sense that the mother (the original "object" of the child's love) is always the same and available to the child (she is "constant"). Children at this age who have not experienced developmental delays or disruptions have a strong enough mental image of their mothers to make them feel safe and protected even when away from their mothers. By age three, most children can easily tolerate brief separations from their parents, such as while at day care, without an undue amount of fear or stress. In addition to carrying the child through brief separations, this mental image helps the child feel secure that the mother is available and dependable even when the child is angry with her, or when the mother is angry or not providing satisfaction from the child's viewpoint.

Object constancy eventually enables children to see that one person can have different moods and feelings without being a characteristically different person (for example, "Mom is a loving person who is angry at the moment," instead of "Mom is angry; she's a bad person or no longer loves me"). While bonding and attachment enable the child to trust the parent and feel safe knowing that his basic needs will be met, achievement of object constancy reassures the child that he is safe and loved—and thus competent and lovable (self-constancy)—even when his parents are not immediately available to him. Achievement of object constancy leads to development of healthy self-constancy. The term *self-constancy* refers to the child's sense that he is always the same person, regardless of the setting in which he finds himself or the emotions he is experiencing at the moment. In other words, the child begins to understand that he can have different emotions yet still be the same person. This blossoming awareness of self also marks the point at which the core identity (discussed in Chapter 4) emerges for the first time.

Later by about age five or six, adopted children begin to deal with the dichotomy of the "chosen-child" message, that is, in order to be chosen by her adoptive parents, the adopted child first had to be "rejected" by her birth parents. Healthy self-constancy will help the child through this struggle and eventually make way for the child to see that her birth parents did not "reject" a bad child who later turned good, making her worthy to be accepted by adoptive parents. Achievement of self-constancy helps the child eventually understand that she had the same basic character before the adoption as she has now, thereby creating a sense of continuity about herself. It also enables her to integrate her life before the adoption as part of her life story and identity since placement. Though the task of addressing the dichotomy of the "chosen-child" message is never entirely easy for adopted children, it's much more difficult if they have not achieved self-and object constancy.

Of course, at the same time the child is working on object and self-constancy, other developments are also taking place in her growth, including the following:

Equilibrium versus disequilibrium. Around age two the cycles of equilibrium and disequilibrium begin to alternate about every six months. At the beginning of the consolidation of individuation, most children are in a period of strong equilibrium; their desires are temporarily in sync with their abilities. In the second half of the year, however, disequilibrium returns. Some of this may stem from limitations of verbal skills, as the child wants or needs to express feelings but cannot because of limited vocabulary and language. Children at this age are also heavily into ownership, yet they are now beginning to be truly able to play *with* other children (cooperative play, which calls for sharing of toys) as opposed to *alongside* other children (parallel play). Anger and rage often stem from not getting what they want or from having their efforts to do something thwarted. Two-and-a-half-year-olds tend to be more destructive in their anger and show more aggression than do children at other ages. It is not unusual for children to return to behaviors such as head banging, hitting, or kicking while in a tantrum. Though children at this age cannot always self-soothe or delay gratification, the times when they can do this continue to grow in duration, moving from several minutes to fractions of hours.

Awareness of family relationships. Sometime during this stage, children become aware of their place in the family in terms of birth order and that they are children as opposed to parents. While they can grasp the concepts of relationships within the immediate family, they do not always fully understand extended relationships within the family, such as cousins, or aunts and uncles. For example, a child might understand that she has grandparents, but she may not understand that Grandpa is her mother's father.

Interest in personal life story. This is an especially good age for bringing out the family storybook and telling your child's personal life story, including at least something about her life before placement. By telling your child about the adoption now, she will grow up feeling she has always known about it. In telling your child's story, be accurate about the basic events, mentioning but not overemphasizing feelings. Your two-year-old is likely to be confused by the idea of "other parents." Terms such as *birth mother* can be especially confusing at this age. To minimize confusion, describe the relationship in concrete terms, such as "the woman in whose womb you grew."

While it is important, as part of their life stories, to tell children from the beginning about their adoption, at this age you should limit your explanations to the questions your child asks. For example, you can talk with your child about being born and how the woman whose tummy she grew in wasn't able to take care of her and how you came to adopt her; but you don't have to go into the details about why the birth parents couldn't take care of her (though if you adopt your child at two years of age, you may have to address this, too). If you are driven to deal with the details of adoption, it may be better to make up adoption stories about animals to give your child a concept of adoption through concrete examples. If you prefer stories about people, Sesame Street's *Susan and Gordon Adopt a Baby* is a good book for this age group (see reading list at the end of this chapter).

Awareness of similarities and differences. At this age, children become much more aware of gender and physical differences, including skin color and race. All children need to feel like their parents, as well as have their unique differences reinforced. Pointing out similarities between your child and other family members—especially parents—will help your child develop a sense of belonging within the family, build a safe atmosphere for your child to work on individuation, and enable your child to continue to internalize attributes of each parent. Positive recognition of differences will help your child in the natural task of developing an identity separate from you (individuation). If, however, the majority of the comments a child hears are about differences, she will have more difficulty working on individuation because she will not feel she belongs in the first place.

Children raised within genetically related families hear fairly regularly from parents and others about how they are like their parents and other family members. Even when a child has a prominent feature that no one else in the immediate family has, such as a different color or texture of hair, families usually do a cross-generational search to "park" the origins of the trait with someone in the extended family, such as a great-grandparent or an aunt or uncle. But even in same-race adoptions, adopted children are less likely to have features, tastes, talents, habits, or interests similar to those of their adoptive parents, and they will probably hear fewer comments from others pointing to the similarities that do exist. While this may help the adopted child separate and become an individual, balance is needed if the child is to develop a sense of belonging—which is crucial to attachment.

As a parent, you can provide this balance and reinforce claiming by recognizing your child's similarities—physical or otherwise—to both you and your child's birth parents. To reinforce your own claiming of your child and her sense of belonging, try to comment at least once a day on a similarity between you—or another family member—and your child, as well as praising the child for differences in both accomplishments and non-accomplishments (physical traits or something else she has no real control over).

If you know your child's birth parents through search or open adoption, you might comment on physical characteristics or mannerisms your child has in common with them. But simply by living with you, your child will pick up mannerisms from you as well. Though you don't need to point all of these out as they occur, make a mental note of them and bring them up at another time, perhaps when your child is trying to find ways in which he is like you.

Family Life Cycle

By the time your child reaches about age two or three, several interesting things begin to occur. First of all, he will begin to understand the triad relationship of mother-father-child. It is at this age that children noticeably try to either interrupt or become a part of Mom and Dad's relationship.

The two- to three-year-old also begins to include both Mom and Dad simultaneously in play or when seeking attention. Prior to this age, children focus on self or one-to-one interactions. But sometime between ages two and three, children begin to understand the concept of "everybody." For example, if you were to point to your home and ask your twenty-month-old child, "Whose house is that?" the child would probably answer with his or her own first name. A child just a year older, however, is more likely to respond saying it's "our house" or "Daddy's house and Mommy's house and my house."

Most married couples spend the first two years of marriage merging their lives and getting accustomed to their new roles in the relationship. The same holds true after the arrival of a new child; it generally takes two years after the arrival of a new child for the parents to adjust to their roles as mother and father and to integrate these new roles into the old ones of husband and wife. In addition, as the child grows in independence, both physically and emotionally, the parents begin to have a greater sense of separation from the child, which allows them to focus more attention on their marital relationship and get beyond some of the rough spots they may have been experiencing since the child's arrival.

When children are adopted at birth or born into the family, parents often wait two to three years before adding another member to the family, simply to avoid having two children in diapers at the same time. But even if children are adopted at an older age, waiting two to three years before adopting again is a good idea because it allows all members of the family time to adjust to their new roles and interrelationships. This amount of time is helpful after each child, not just the first.

Another issue families tend to face at about the time a child reaches this age is the mother's sense of loss. It is natural for the mother or other primary caregiver to be seemingly immersed in the infant and her needs. As the child achieves her first real sense of separateness from the mother and gains increasing physical and emotional independence, the mother's role takes on a different nuance: the baby is "growing up." At the same time that the child's need for the mother's care is diminishing, the father is likely to be gaining interaction with the child. Women often experience this loss earlier on, for instance, when the child first begins to crawl, feed himself, walk, or talk. But if the mother hasn't experienced the loss yet, she is certain to do so to some degree by this point. As the child begins to build greater independence, it is important that the mother also begin to build a sense of self separate from motherhood. This doesn't mean she must find a job outside the home. The real goal is for the mother to feel competent and take joy in life again as an adult outside of—as well as within—her role as parent. Some examples of this include renewed attention to her marriage, taking a class for personal or professional growth, or resuming hobbies.

If Moved During Consolidation of Individuation

The lesson the child learns from consolidation of individuation is that Mom and Dad love him even when they are angry with him and that they will be there when he needs them. This lesson moderates the child's fear of separation from the parent, which began in infancy with the first experiences of being a separate person from the parent.

Children who are moved at this age have had their greatest fear realized: that of losing a parent. Again, one of the primary end products of object constancy is that the child feels safe because her parents, through their reliability, availability, and unconditional love, make her world a safe place. The loss of a parent (or other primary caretaker) at this point in a child's development can leave the child feeling very vulnerable that she will lose someone again, even if a new parent takes the previous parent's place. As the child grows and new age-appropriate fears arise, this lack of security leaves her less able to mitigate those fears. The child may also be less able to work on other areas of development because she does not feel safe to separate from her adoptive mother (because she was forced to separate from her birth mother about fifteen years too early!).

Despite the difficulties created when a child is moved at this age, the good news is that because the period of consolidation of individuation is really just the beginning of a lifelong process, this is one stage that can be worked on later with relative ease. As a parent, you can help smooth the transition by following the advice given for moving toddlers (see section "If Moved During Rapprochement" earlier in this chapter). Transferring trust, maintaining contact with previous caretakers, recording the circumstances of the move, and getting pictures of previous caretakers or birth parents are just as helpful and important for the two-year-old as for the younger toddler. We might add, however, that it's a good idea to have copies of photographs, rather than the originals, available for your child to protect these treasures from being destroyed during a temper tantrum.

Other things you can do include the following:

Be realistic in your expectations. A two-year-old who has just arrived in your family will not love you immediately. It is likely that he may even be fearful of falling in love. Still, he will need love from you. You can help your child accept your love and comfort by first acknowledging and helping your child label his feelings with statements such as "It *looks like* you feel (angry, sad, frightened, or whatever)." You can also talk with your child about how puppies are frightened when they come to a new home, but that they still want hugs and kisses.

Allow for regression. Regression to earlier stages of separation anxiety (among other stages) is normal. Children who are moved or placed at this age are often less able than other children their age to tolerate separations from parents. When leaving your child with a baby sitter, in the nursery at church, or at day care, feel free to take extra time to calm him before you leave. Even though he has stopped crying or clinging, he will probably begin to cry again when you actually do leave, but this is normal. A quick drop-off at the baby sitter's, however, can be particularly difficult for a child who is fearful.

Avoid overprotection. Adoptive parents are sometimes more vulnerable to becoming overprotective when it comes to separations. As we've pointed out earlier in this book, separations allow your child to work on individuation and object constancy. By your leaving and then returning, your child learns that you will return and that she is safe even when you are not present (object constancy). Without experiencing at least occasional separations of a few hours, you child learns she is not safe without you, a message that interferes with development of object constancy.

Use the one-minute scolding technique to reinforce object constancy. Gerald Nelson's (1985) one-minute scolding technique reinforces for the child that you still love her even when you are angry—one of the primary lessons of object constancy. In fact, for many children, the technique may actually be more effective for developing or reinforcing object constancy than it is for actual discipline. The technique is basically as follows: While touching your child lightly on the arm or shoulder, begin by saying, "I am angry. Do you know why I am angry?" If your child doesn't respond, repeat the question. If your child still doesn't answer, explain why. If she does answer, confirm what she has said if she is correct ("Yes, I don't like it when you hit your brother. Don't do it anymore"), or correct her if she is wrong ("No, I'm not angry because I don't like you. I'm angry because you hit your brother"). After briefly discussing with your child what happened, end the scolding by moving your arm from the light touch to a hug, tell her you love her, and comment on something positive: "I love you very much. I like it better when you play nicely with your brother, like you usually do."

In some situations, you may find that other forms of discipline, such as consequences, or removal of privileges, are better suited to the seriousness of your child's action. If you choose another form of discipline, when it is over, still tell your child you love him, while reinforcing your statement with touch. The other key to the one-minute scolding technique is to let go of your anger once the "sentence" has been given, even if it hasn't been carried out yet. For example, if you decide the "punishment" or consequence of your child's action is to turn off the television or have the child help clean up a mess he made, don't continue to huff and puff in anger until the set is back on or until the job is done. Of course, it won't always be easy to let go of your anger, but do your best.

For some adopted children, timeouts can trigger their fear of abandonment. If you do choose to use timeouts for disciplining your child, be sure to state that it is your child's behavior that you dislike, not the child himself. During the timeout, remain in the child's view; the child will still experience the "punishment" and know you disapprove of whatever his action was, but without the extra anxiety of feeling abandoned.

Issues That May Arise

We discussed earlier how children first learn to trust their caregivers, themselves, and eventually the world around them through the bonding cycle. Achievement of object constancy during consolidation of individuation is the first step toward translating the child's trust in the primary caregiver to trust in the world around her. It is possible for a child to have developed a healthy bond and attachment and yet not develop object constancy (which leads the way for self-constancy). A child who has bonded with a parent but who has not achieved an adequate sense of object constancy will, as in infancy, feel safe when in the parent's presence, but insecure when the parent is absent or upset with something the child has done.

Of course, all children—and even adults—have some degree of difficulty with object constancy. Consider, for example, how you feel when you and your spouse or another important person in your life have an argument. You may well be at a point in your relationship with that person that you feel fairly secure that the issue at hand will pass and your relationship will not be permanently marred by the incident. But if you think back to an earlier time in your relationship, you may well remember having felt fearful, either during or after an argument, that the relationship might be over, or that the other person might leave you forever. As with bonding and attachment, achievement of object constancy with the primary parent enables the child to feel secure in future relationships with other people, as well as secure in herself as a "good" person (healthy self-esteem). Achievement of object constancy carries us not only through the challenges of childhood, but also through the rigors of adulthood. Edward, Ruskin, and Turrini explain the importance of object constancy this way:

> At least a minimal level of object constancy is required to enable the adult to adapt independently. Throughout the life-cycle, some degree of separation anxiety can be anticipated in reaction to life events that promote a new level of separated development. The child who goes to camp, the adolescent who takes a hostelling

trip, the adult who enters college or employment are all confronted with a new level of separation. Unconsciously, perhaps consciously at times, these changes are eased by drawing on all that has become associated in the mind with the "idea of mother." (1981, 30)

For the adopted child, this idea of mother draws on the child's experience with the adoptive parents, but also on the fact that the birth parent is gone, or in the case of open adoption, not always present or available to the child. The idea that a parent can go away fights against the concept that Mom and Dad are always available. Though your two- or even three-year-old is unlikely to actually ponder the mixed message about the availability and reliability of parental figures, having actually *lost* his birth parents, his fears of losing you may be more intense than the same fears in children who are being raised by their genetically related parents. (Again, this does not mean that you don't tell your child about the adoption.)

So what does this mean for your child's development? First of all, it's important to realize that object constancy is not necessarily something a person either has or doesn't have; most people achieve a degree of object constancy that falls somewhere between very strong to very weak or almost nonexistent. Weak object constancy is likely to manifest itself in the following ways:

Difficulty feeling safe in intimate relationships. When a relationship begins to become close, the child or adult with weak object constancy is likely either to become very clingy out of fear of losing the other person or to begin to distance himself from that person to prevent the pain of the loss that he feels, though perhaps unconsciously, is inevitable (i.e., "if I love someone too much, that person will go away").

Lack of sense of belonging in the family and in other situations, especially later in life.

Difficulty mitigating anxiety. Without a healthy degree of object constancy, a person may be easily overwhelmed even in mildly or moderately stressful situations.

Because of the above difficulties, weak object constancy is also an inhibitor that can weaken an existing attachment or prevent the transfer of trust needed to form a new one. Difficulty with object constancy may also be a factor in why so many adopted children are diagnosed—whether accurately or not—with attention-deficit disorder (ADD). For some of these children, the inability to calm themselves or self-soothe when away from their parents may contribute to attention deficits; other children may not sit still long enough to concentrate on any one thing because when they do the pain and fear come back.

Whether your child is age two now, or is older but still struggling with object constancy, here are some things you can do to help:

- Show joy in your child even when she isn't doing anything particularly special at the moment (for example, give your child a hug, smile at her, or tell her you love her simply out of the blue).
- When disciplining, stress your disapproval of your child's behavior, not of the child himself, to reinforce that you still love him even though what he has done is not good.
- Include planned absences in your routine: go to dinner or a movie, or both, if for no other reason than to show that when you leave you do come back as promised.
- Develop a plan for times when unplanned separations occur—for instance, if you must stay late at work, your child knows that Grandma will pick her up from day care and stay with her until you come home.
- Validate your child's feelings about losses (even if they seem to you to be blown out of proportion).

Reparenting: A Technique for Bonding and Attachment

Whenever a child is placed in an adoptive home, with the exception of immediately after birth, both parent and child have missed sharing some developmental stage together. Some children will be on track developmentally; others will not. A child who seems to be struggling developmentally, in her relationship with her adoptive parents, or in feeling part of the family, may need to *repeat* earlier stages to help counteract a history that may be inhibiting healthy bonding and attachment, and thus interfering with other areas of development. A technique called *reparenting* is one way to enable the child to go back through the phases of infant/mother development from fog to consolidation of individuation.

The reparenting technique involves interacting with your child with increasing frequency in ways similar to those in which infants and mothers normally interact at various stages of early development, and then to move forward again through the developmental stages to the child's current developmental age. No matter how old your child is now, it is possible to go back through the phases of infant/mother development, from fog to consolidation of individuation. It's been said time and again that the first three years of life are the most crucial in determining the person a child will eventually grow to be. While the reparenting technique will not reverse a child's experiences during this period of life, it can *help* heal old wounds and lessen some of the inhibitors that might be interfering with your child's attachment to you, his sense of belonging in the family, or other aspects of development.

The technique focuses on three areas:

- *establishing or transferring trust* in order to enable your child to bond with you;
- *positive interaction*, which leads to attachment; and
- *claiming and belonging*, which enhances attachment and frees the child for consolidation of individuation by reinforcing object constancy.

Application

The first step in reparenting is to choose a developmental stage to which you and your child will regress. Symbiosis is a comfortable starting point for many parents and children. You'll remember that symbiosis is the stage in which mother and baby "fall in love." Eye contact is an essential element of this wooing process. One of the most nonthreatening and enjoyable ways—for both parent and child—of evoking eye contact is by playing such childhood games as peekaboo and pat-a-cake. Once comfortable with making eye contact, many children want to go back further to be held, rocked, or cuddled as one would a newborn in the fog stage. Your child will move forward again naturally, with little or no prompting. In fact, for many parents, especially those experiencing closeness with their child for the first time, this progression comes sooner than they would like.

Whatever the type of interaction you (and your child) choose to begin with, the goal is to set aside time everyday for that sharing. How often you do it and for how long depends on your child's age and willingness to participate, and your level of frustration. The older your child is the more leery he may be of acting or being treated like "a baby." For this reason, you need to protect your child's privacy by reserving reparenting "sessions" to times when people other than immediate family (or your therapist) are not around. Tell your child fairly often that the reason you are playing "baby games" is because she missed out on this when she was a baby or that the two of you never shared it together. Once the initial fear, if any, subsides, most children and parents truly enjoy the comfort and closeness of the interactions.

While this technique can be used for older children as well as infants and toddlers, it should be done only with supervision from a social worker, psychologist, pediatrician, or other trained professional if your child is already three years old or older. You will still work with your child at home, but the supervision will help ensure that problems do not arise. Unlike some other techniques, such as rage-reduction (holding) therapy, reparenting cannot cause any harm to your child or your relationship so long as you don't force the child to participate if he resists.

All interactions between you and your child should be mutually respectful. If your child says no or that he doesn't want to play, be hugged, or whatever, respect his wishes and find another way to interact that accomplishes the same goals but in a way your child enjoys. For example, if your eight year old is embarrassed playing peekaboo, saying she's too old, find another way to achieve brief eye contact in a playful way, such as by playing hand-clapping games like Miss Mary Mack or simply making goofy faces at each other across the room. Likewise, if your child acts in a way that doesn't feel good to you, tell him so—for example, "That isn't a loving hug."

Though reparenting involves regressing the child to an earlier stage of life, it is not a complete regression; it is a regression only in the way you and your child interact. For example, you should never regress your child's toileting habits. Furthermore, reparenting involves only a small portion of the day, ranging from a minute or two here or there throughout the day to fifteen minutes to an hour before bedtime.

Below are some specific suggestions for reparenting toddlers and infants.

Revisiting symbiosis. Eye contact is an important part of intimacy in relationships, whether between friends, husband and wife, or parent and child. Eye contact is integral to the wooing that occurs between mother and infant during symbiosis. When parents play with their baby, they watch the baby's face for the response. The baby takes pleasure in the game and parents take pleasure in watching their child laugh. And most importantly, they watch each other's faces to see the response. Even during quiet times, mothers and infants in symbiosis often spend long moments looking into each other's faces. The pleasure that comes from the shared moments of interest and enjoyment completes the positive-interaction cycle for parent and child alike. Reenacting these types of moments is the goal of revisiting symbiosis as a part of reparenting.

For children under the age of three, it is fairly easy to elicit eye contact and enjoyment through games such as peekaboo, pat-a-cake, or gentle tickling. Once your child has become comfortable with eye contact during games, you can try making eye contact during quiet times. Cradling your child in your arms (the "nursing position") while rocking before a nap or at bedtime is one way to achieve this.

Moving back to the fog. The focus of the first month of life is establishing trust by meeting the child's physical needs and providing relief from distress. The infant grows to associate comfort and security with the mother through a variety of sensory means: touch, smell, rhythm, visual contact, sound, relief of hunger, and relief from discomfort. The goal in revisiting the fog stage is to similarly provide soothing for your child through the different senses. Below are some suggestions for doing this:

- *Hold your child* while wrapped in a flannel blanket or afghan and rock. You might begin by doing this once or twice a week and then working up to once a day and finally, several times a day. If your child resists cradling, let him sit on your lap facing outward toward the room. Cradling and rocking facilitate the kinds of rhythm, touch, and visual contact parents and infants experience together. One couple we know built a loveseat-size rocking chair with soft cushions and used this as their special place for reparenting moments. This allowed the older adopted children in the family to join in on these special moments and benefit from them in terms of attachment, without their feeling "babied."
- *Play together with food.* You can make a game of feeding your child and her feeding you or simply playing together with food (for example, building roads in a blob of pudding). This activity is especially good to use with an older child who would otherwise resist your "feeding" her.
- *Feed your child.* While reparenting a child, "sit down" meals are particularly important. Buffet-style dinners or eating casually in the living room will not lead your child to associate the relief of hunger with you. Even if your child is able to serve herself (which most children under age three will not be able to do anyway), you should prepare her plate and sit with her while she eats her meals, even if you are serving fast food from a take-out restaurant.
- *Give back rubs.* A gentle back rub incorporates touch, rhythm, and relaxation. Younger children may enjoy skin-to-skin contact; older children may prefer a back rub through a shirt.
- *Sing and talk to your child,* while following any of the other suggestions in this list, as a way of providing auditory stimulation. Especially important is talking with your child about feelings when he is sick, hurt, at the end of the day before bed, or during the rougher moments of the day when he is angry or frustrated. Listen to what he says about his feelings and help him identify them when he can't seem to do it for himself (i.e., "You seem angry," "You seem tired," "You look very happy").
- *Offer comfort.* A child who has not bonded or attached to her parents usually will not seek comfort when hurt or in distress. Even if your child doesn't cry when she falls, offer comfort regardless, saying, "Oh, that must have hurt," and giving a hug or helping hand. Tell your child to come for a hug when she is frightened or hurt.

Moving forward again through separation and individuation. Once your child has attached and bonded with you, it will be time to begin his lifelong journey of separation. Usually this trek will require no prompting from you; once your child feels safe he will begin to do this on his own. You will probably notice your child exhibiting separation anxiety, as well as other behaviors common among toddlers, such as shadowing and darting, checking back, and wooing and coercion. The techniques described throughout this chapter for helping your child at each developmental stage apply even if your child is already beyond the usual age at which such behaviors appear. Establishing hello, good-bye, and bedtime rituals are particularly helpful as well.

Claiming and belonging. Throughout reparenting it is important to reinforce your child's sense of belonging and your claiming of her. Again, pointing out similarities between your child and other family members, including yourself, expressing joy and pride in achievements, and showing your pleasure in your child's very presence are all ways of helping your child feel loved and good about herself.

For Further Reading

• *In Time and With Love: Caring for the Special Needs Baby* by Marilyn Segal, Ph.D. New York: Newmarket Press, 1988.

A sensitive, caring discussion for parents raising and loving infants with special medical and developmental challenges.

• *The Essential Partnership: How Parents and Children Can Meet the Emotional Challenges of Infancy and Childhood* by Stanley Greenspan, M.D., and Nancy Thorndike Greenspan. New York: Penguin, 1989.

This book is an excellent companion to *First Feelings* (recommended in Chapter 8) giving parents practical techniques for nurturing their children's relationship skills.

• *Toddlers and Parents: A Declaration of Independence* by T. Berry Brazelton, M.D. New York: Delacorte Press, 1989.

Dr. Brazelton guides parents through the normal developmental needs of toddlers. Through clear and concise explanations, parents learn how to create an environment that encourages toddlers to explore the world around them and expand their individuality.

• *Who's the Boss: How to Cope with Your Child* (previously published as *The One-Minute Scolding*) by Gerald Nelson. New York: Random House, 1985.

Nelson's technique reinforces bonding and attachment, while enabling parents to address their children's discipline needs. We highly recommend this book for all parents, but especially for those who are working on reparenting.

• *Susan and Gordon Adopt a Baby,* based on *Sesame Street* scripts written by Judy Freudberg and Tony Geiss. New York: Random House, 1986.

Big Bird and the "Sesame Street" gang welcome Susan and Gordon's newly adopted baby to the neighborhood. Children love to read about their Sesame Street friends, as well as about the adoption.

Table 9.1.
Signs of Healthy Bonding and Attachment

Developmental Stage	Child's Behavior	Parent's Behavior
Fog: First month	Cries to signal needs.	Responds to baby's signal and successfully identifies needs most of the time.
	Ceases crying and returns to relaxed state when need is met.	Returns to relaxation along with baby; feels good about self and child.
	Good sucking response.	
	Accepts cuddling.	Offers nurturing.
Symbiosis: 2 to 5 months	Smiles; makes eye contact; stares at mother's face for few seconds at a time; makes happy sounds.	Begins wooing child; initiates positive interactions; calls baby by name (claiming).
	Length of eye contact/loving exchanges with mother increases from seconds to minutes.	
	If eye contact is interrupted by sudden noise or other distraction, child is increasingly able to return to the gaze.	
	Child appears responsive and exhibits full range of emotions.	Responds to child's full range of emotions.
Differentiation: 5 to 10 months	Explores parents' faces visually and through touch.	
	Enjoys and engages in peekaboo games.	
6 to 7 months	Differentiates between parents and strangers.	
	Begins checking back to parents for reassurance when strangers are present.	Offers visual, verbal, and tactile reassurance.
8 to 9 months	Exhibits anxiety, anger, or flattened affect when parents leave or are not present.	

Table 9.1.
Signs of Healthy Bonding and Attachment (continued)

Developmental Stage	Child's Behavior	Parent's Behavior
Practicing: Early 9 to 18 months	Checking continues and is used to help child feel safe when exploring.	Encourages safe exploration.
	Shows glee at accomplishments.	Exhibits joy at child's accomplishments.
	Continued increasing interest in father.	
	Returns to parents to refuel (get hug, kiss) during play.	Provides reassurance; encourages return to play.
	Easily turns to parents for comfort when tired, hurt, or ill.	Offers comfort.
	Accepts comfort most of time.	
	Ability to delay gratification increases slightly.	
	Self-comforting skills increase (thumb-sucking, transitional objects).	
Rapprochement: 15 to 22 months	Wooing and coercion.	Responds to need and redirects; does not usually overreact to coercion.
	Shadowing and darting.	
Consolidation of Individuation: 21 to 36 months	Previous behaviors continue: full range of emotions; able to handle increasingly longer periods of separation (in hours) without anxiety; increasingly longer periods of independent play.	Continued responsiveness to child's needs; encourages growing autonomy and praises accomplishments.
	Increasing ability to accept redirection, discipline, and authority.	
	Imitates parents in play.	

Note: While this table focuses on infant behaviors, older children—even through adolescence—will demonstrate similar behaviors if they are progressing through the stages of building attachment.

10

⚘

The Preschool Years:
Three to Five Years

*T*he preschool years are a magical time for children. Their imagination
is able to soar because their logic is not yet sophisticated enough to
interfere with creativity—in other words, anything is possible. But imagination unhindered by logic can also lead the three- to five-year-olds to "scary"
interpretations of things they don't yet fully understand, including facts
surrounding their adoptions. Understanding how preschoolers think can
prepare parents to better help their children deal with these issues. Common
characteristics of preschoolers include the following:

Egocentrism. The world of the preschooler is very egocentric ("I"-cen-
tered). The child's universe has grown beyond including just mother and
self; but the child remains the center of the universe, with all else revolving
around him and moving as a result of his actions, just as the turning of the
hub of the wheel moves the spokes and rim. As a result of this, preschoolers
often believe that anything they experience, others experience as well. A
good example of this is the three-year-old who asks his mother to touch a
bruise on his knee, saying, "Does it hurt?" and believing full well that his
mother can *feel* the pain of his bruise. Likewise, preschoolers are often
vague when answering questions about what they did while away from
their parents because they think their parents already know. When you tell
your child about your experiences while the two of you were apart, you
help your child move beyond egocentricism by teaching that you each have
different experiences.

In the preschool years, from ages three to five, it is normal for adopted
children to begin to believe they caused the loss of their birth parents. A

child who is moved while still working on merging the "good" and "bad" child into a unified sense of self will be more likely during this time to generalize his belief that he caused his birth parents to leave into a belief that he causes bad things to happen. This can also lead him to fear his own power (for example, "If I wish or think something bad, it will happen").

The egocentric nature of preschoolers also makes them easily distracted. While this may be a drawback if you are trying to teach your child her ABCs or get her to pick up her toys, it can be an advantage in situations in which you want to redirect your child's attention, such as while going through the supermarket checkout (that is, if you're savvy enough to be able to pull it off!).

Animism. For very young preschoolers especially, the line between reality and fantasy is often quite blurred. One example of animism is that of a child who is scared that a monster is under his bed. Telling the child that monsters are not real is never enough; you still have to look under the child's bed to prove that the coast is clear, because to the child a monster doesn't have to be "real" to hurt him. Though older preschoolers know when they are pretending (for example, they know they aren't really a mutant ninja turtle or Dorothy from *The Wizard of Oz*), objects they have anthropomorphized, such as a named teddy bear, doll, or even an imaginary friend, are often as "real" as any living person around them. Children create imaginary characters and give life to inanimate objects to fill their own needs, whether for companionship, or as a way to embody fears and anxieties. Once a fear is tangible, the child can then conquer it. Animism and imaginary play, however, do not help in mitigating fears when the source of the fear is real, such as in the case of abuse.

This ambiguity between what is real and what isn't can raise problems for adopted preschoolers when language such as "real parents," "real children," or "real family" is used to explain the child's relationship to her adoptive family and parents and to her birth family and parents. Problems occur most often when people outside the family use these terms to ask questions or talk about the child's birth parents ("Why didn't your real parents keep you?"). The connotation of the word *real* is often lost on the child, whose concrete thinking interprets the word to mean the opposite of *pretend*. For this reason, use of such terms as *real child*, *real parents*, and *real family* can lead the child to confusion about whether he is a "real child" or a "fake child," or lead him to think that, like other pretend play, his membership in the family is only temporary. Such confusion can have an inhibiting effect on attachment and identity. You can avoid this confusion by referring to birth parents by first name or descriptive terms such as "the woman in whose tummy (or womb) you grew." If another person asks you in your child's presence if she is "your real child," you can give an honest answer such as, "Yes, she is my real daughter. We adopted her when she was a baby." If such an answer proves confusing to the other person, so be it; your child's sense of belonging will have been reinforced, and that's all that truly matters.

Magical thinking. Animism and egocentricism lead to the third characteristic of preschoolers: magical thinking. If a child is the all-powerful center of the universe, and nothing happens that he does not cause or experience, and if fantasy is sometimes the same as reality, the next logical step is that the child believes she can *cause* things to happen simply by wishing them so. Furthermore, the child believes she somehow has a hand in everything that happens around her. Thus, when parents divorce, the child is placed for adoption, a grandparent dies, the new baby in the family is a girl, or any other significant event occurs, the preschooler's natural response is to figure out how she caused that event to happen. And she will look for the answer by exploring her thoughts, actions, words, wishes, and feelings.

Preschoolers will apply magical thinking when sorting out why they were adopted. While three- to five-year-olds will not yet cognitively understand the dichotomy of "I was chosen by my adoptive parents"/"My birth parents chose not to parent me (they rejected me)," they will explore at least one half of the dichotomy; and which half they focus on can affect whether their answer has a positive or negative impact on their identity. If the child explores how he "caused" his adoptive parents to choose him, the effect will usually be positive, since he must have been a good child. If, on the other hand, he dwells on answering the question of what he did to "cause" his birth parents to choose not to parent him, the answer may inhibit development of a positive sense of self. Fortunately, because the preschooler's logic is not yet very sophisticated, children often focus easily on the "chosen-child" message without the flip side of the coin dawning on them for several years. (See "Issues That May Arise" later in this chapter for further discussion of this dichotomy.)

Another casualty of immature logic is that, at the same time the preschooler feels all-powerful, he also believes his parents to be omnipotent. Parents often miss that the child feels himself to be omnipotent because they can see his belief that they are omnipotent. The paradox is lost on the child. Furthermore, though preschoolers believe they are to blame or to credit for the events in their lives, they also feel powerless and unable to direct their own destinies. This sense of powerlessness leaves preschoolers feeling very vulnerable to the world around them. While most children experience this vulnerability, adopted children may feel it more acutely because of the losses entailed in adoption. Even so, telling children about their adoption remains the best route since the "injury" incurred at this age is still less acute than if they learn about their adoption at a later age.

Generalization. Young children through the preschool years sort and label things in the world around them by looking for general similarities rather than specific differences. This process of generalization is perhaps most apparent as children first begin to talk. An example is that of a very young child who knows what a dog is but who has never before seen a cow. When she sees a cow for the first time, she considers that it has four legs, a tail, and a general silhouette similar to that of a dog, and she points to the cow and says, "dog." The adults around her then say, "No, that's not a dog, it is a cow," and proceed to point out specific differences between cows and dogs. The child has probably already noticed the differences, but because she doesn't have a category for cows, she places the cow in the next best category—the dog group—even though it doesn't fit.

While three- to five-year-olds usually know a cow from a dog, generalization remains their primary mode of categorizing the world. Finding ways in which they are like their parents and other family is very important at this age because it is through their likenesses that they are able to feel they belong in the family. When those likenesses are difficult to find because they look different from their adoptive parents and because they hear other people comment on their differences, with fewer comments on their similarities, it becomes harder for children to *generalize* themselves into their families. And even if the child never hears comments on his differences, as he learns his life story he will learn that there is someone someplace whom he resembles more than he does his adoptive parents.

To counteract the inhibiting effect differences can have on your child's sense of belonging, you need to celebrate both your child's differences and similarities. Denying or minimizing differences does more harm than good. For example, if you have a child of color and you are white, and you tell your child, "You look white to me," the message your child will ultimately take in is that the only way she can really belong is if she changes. By about age two, children can easily identify differences in physical characteristics of people, including race, and they know that society, too, separates by differences.

By age three to three and a half, children are already aware that different skin tones are valued differently in our society (in other words, that darker skin color is somehow valued less than lighter skin tones). Though young children naturally embrace differences, they pick up from other people that some differences are undesirable. Telling your child that her skin looks like yours when she can clearly see that it doesn't, reinforces for her the belief that she is not good enough as she is now. A better approach would be to tell your child, "You have such pretty brown skin," to celebrate the differences, and "You are so good at (drawing pictures, catching a ball, singing, or whatever), just like Daddy," to celebrate the similarities. When she is older, helping your child "park" other characteristics somewhere in her birth family will help her develop a sense of roots and a genetic connection to the human race. For example, from pictures you might see that your daughter got her nose from her birth mother. If you are unsure what characteristics she inherited, comments such as "Linda (the birth mother) probably drove her mother crazy with tapping her fingers, too," can serve to park traits. This advice about celebrating similarities and differences is as important to follow in same-race adoptions as it is in interracial or international adoptions.

Modeling. Children learn through play. During fantasy play, children actually take on the characteristics of the people or characters they are imitating. Even after play is through, some of the characteristics remain, and the more the child feels like the character she is imitating, the more she will take on the attributes of that character. For example, after pretending to be Batman, a child will still feel powerful and strong, though more calm than during play. Three- to four-year-olds are more likely to pretend they are fictitious characters from television, movies, or books, or people who are "real" but whom they don't actually know, such as sports stars or other celebrities. But as they get closer to age five, they begin to spend more play time imitating people they know, especially their parents.

Modeling is one of the means through which children internalize their parents' characteristics and values. Just as a child becomes more engrossed in playing Superman when she has a cape than she would without it, the more characteristics she feels she shares with either parent, the better able she will be to internalize that parent. Again, since adopted children are less likely to hear comments from others on how much they are "like" their parents and other family members, adoptive parents need to make it a point to comment at least once a day on shared characteristics: interests, mannerisms, likes or dislikes, as well as physical features. The more characteristics you can identify over time, the better. Grandparents are often great at helping point out similarities between parents and children, especially childhood similarities.

Awareness of parents' relationship. Sometime during the preschool years children recognize for the first time that their parents have a relationship with each other that does not include them. Until this point, children have a dyadic (one-to-one) relationship with each parent. And though they may recognize each parent's relationship with other siblings (since these dyads are similar to their own), they usually fail to see the third side of the family triad—the parents' relationship with each other—until sometime after the third birthday. At first they feel their relationship with each parent is in competition with the parents' relationship with one another. Since they are modeling and internalizing the same-sex parent, they begin to feel a sense of competition with that parent for the attention of the opposite parent. While Freud described this phenomenon in terms of "sexual" desire for the parent (Oedipus and Electra complexes), in most cases the real issue is that in order to grow up to be like the same-sex parent, on whom the child is already modeling, the child needs to marry just as that parent did. Because preschoolers think concretely, the only partner they can imagine marrying is the one their parent already has. Of course, children know that they can't marry that parent unless the other parent is gone. Magical thinking, combined with the child's sense of omnipotence, can lead to fear that the same-sex parent will disappear.

If the child loses the same-sex parent, her magical thinking is confirmed. If she loses the opposite-sex parent, she may feel that she is being punished for her thoughts. The Oedipus/Electra theory holds particular relevance in adoption if a child is moved during the preschool years, though it can also be an issue in the event of divorce or the death of a parent.

Grouping three- to five-year-olds into one broad category is a bit misleading. As at earlier ages, preschoolers continue to alternate about once every six months between times of equilibrium and disequilibrium; they also continue to stretch their abilities. Throughout these years, there are a variety of less-than-desirable behaviors most children try at least once—and in most cases, quite a bit more often. Adoptive parents often worry that some of these behaviors are signs that their children are having problems related to adoption.

The first of these behaviors is the three-year-old who repeatedly asks the same questions about his adoption. Adoptive parents are sometimes concerned that their children are either obsessed with adoption or that they, as parents, are failing to answer the questions in a way their children can understand. In fact, however, three-year-olds just like to ask questions over and over again, in part simply to see if they will get the same answer as before. But children will also ask a question they've already had answered because they are thinking about the topic, want to discuss it again, but don't have the ability to carry the conversation on the topic further than asking the same question and repeating the earlier discussion.

At about age four and a half, children enter another period of disequilibrium. Older four-year-olds are often called "out of bounds" (Ilg, Ames, and Baker 1981, 32): they often seem emotionally, physically, and verbally out of control. Temper tantrums may return; and a growing imagination leads to growing fears of such things as the dark, imaginary creatures, or strange noises. But particularly upsetting to adoptive parents is when their children in anger say things like "I hate you," "I wish you were dead," or "You're not my *real* mom or dad." Adoptive parents easily overreact to these outbursts, interpreting them as personal rejection or as evidence that there is no attachment. But these outbursts are usually just expressions of anger and frustration, not actual commentaries on the state of the parent/child relationship.

If you overreact to your child's outbursts, they will become a "button" your child can easily push to upset you or coerce you into giving in to his wishes. The best approach is to deal with the issue triggering your child's anger. Statements such as "It looks to me like you are very angry" or "I know you are angry that . . . ," help define and acknowledge your child's feelings without getting into a hassle over whether the child has a "right" to feel that way. While it is often better to address the adoption-related elements of "You're not my real parent" at another time, if you feel compelled to comment on it immediately, you can say something like, "You are my son. I didn't give birth to you, but you are my son. I know you are angry." Whatever you do, don't get caught up in the fruitless I-*am*-your-parent argument at the moment when your child is angry. By dealing with the real issue at hand, you will demonstrate that you are your child's mother or father because you are *parenting*.

Three- to four-year-olds, particularly girls, who are exposed to pregnancy will be more apt to have questions or ideas about their own origins, but may not always express them. Your child may assume she grew inside you (assuming you are a woman). While it may seem less confusing and complicated to delay adoption explanations until a later age, it is better to begin to get the story straight now. To help minimize potential fears your child may have that she will have to leave you just as she left the woman who gave birth to her, it may help to tell her that adoption means she will be your daughter and live with you until she grows up; and even after she is a grown up, she will still be your daughter and you will still see her often and love her as much as you do now, if not more. We suggest avoiding the expression "forever child" because *forever* is an abstract concept that very few preschoolers truly understand.

Preschool girls also tend to actively search for their birth mothers and are more likely than boys to get caught in yearning and pining. It is not uncommon for preschool girls to approach strangers and ask, "Are you that other lady?" When this happens, parents sometimes fear that their children are actually seeking to replace them. What they are more likely looking for is tangible evidence of the missing character in their story (i.e., birth mother) and proof that they, too, were *born* just like all the other children they know. In fact, a child may be searching and at the same time afraid that her birth mother will actually come back and take her away. Reinforcing through actions and words that your child belongs in your family can help alleviate fears your child may have. Parking the image of the birth parent by showing your child photographs of the birth mother, having your child draw pictures of her if there are no photos, and giving the birth mother a name (using her first name if you know it, or making one up saying, "I don't know her name, but let's call her . . . ") will answer your preschooler's questions and lessen her urge to search by giving her the information she is looking for.

Even if your child is not overtly searching, it is important to tell stories about her life before placement, beginning with her birth. One therapist working with about ten adopted teenagers in a residential psychiatric treatment program found that none had ever been told anything about the circumstances of their birth. While this is anecdotal, we do see a pattern of adopted children having greater psychological problems at older ages when they know nothing about their birth, while children who know facts or have discussed the lack of facts about their births seem to have fewer problems. Furthermore, some children, in their concrete thinking, believe they came from an adoption agency, orphanage, or country, as opposed to a womb; this can have a dehumanizing effect and a negative influence on their feelings about themselves, their bodies, and eventually their sexuality.

Children in open adoptions may also exhibit searching behaviors as they look for more facts or a parent/child relationship with their birth parents. Adoptive parents and birth parents need to be clear in words and actions as to who are the "real" parents—the ones responsible for raising the child—and who are the people who gave birth, care about, and visit the child, but who are not active "parents." Preschoolers who go on outings or day-long or overnight visits with their birth parents are easily and understandably confused about the role these people have in their lives, and often fear that they will have to leave their family to return to the birth parents.

Search also becomes a source of fear for preschoolers who are interracially or internationally adopted, particularly when they are taken to cultural gatherings with many adults of their ethnic or racial heritage. Often preschoolers are afraid their birth parents are among the crowd and waiting to take them back. This fear is based primarily on the preschooler's fear of losing her adoptive parents (the only parents she's ever truly known unless she was moved as a toddler or older) and fear of the birth parents as strangers; rarely is it on racial or ethnic biases or fear of the birth parents as individuals the child actually knows.

Exposing your child in positive ways to his ethnic heritage promotes healthy self-esteem. But before attending cultural gatherings, you should alleviate possible fears by explaining that he will go with you and return home with you afterward. You might tell him in advance that there will be a lot of people who look like him, but that they have families of their own and are not related to him. During the event, reassure your child of your claiming of him by holding his hand, letting him sit on your lap, or giving other physical and verbal assurances. If your child asks if a certain person is his birth parent (and that person is not) say something like "No, she is (African-American, Korean, or whatever other ethnic or racial group) like you, but she isn't related." Another possible answer is to tell your child, "No, I think your birth mother is still in (fill in the country, city, or state), and that's very far away."

Imaginary friends and tall tales are another part of preschool life. Imaginary friends always serve a need in the child's life, whether that be for a playmate or to help the child deal with other issues. Frequently in transracial adoptions the imaginary friends will be the race or ethnic background of the adoptive family. Children blame imaginary friends for things they themselves do wrong, and they give imaginary friends powers they wish they had. Imaginary friends also tend to take on fears and vulnerabilities the child feels; for example, the imaginary friend who doesn't want the light turned off at bedtime. Adopted children who are told their parents are not their "real parents" or that they are not their parents' "real children" will sometimes say they are imaginary like their imaginary friends. This of course is very scary because preschoolers—like everyone else—know their imaginary friends don't exist, and if they, too, are imaginary then they don't exist either. They may also think their membership in the family is pretend and therefore temporary.

Some parents are disturbed when their children blame an imaginary friend for something bad they themselves did. Imaginary friends help children work out the different sides of themselves, especially the good and the bad. Since self-constancy is not yet mature at this age, blaming an imaginary friend for bad deeds enables the child to maintain his sense of being a good child. This, however, does not mean that you do not impose consequences for your child for misdeeds; instead, you consequence both the child and the imaginary friend—for example, "You and Amy have to take a timeout," or "Well, since Joey ate so many cookies, there aren't enough left for you." By grinning or winking at the child when you say that the imaginary friend will have to pay the consequence also, you let your child know that you know his imaginary friend isn't real. Preschoolers usually accept the joint punishment with little further argument about who did what.

A preschooler's use of an imaginary friend should not be confused with lying. Children do not knowingly lie until they are closer to age six. A child who is called a liar is likely to become one out of self-fulfilling prophecy. At the same time, children who continue beyond the preschool years to blame their misdeeds on imaginary friends may have problems merging the good and bad aspects of themselves to achieve self-constancy.

Preschoolers are also great tellers of tall tales, particularly when they are caught doing something wrong and have difficulty accepting that they did a bad thing. They even tend to believe their own tales. But explaining misdeeds isn't the only use for tall tales; children tell such stories about any number of things. Adopted children often make up stories about life with their birth parents or previous caretakers. In most cases, particularly if your child joined your family in infancy, the best approach is to simply nod and give an interested "Oh," rather than get caught up in facts and accuracy—you won't be able to change the child's fantasy anyway. If the tale is about something that has recently happened, correct the child's facts; if you are unsure of the facts, don't worry about it. If you feel compelled to correct some of the taller tales, do so by saying something like "That would have been nice if it was like that, but it probably wasn't." Keep in mind, however, that if your child joined your family as a young toddler or older, she may actually have pieces of memories about her life with previous caretakers; write down what your child says and save it to talk about when she is older (middle childhood, around age eight, is a good time for this). Furthermore, tall tales fill the child's need to see herself in a certain light; refuting them directly can leave her feeling defenseless.

Last, but not least, play is a crucial part of the preschooler's life. The most common themes of preschool play tend to be babies, birthdays, superheroes, and bad guys (Fahlberg, *Child Development*, 1982, 34, and Paley 1988, 3). Through these themes, children explore both dependency (playing babies) and individuation. They fulfill their need to be in control and have a sense of power; and they experiment with adult roles, from astronauts to parents, doctors to truck drivers, cashiers to paleontologists. Play provides a way for children to manage their feelings, especially of fear, powerlessness, and anger. Through play, children can take control of the bad guys, determine outcomes of events, and even revisit their babyhoods.

Parents often misinterpret aggressive play as proof that similar behaviors have been done to their children; in many cases, however, such play is more a reflection of the children's need to be in control than of behaviors they have personally encountered. Parents also sometimes become concerned when their children play games about adoption, especially if the game does not accurately reflect the facts of their adoptions. Through such games, however, children are able to, at least in part, work out their fears and feelings of helplessness about what happened by rewriting the script and controlling the actors involved. Even when the "bad guys" are after a child, the child remains in control because she determines the limits of what they can do. Adopted children sometimes feel a greater degree of powerlessness than other children, and thus will sometimes tend to play superheroes and bad guys—with the child in either role—more frequently and intensely than other children.

Birthday play can be difficult for adopted children, especially when pretending with other children. Birthday play may focus on cake, ice cream, and presents, or on being born. The unwritten rule about birthdays that persists even into adulthood is that only happy things can happen on one's birthday. For many adopted children, of course, something sad did happen on the day of their birth: their birth parents chose not to keep them. Furthermore, for adopted children there is often a chasm of unknowns about their day of birth and a pronounced absence of stories about how happy their parents were when they were finally born—the type of stories they may hear from other children during birthday play. You can help your child by acknowledging that something sad may have happened the day your child was born, but that the child's birth was a miraculous and happy event, just as the births of all new babies. Reading books such as *On the Day You Were Born* by Debra Frasier (see reading list at the end of this chapter), is one way to rejoice with your child and help him feel that his birth is something you rejoice in.

Body Image, Gender Roles, and Sexuality

Just as children—even adult children—tend to view their parents as asexual, one of the last things parents like to think about is their children's sexuality. But the facts of life are that, like all creatures on earth, humans are biologically programmed to be sexual. The roots of sexuality begin to grow from infancy on, even though children are not intended or ready for sexual activity until they have reached physical and emotional maturity. For preschoolers, sexuality is fairly synonymous with body image, gender roles, enjoyment of their bodies, and knowing they were conceived and born in the normal human fashion. Young preschoolers are already very much aware of gender differences, and throughout the preschool years they continue to explore and learn about the roles of men and women, of girls and boys.

The preschooler's body image is often very much based on the adult on whom the child is modeling himself. For example, a boy who is pretending to be a basketball player like Michael Jordan will *feel* tall even though he isn't and, based on the physical stature of those in his genetic family, he probably never will be. Still the child's growing fine and gross motor skills, as well as the pride and sense of capability he derives when pretending to have skills (such as pretending to shoot baskets like Michael Jordan), all are factors in body image.

By age four, most children know where babies come from, though the majority will not know all the specifics. At this age, children are satisfied with knowing that babies are born from mothers, usually without questioning how they got in the mothers in the first place. The knowledge that one was born of two parents, the same as all other people, helps tie individuals to the human race. Adopted children, however, sometimes miss this dimension. In fact, it is not unusual for young children who have been adopted internationally to believe an airplane gave birth to them, since the life stories they are told often begin with the plane trip or a meeting at an airport. In international adoption, too, agencies often claim and label children as their own, for example "Orphanage or Agency X's children." Because preschoolers lack abstract thinking, they interpret this literally to mean that the orphanage or agency gave birth to them. Such beliefs at a time when they are learning that children are born of parents can make children feel less than human.

Children's myths about their origins may also be reinforced when the next sibling to join the family comes through adoption. Like any other child, the adopted child needs to be told that there was a man and a woman who made a baby and that baby was she. This is especially important for adopted children since their conception will be a factor in their own growing sense of sexuality, identity formation, and grief surrounding adoption, especially in adolescence.

Many adoptive parents find it difficult to talk with their young children about their birth. Some parents feel they don't know enough of the specifics to be able to discuss their children's birth; for others, the topic raises their own issues of loss, especially when infertility is a factor. And for any adoptive parent, it is far easier and more enjoyable to talk about the child's life since joining the family, because that is the part in which they too share. Sometimes parents may need to create moments to talk with their children about their birth. Pregnancy—whether the mother's, a friend's, or a relative's—provides a wonderful opportunity for opening such discussions. Likewise, the pregnant hamster at preschool or the neighbor's pet cat and newborn litter can be used as launching points for telling about human birth and the child's own story.

Gender roles are another important part of sexuality for the preschooler. Children need definitions of what men and women are and how they are different in their social and work roles, functions within the family, mannerisms, and dress. This doesn't mean children should necessarily be taught traditional gender roles; but they do need some definitions. Mr. Rogers' song about how "a girl will grow up to be a woman and a boy will some day be a man" sums up well what preschoolers most need to know about gender.

Sometimes adopted children, especially those who have been told that their parents adopted because they couldn't conceive, believe they, too, will be infertile and thus will build their families through adoption. It is normal for preschoolers to believe they will follow in their parents' footsteps, but adoptive parents need to reinforce for their children that they will probably be able to conceive children. One way to do this is by saying, "When you grow up you can choose to have children. You may choose to adopt. Or you may choose to make a baby with your (husband or wife). Most grown-ups can make babies."

Throughout the preschool years, children continue to discover the many things their bodies can do, what they look like, and the many ways in which they can sense the world around them. Often to the chagrin of parents, they do things like pick their noses, pinch themselves and others, and make messes with water, dirt, flour, or anything else they can get their hands on. In this same vein, it is very normal for boys and girls to mastur-bate at this age. This is often disturbing to adults, but the preschooler does not perceive masturbation as a sexual act; it is simply a pleasurable feeling they have discovered that is as innocuous as being tickled. Telling a child not to touch his or her genitals or that doing so is bad leads to shame about their bodies and eventually about sexual sensations. Feeling good about the good feelings your body can give you is an important aspect of positive sexuality as an adult. Rather than shaming the child for the touch, parents need to teach children about privacy and respect for themselves and others. In other words, you can do that in your own room, but not in front of other people. Your child needs to be told that there is nothing physically harmful about masturbation, but you should also talk with your child about your values and why you feel as you do about it (Children's Television Workshop, 1992).

Avoiding shaming the child is particularly important for the adopted preschooler who may already be thinking she was a "bad" baby and that is why her birth parents chose not to parent her. A child who believes she was a bad baby will also believe she has a bad body. When drawing pictures of themselves, children who feel this way often will draw themselves with damaged bodies—even though they have no physical disabilities or injur-ies—and draw other people fine. Helping the child feel good about her body through complimenting motor skills and appearance, teaching her that she was born in a normal way, and not shaming her if you do find her masturbating will help overcome feelings she may have about being a bad baby.

Special Issues for Interracial and International Adoptions

We've already mentioned that children from a very early age are aware of the physical differences attendant to race, that even preschoolers sense that nonwhites are devalued in our society, and the importance for children of feeling like their parents without having their differences ignored or denied. But no matter how much love and unconditional acceptance interracial families have at home, they are bound to encounter what we call "grocery-store scenes," in which parents or other family members are approached in the presence of the children and asked directly about their origins. Typical questions include: Where is she from? When did you get him? Is he adopted? Is she your real child? Whose child is he? and even How much did she cost?

Whether questions are asked outright or indirectly through stares, the effect is the same: an uncomfortable situation that points out the child's differences, undermines her sense of belonging, and devalues her by addressing her as property. Sometimes questions are asked politely and with no intention of causing pain; sometimes people simply don't realize that approaching a family and publicly pointing out a child's differences does hurt. Adoptive parents often get caught up in answering the questions out of a desire to promote adoption and talk about how good their experience has been. But answering such questions in any depth at all tells the child that he needs to be explained or justified. Instead of focusing on answering the question at hand, parents need to take charge by directing the conversation in a way that will support their child even if it doesn't address the stranger's question. Here are some effective ways to answer common questions:

- *Where is your child from?* A simple answer is the name of the city in which you live. Another approach is to give the lineage of the entire family, beginning with the oldest member (not with the child about whom the question was asked) and working through the family in order of age. For example, "Well, I was born in Illinois, but my grandparents on my mother's side came from Germany. My husband was born in California, but because his father was in the military, they moved from there to Hawaii, then to Japan, Korea, West Germany, Texas, and Washington, D.C. He then moved to Minnesota for college and that's where we met. Our first son. . . ." By the time you get to the child in question, the asker will either have gotten the message or become bored or irritated with the answer. But most important, your child's need for claiming and belonging will have been protected.

- *Whose child is he?* Mine!
- *When did you get her? Where did you get her?* I picked her up after school to come to the store. We left the house together, like we usually do.
- *How long have you had him?* It's hard to remember a time when he wasn't a part of our family. It seems like he's always been with us.
- *How much did she cost?* Oh, she's priceless. Or: How much did your child cost?

Other ways to answer intrusive questions are to turn the question back on the asker, as in the last example above. You can also debate out loud whether you should answer the question, especially if you have someone else with you. As your child gets older you can transfer control of the situation to your child by asking, "Should we answer that?" or "Would you like to answer that?" Let your child know that the family rule is that he can decline to answer and that you will respect his decision. Any of these questions can also be answered by simply saying, "I don't care to answer that question."

Choosing not to answer a question is one way to teach your child how to protect her personal boundaries. While people may approach you about your child because they truly are drawn by the child's good looks or character, there can also be an element of racism in such encounters, just as it can be in stares. A white woman with a child of color is more likely to be approached than a white man in the same situation, with the underlying curiosity being whether the woman has slept with a man of color. White men are less likely to be approached on the same grounds because of the gender and racial hierarchy in our society (in other words, he will be less likely to be challenged because his race and sex afford him more freedoms). Because of barriers institutionalized in our legal system (such as economic criteria for adoption) and biases in many agencies, the opposite situation—that of a person of color adopting a white child—is relatively rare. When it does occur, however, parents often find themselves accused of having kidnapped their child, or the mother is assumed to be the child's nanny or other family domestic servant.

Maintaining personal boundaries can be problematic for any adopted child, but it is a particular issue for children of color. People feel fairly comfortable approaching a baby, but the older a child gets, the less frequent such encounters usually become. They tend, however, to persist to a later age for children of color than they do for white children. This, combined with the tendency for large portions of society to view adopted children in general as somehow not "belonging" to their parents in the same way genetically related children do, creates an atmosphere in which any adult can feel freer to exert authority over an adopted child or disregard personal boundaries—especially by touching the child—well beyond the toddler years, after which such "freedoms" normally end. A common example is a stranger rubbing or touching a child's hair. Some people do this out of curiosity (for example, to see how soft or coarse the child's hair is); others do this to show their "acceptance" of the child. Either situation carries an element of racism, just as rubbing a redhead's hair for good luck has elements of stereotypes and superstition.

Regardless of how you interpret such situations, your first response must be to validate your child's feelings. If your child is nonwhite, it is inevitable that at some point he will encounter more overt forms of racism than the types of condescension described above. He may be called a name, picked on, or excluded by other children—or worse, by adults. Most white parents wait until that first injury to talk with their children about racism. Most African-American families, and other people of color, warn their children about the cruelties of racism before they encounter it firsthand. If you don't share your child's race, you may find this latter approach difficult. After all, if you tell your child that someone may one day call him a "nigger," "gook," "spic," or other such deplorable name, are you somehow implying a degree of validity to the slur? Regardless of what your gut reaction to this approach may be, it holds a great deal of wisdom. Telling your child about racism before he encounters it is like having your child vaccinated for measles before he is exposed to the virus. Exposure is highly likely, if not inevitable, so the best thing you can do for your child is to increase your child's resistance and thus decrease the subsequent pain. If you cannot find it in yourself to discuss such harsh realities, you might ask an adult friend (or even a mature teenager) who shares your child's race to talk with your child about racism.

No matter who tells your child, the basic points to cover include the following:

- that such things happen and do hurt;
- that your child does not deserve such treatment and is a good person just as he is; and
- that people who act this way don't really know your child and therefore have no right to comment on what type of person he is.

Teaching your child ways to take control of the situation is also important. Children can respond effectively to playground taunts by saying, "My mama says that people who say that are ignorant." Granted this may not be the nicest thing to say, but it is effective. First, your child has communicated that what was just said about him is not acceptable; second, he has quoted an authority figure (his mother) to back up the statement; and he has taken control of the situation. The argument is not likely to last much past a relatively weak retort of "Well, your mama is stupid."

Since your child may also encounter uncomfortable stares, you need to give her techniques she can use to guard herself from feeling self-conscious, belittled, or otherwise hurt. Again, the goal is to empower your child when such situations arise. One way to do this is to tell your child that people who stare are rude. Another way is to teach her to confront the starer in a safe way. Staring back at the starer's clothing, especially around the trunk of the body, is often enough to avert the stare by letting the person know the child is aware of what is happening and also by returning the uncomfortable feeling of being stared at—without making direct eye contact. Families can practice this together at home to help their children build the skills. When a child or the entire family is being stared at in public, waving or staring back in this way as a family can both empower you and build a sense of unity—not to mention that it is that much more intimidating to the person who was so rude as to stare in the first place.

In addition to helping your child, however, if you are white, you must also be aware that as a parent of a child of color there will be times when you, too, encounter racism by association. For example, you may find that when you go to a store alone you are treated with respect, but when shopping the same store with your children present, the security guard follows you or the cashier runs extra checks on your credit card or asks for more than the usual amount of identification for the check you've just written. How do you react? How do you feel? Anger is a natural reaction, as is embarrassment. But if either emotion leads you to hide or deny your relationship with your children or to go out of your way to avoid such uncomfortable situations, it's time to take a closer look at yourself, especially your attitudes and values.

In interracial families where some of the siblings are white and others are of color, the white children may feel a sense of guilt that they can walk away from the stares and loss of privilege. Some children draw closer to their nonwhite siblings as a result of this guilt. Others try to deny any relationship to their brothers or sisters and then feel guilty for doing so. These children need to be taught some of the same coping skills one would teach a child of color. Though the attention the child of color is getting is negative, other children in the family—including cousins—sometimes feel jealous over the attention the child of color receives, particularly when strangers and acquaintances are asking questions about the child of color, but never ask about the "plain old white child."

Until now, we've focused on ways to cope with racism from outside the family. But one of the most difficult and painful encounters interracial families can have is when extended family or close friends do not accept the child because of race. You must choose how much of the family dispute and racism you will allow your child to be exposed to. Your first responsibility is to support your child; in some cases this may mean breaking ties with a family member or friend you have been close to in the past, at least until they can grow to accept your child. These can be difficult and painful choices, but only you can protect your child. While children of color inevitably will encounter racism in the outside world, the one haven from racism they should be assured to have is at home and with family.

Family Life Cycle

Unless you've since added another child to your family, by the time your child is three years old you've probably finally begun to catch your breath. In theory, at least, your child's growing independence has freed some of your time for focusing on your marital relationship and socializing with other adults. For many parents, the fun of building a new family is old hat, but parents often remain so focused on parenting that they lose sight of their marriage. Depending on your age and occupation, this may also be a time when you are still saving and trying to establish yourselves financially, making it all the easier to say that you can't afford a baby sitter and a night out. By now you may even have grown accustomed to *not* going out and no longer feel you need dates or evenings out as you once did. But by taking good care of yourself and your adult relationships, you teach your children by example what it means to have good self-respect and self-esteem. Even if your child doesn't like being left behind with the sitter for an afternoon or evening, doing so teaches your child about healthy adult affection and emotional intimacy. Single parents, too, need time away from their children to spend with other adults, whether that means going to a movie with a friend, dating, or participating in some kind of a recreational club, study group, or even a class.

If you truly cannot afford a baby sitter, find ways to have privacy at home. If your children regularly go to bed at eight o'clock and you stay up until ten or eleven, finding time alone won't be too difficult to do. But if your children tend to be night owls, the job becomes more challenging. One solution is to have "room time," during which everyone—parents included—spends time in their own rooms with the doors closed. No one is required to go to sleep during room time, but they do have to stay in their rooms or in bed, quietly playing, reading, talking, listening to the radio, or watching television.

Teaching your children to respect closed doors is another key to ensuring adult privacy. By the preschool years, children have usually already learned this about the bathroom door. Taking the rule that you always knock and wait for permission before opening a closed bathroom door and applying it to all closed doors—or at least bedroom doors—is usually fairly easy to do, especially if you remind the child about the rules whenever they are violated. You can reinforce this lesson in respect for others by following the same rules you set for them: knocking before entering your children's rooms to let them know you are coming (you don't necessarily have to wait for their permission).

Parents often begin to get caught up in their careers at about this time as well. This focus on career is a natural part of the adult's life stages, but it can also be a way of maintaining identity apart from parenting for the parent who is providing the primary care for the children. Unfortunately, women in our culture often feel devalued if they are full-time homemakers and parents. But whether your career is in the home or out of the home, finding time to focus on your relationship with your partner remains crucial to keeping that relationship in good shape. Showing your partner that you still enjoy and love him or her doesn't always have to be as goal-oriented as setting aside time for sex, though this is important, too. Brief interactions throughout the day, such as a call from work just to say hello, or a spontaneous hug, kiss, or pat, can help maintain intimacy and serve as a warm-up for more intimate interactions when the two of you are finally alone.

It is especially important at this stage in the relationship to keep each other's needs in mind, as well as your own. Many men view sexual intimacy as the proof and enactment of emotional intimacy; women on the other hand often view sexual intimacy as a *result* of emotional intimacy established in other ways. In his book *His Needs, Her Needs: Building an Affair-Proof Marriage*, William Harley, Jr., reminds readers that men and women desire different things from their relationships. Harley boils these needs down to two basic lists, as follows:

The man's five most basic needs in marriage are:
1. Sexual fulfillment
2. Recreational companionship
3. An attractive spouse
4. Domestic support
5. Admiration

The woman's five most basic needs in marriage are:
1. Affection
2. Conversation
3. Honesty and openness
4. Financial support
5. Family commitment (1986, 10)

While your needs may vary from these lists, the important point to remember is that you and your spouse, no matter how well suited to one another, probably look to each other to fulfill different needs. Clarifying and communicating these needs is important for keeping your relationship strong. And keeping your relationship strong is a key not only to your personal happiness, but also to your children's happiness.

By age three, your child has already developed a distinct personality, mannerisms, habits, and interests; how well these fit with your expectations, likes, and dislikes affects the quality of your parent/child fit. A classic example of poor parent/child fit is the story of the ugly duckling; the duckling was considered ugly because it didn't fit the characteristics of the rest of the family. Of course, the real problem was that the "duckling" was a swan, not a duck. Parents and children who are genetically related can have poor parent/child fit, but if the family system is healthy there will usually be other relatives who can help the parents park the characteristics the parents find problematic or irritating by pointing to another family member who had the same traits ("Oh yes, your brother did the same thing at that age"). This parking helps normalize the characteristic for the parents, and parents often find helpful advice on managing it from other members of the family.

The types of differences that contribute to problems with parent/child fit are more apt to arise when parent and child do not share genetic lines. Some examples might be the athletic family with the nonathletic child, a fast-paced family with a child who is naturally easygoing (or the other way around), or simply mannerisms and ways of expression that don't fit with what the parents are accustomed to. Issues related to parent/child fit may be accentuated for adoptive parents because of the loss of not sharing genetic ties with their children. Even in cases of preferential adoption, where the parents have birth children as well as adopted children, lack of genetic ties with the adopted children can still be a loss. For this reason, it is important that parents check in with themselves: Why does the particular trait bother you? Does it conflict with the way you were raised or the values of your family of origin? Does it bother you because you had hoped your child would be "better" than she is? (Were you hoping for a perfect child?) Does it remind you of something, or someone, from your childhood? Is the trait harmful—will it hurt the child or other people, or lead to criminal behavior—or is it just irritating? We ask parents to take a look at themselves in these situations because problems of parent/child fit usually stem from the child's inability to meet the parents' expectations. We can only shape and mold our children within the parameters of their personalities and innate potentials; as in other interpersonal relationships, the most effective way to solve the problem of someone else not meeting our expectations is to try to change *our* expectations.

Finally, it is often sometime during the youngest child's preschool years that parents decide to add another child to the family, if they desire more children. Children naturally feel somewhat displaced when a new sibling arrives, but for adopted children these feelings are sometimes intensified. Adopted preschoolers often fear that the new addition means they are no longer needed or wanted, and that they will literally have to move on. This is especially common for children who have been told that Mommy and Daddy were sad because they couldn't make a baby and, in brief, that their adoption filled the void; if the parents conceive, then the children may believe they are no longer needed because what their parents really wanted was a genetically related child.

There probably is no easy way around the complexities of this type of situation. You need not go out of your way to modify the way in which you tell the family story in order to ensure that you don't encounter problems later, in the event you decide to add another child to your family. But you do need to be aware of and sensitive to your child's feelings and interpretations of the situation and reinforce for your child that you will always love her and that she will always be your child, just as the new family member will be. Furthermore, don't become overly concerned if your child shows hostility to the new sibling during imaginary play (for example, by pounding lumps on a doll he is calling Joey, the new sibling's name); such games, believe it or not, are normal and provide a way for the child to work out his feelings without needing to take them out directly on the new sibling. With some time, support, and understanding of their feelings, children usually come around to feeling more positively toward their siblings. Preparing your child in advance for being a big brother or sister (or even a younger brother or sister) can also make a world of difference when the new sibling finally arrives. Hospital-sponsored prenatal classes often have lists of resources and handouts with tips on preparing children for new siblings and on reducing sibling rivalry. Even if you are adopting again, it would be well worth a call to see if they would give or sell these resources to you; if they don't exactly fit your family's structure, adapt them.

If Moved During the Preschool Years

The preschool years can be a difficult time for children to be moved from one family or home to another. Magical thinking typical at this age increases the likelihood that the child will believe he did something bad to cause the move and the loss of the previous caretakers, whether birth or foster parents. And at just the age children are normally firming up object constancy, the permanent loss of a caretaker can interfere not only with object constancy but also with self-constancy. On the positive side, however, preschoolers are verbal; thus with some insight and caring, parents can help their children begin to understand what is happening and why.

Moves raise slightly different issues at each age within the preschool years. Children moved at age three often become stuck in the behaviors of a three-year-old. Negative behaviors, in particular, which would otherwise be a phase for the child, may develop into long-term trends. When moved between four-and-a-half and five, children often blame themselves for the move. And moves at age five can interfere with the equilibrium normally seen at that age. Five-year-olds generally identify very strongly with their parents, which is why this stage is so smooth. Loss of parents at this age not only disturbs the equilibrium, it also interferes with the accomplishments normally achieved at this age. In addition, since five-year-olds are working so hard to be what they believe their parents want them to be, a move at this age can lead to a shame-based identity because magical thinking tells them not only that they caused the move, but that they failed to meet their parents' expectations. In the new adoptive home, some five-year-olds will cover their feelings in an attempt to please their new parents; others will do little or nothing to temper their emotions.

Whenever children are moved during a stage of equilibrium, the initial move is often relatively smooth, leading to a false sense of security that all is well with the child. Because children won't always show that they are having difficulties, parents need to raise potential issues for discussion with their children. A good way to do this is by reading or telling stories about animals or children who have been adopted, and then talking about how the characters must have felt. The key is to stay concrete in your examples and to talk about the characters' feelings. One analogy that works well with preschoolers is talking about how puppies at the pound feel when they are first taken home. They may be scared, miss their old home, and worried that they won't be able to learn the rules of the new home. Though parents sometimes feel uncomfortable drawing analogies between their children and animals, the examples do work for the children. Stories can be followed up by discussions with the child about how he might have felt the same way when he came to live with his new family. Again, the key is to help the child identify how he feels and then to validate those emotions.

The advice given for moving toddlers holds true for preschoolers as well (see sections on "If Moved" in Chapter 9). The focus should be on transferring trust before the move and maintaining contact with previous caretakers after the move. If possible, visits with the previous caretaker after the move are still recommended. Visits should take place with the adoptive parents present, in either the child's new home or a neutral place. During visits, the previous caretakers need to continue the transfer of trust by deferring to the adoptive parents to comfort, assist, and correct the child.

In addition to facilitating transfer of trust, visitation with previous care-takers helps to challenge fantasies the child may be building about the caretakers in their absence (particularly perfect-parent fantasies), keeping the child in check with reality. Visits should be spaced often enough to challenge the child's fantasies, but not so often as to interfere with progress in the new family. Depending on the child and the specifics of the situation, once a month to four times a year is usually enough; weekly visits are not advisable. Gradually, visits should dwindle, with contact being maintained through letters or telephone calls. If visits or other contact is impossible or extremely difficult, such as in the case of many international adoptions, talking with the child occasionally about the previous caretakers (where they are now, how much they miss the child or the child misses them, memories about them, and so on) may serve the same purpose. It is natural for the child's grief to resurface following these visits. Though painful, this resurgence will actually help the grief process to progress and the child to heal.

Wooing, similar to that done with younger children, is also helpful when a preschooler first joins the family. Engaging the child in brief, playful moments of eye contact, as described in Chapter 9 for toddlers, and then gradually gaining closeness with cuddling, rocking, back rubs, or patting can help the child begin to transfer bonds and build attachments with the new parents. At the same time that reparenting is taking place, the pre-schooler should be given ample opportunities to play and develop at a level appropriate for her age.

Adoptive parents should also find out about the child's position in the previous family, what her responsibilities (chores), daily routine, and per-ceived capabilities were, as well as how feelings were expressed. In some cases, the child's roles in the previous family or home may not be acceptable in the new adoptive family. An example of such a case is that of a girl who was the only girl in an orphanage with about eight boys. It was her job to wash dishes following meals, and she took pride in her ability to do this chore. Though her adoptive parents were taken aback by what they per-ceived as sexism, their daughter didn't know how else to conclude a meal.

Before taking away your child's former role, wait until your child has new accomplishments and capabilities in your family. Then redirect her attention by telling her that while you appreciate her other work, you really need her help in another area, and reinforce the new direction with praise.

One sign that a child is experiencing problems following placement is that he does not play. If your child does not resume playing after the initial shock of the move (after the first month), consult a professional, such as a pediatrician or counselor. Lack of play can be a sign of emotional neglect in the early years, or of childhood depression. Even if a child was too impoverished to have toys, and thus doesn't know the intended use of the toys you provide, he should still be able to play in some way: imaginary play, gross and fine motor activities, and exploration. If your child has experienced neglect in the past, enrolling him in a good part-time preschool program may help him learn to play. At home, brief forays of infant games, such as stacking blocks, running cars on the floor, dressing dolls, playing catch or Nerf® basketball, or dancing to music, can help your child learn to respond.

No matter how healthy your child is when she joins your family, we recommend—if at all possible—that one parent stay home with the child for the first year to help promote healthy attachment. Of course, this is not financially possible for all families. If you are unable to have one parent stay at home full-time, consider working part-time rather than full-time. If this is not an option, look for a loving day care program with a low ratio of children to adults and a low turnover rate of both providers and enrolled children; and then avoid changing day care programs.

Issues That May Arise

The older children get and the more life experiences they accumulate, the harder it becomes to pinpoint single life events that may have contributed to emotional, psychological, or developmental difficulties. Unmet needs during the first six to twelve months of life leave relatively clear telltale signs in the child's overall development; by the toddler years, the signs can become less pronounced, in the absence of severe abuse or neglect. By the time children reach the preschool years (ages three to five), potential difficulties that may arise as a result of poor parent/child fit or inadequate parenting are much more difficult to list in any meaningful or useful way.

Without help from parents or professionals, however, any child who has experienced a significant loss or trauma during the preschool years runs the risk of becoming fixated in magical thinking. The longer the child believes he caused the trauma or loss, the more likely it is that the magical thinking will turn to feelings of guilt and eventually to a shame-based identity. The child's thought progression begins with fear of his own power: "I caused *this* bad thing to happen because of something I did" (a particular thought or action). If the magical thinking is not corrected, the child's fear turns to guilt; and if the guilt persists for too long, the child's thoughts about that one event may eventually (in middle childhood years) be extrapolated to the child as a whole (shame): "I cause bad things to happen because *I* am bad."

Some children who become stuck in magical thinking progress in other areas of cognitive and emotional development, but remain in the magical thoughts about that one trauma or loss. Such children may have a realistic sense of the power of their thoughts and feelings in every other area of their lives, but not when it comes to the loss or trauma they experienced while a preschooler. Others may be able to see cause and effect in other people's lives but not in their own. In the most severe cases, children are unable to see cause and effect anywhere, lacking both hindsight and foresight. It is important to note here that absence or delays in the development of cause-and-effect reasoning can also be a result of fetal alcohol syndrome, or cocaine or other drug use by the birth mother during pregnancy.

For Further Reading

• *Our Baby: A Birth and Adoption Story* by Janice Koch. Indianapolis, IN: Perspectives Press, 1985.

This book is a great resource for helping adoptive parents talk with their young children about their birth and adoption. Koch gives a simple and accurate explanation of the "facts of life" to help parents answer the question "Did I grow in Mommy's tummy?"

• *On the Day You Were Born* by Debra Frasier. New York: Harcourt Brace Jovanovich, 1991.

The earth and the rest of nature pass through the glorious cycles of a day in celebration and welcome for a newborn baby. That baby is any and every baby. *On the Day You Were Born* lets children know their day of birth was special and a day worthy of rejoicing.

• *It's My Body* by Lory Freeman. Los Angeles: Parenting Press, 1982.

A short, fun text to aid parents in teaching children healthy boundaries about their bodies.

• *Sometimes I Get Angry* by Jane Werner Watson, Robert E. Switzer, M.D., and J. Cotter Hirschberg, M.D. New York: Crown Publishers, 1986.

Parents and children together can explore ways to handle frustration and anger.

• *How Babies and Families are Made: There is More Than One Way* by Patricia Schaffer. Berkeley, CA: Tabor Sarah Books, 1988.

A great book for teaching children that their families are OK, no matter how they came to be.

• *A Mother for Choco* by Keiko Kasza. New York: Putnam, 1992.

Excellent for preschoolers and older children learning what parents do and how families can be multicultural.

• *All Kinds of Families* by Norma Simon. Niles, IL: Albert Whitman, 1976.

Explores the many variations of families.

Tips for Parenting Adopted Preschoolers

To Enhance Bonding and Attachment:

- Let your child know that your family structure, though different from her friends', is okay and normal. Look for books about different types of families, such as *Free to Be a Family* by Marlo Thomas and friends (New York: Bantam, 1987).

- Use concrete examples to reinforce that your child will always be your son or daughter. You can do this by occasionally talking about the life the two of you will share as he grows up, and the love you will continue to have for each other even after he has become an adult.

- If possible, avoid prolonged separations of several days or more. Talk about planned separations and what will happen, beginning not more than two weeks in advance. Leave little surprises for the child during the separation, such as a taped message from you to your child, which she can listen to at bedtime. Try to call daily; if you promise to call, be sure to carry through.

- Do not introduce or define your child as your "adopted child." Such labeling can distance your child from you and inhibit attachment and belonging. While it's healthy to talk about the fact that your child joined your family through adoption, it should not become a label.

- Let your child know you take joy in her uniqueness, as well as the many ways she is like you. Find times to have fun together.

To Help Your Child Through Grief:

- Continue helping your child learn to label and recognize her feelings.

- Model and teach appropriate ways of expressing feelings.

- Whenever answering painful questions about your child's adoption or discussing feelings, try to touch your child to reaffirm your closeness. If possible, have your child on your lap facing sideways or with her back toward you to avoid forcing eye contact, which can be difficult if your child's emotions are running high. Reestablish eye contact later in an enjoyable way by playing peekaboo, counting and naming freckles, or stealing a nose. *Tell* your child you love her, in addition to demonstrating your closeness and love through actions and touch.

To Nurture Identity:

- Tell your child about his adoption and about his life before coming to you, including his birth and information you may have about his birth parents. Telling your child about his past loss may temporarily stretch his attachment to you, but it will return in strength and closeness with time.

- Read and talk with your child about the family storybook and her own life storybook or baby book. If you haven't prepared a family storybook, involve your child in helping you make one. (See Chapter 5 for more on writing a family storybook.) Be sure to begin your child's story at birth.

(continued)

Tips for Parenting Adopted Preschoolers (continued)

To Nurture Identity (continued):

- When talking to your child about her birth parents' decision not to parent, be sure to include feelings. This gives the birth parents human dimension and shows your child that she is of value, not a throw-away child. *Love* is not always the most appropriate word to describe birth parents' feelings because love takes time to grow. Your child will feel valued if she knows that her birth parents' decision was difficult and painful ("they cried").

- If at all possible have first names for your child's birth parents. Names make people human; use of first names also avoids problems posed when other terms are used, such as "real mom" or "first mom." If you don't have a first name, you can make one up saying, "We don't know her real name, but let's call her ____." The more human your child's birth parents seem, the more human and OK your child will feel.

- Celebrate your child's genetic heritage, blending parts of his cultural heritage into your home life, as you do yours and your spouse's. Avoid focusing on your child's cultural heritage simply because you feel it is exotic or different; as a multicultural family, you should be including and recognizing cultural contributions from each member's heritage, not just that of the child who is most unlike the rest of the family.

When You Need to Discipline:

- If you use timeouts, stay in your child's sight or at least within talking range to ensure that your child does not feel abandoned, especially if your child has recently come to your family or if she has been moved many times.

- To avoid struggles and to help your child feel some degree of control over his life—while maintaining an appropriate level of control yourself—give your child choices. For example, "When you are angry you may pound playdough or stomp your feet in your bedroom," or "You may wear the blue shirt or the red shirt."

11

❦

Middle Childhood: Six to Ten Years

*T*he move from the preschool years into middle childhood represents a major developmental turning point in a child's life. Formal schooling begins and through it the child is exposed to a larger world than she has previously known. But the child's expanding world comes from more than just greater exposure; the child's growing ability to understand and reason brings new meaning and depth to the corner of the world she already knows. Thus, at a time when parents and families are naturally inclined to talk less and less about adoption, it is as important as ever to continue the dialogue and help the child with the variety of feelings she may have surrounding her adoption.

A number of developmental landmarks lead the child to this heightened awareness and understanding, including the following:

Logical thinking. By age six most children have begun to develop the ability to think logically, to see that actions lead to reactions. During the middle childhood years, children still think concretely (they cannot yet think abstractly); but within their concrete thinking they can recognize and predict cause and effect. Of course, at this age, no matter how well developed their logic is, just because they have the ability doesn't mean they will always use it. In some situations a child may choose not to use this ability; in others, stress may interfere with logic, or a situation may simply be beyond the child's experience and thus beyond the realm of his logic.

Movement away from egocentrism. Armed with logic, children begin to understand that their personal experiences are not universal, that when

Mom is at work she is having a different experience than the child is having at home or school. Once a child understands that other people have different experiences from his own, he can begin to understand that they may also have different feelings. This is the beginning of the child's ability to empathize with other viewpoints.

Empathy, in turn, allows children to develop personal-relationship skills and continue their development of moral conscience. A child who has moved beyond egocentricism and learned empathy will be better able to understand that two people can experience the same event and feel differently about it. For example, a child without these skills may well believe, "If I tease you and enjoy it, you must like it, too." A child who has developed these skills will be more likely to understand that teasing, while fun for the teaser, may be painful for the teased. These budding skills, however, can be selective; even as adults, we all have times when we fail or opt not to empathize with others and times when we regress to egocentrism.

Changing roles for family and peer groups. Family continues to play a major role in the child's evolving identity during middle childhood. Children continue to explore how they are like their parents; but at the same time they are also comparing themselves, often in a very competitive way, with their peers. Adopted children tend to feel a greater degree of difference between themselves and their peers, and as they move through middle childhood, they usually discover more and more things about themselves that don't fit the family's patterns. By age eight to ten, most adopted children can name a myriad of things about themselves that no one else in their family shares; this can have an inhibiting effect on belonging and attachment.

In his "eight stages of man," Erikson (1963, 258) says that middle childhood is a time of "industry versus inferiority." The child's task is to ". . . begin to be a worker and a potential provider." As they learn the tools they will need later in life, children also begin to define themselves in relation to their peers, especially on the basis of what they can do, learn, or make. The goal more often than not is to determine who is better and who is worse, with emphasis on superlatives (i.e., the best and the worst).

Through this appraisal process of self and peers, the differences in the ways in which adoptive families and genetically related families are formed become apparent to the adopted child; but perhaps more importantly, it also becomes apparent to their peers. To her peers, the adopted child is the embodiment of the greatest fear of childhood: losing one's parents. The result may be that the adopted child is teased, avoided, and picked on by bullies, especially if the child shows it hurts. Even more painful, however, is when, as often happens, such treatment comes from a best friend. Other children will try to differentiate themselves from the adopted child and thus from the feared loss. They will try to explore and explain how this happened to the adopted child to reassure themselves that it couldn't happen to them. In doing so, they may make negative remarks—ranging from innocent but painful comments to outright teasing—about the child, her family, and adoption. Such encounters are common at about age seven, and tend to pop up again at ages nine, eleven, and thirteen—all years of disequilibrium.

The older children get, the less likely they will be to tell their parents that this is happening. If you suspect it is, use the pebbles technique described later in this chapter to raise the topic. Rather than ask your child directly, mention that sometimes other children tease adopted children because they don't understand adoption or because they are scared by it.

Fear of kidnapping. In generations past, children were taught to fear the bogeyman or being swept away by "gypsies" (based on a racist stereotype). Today's children are taught about "stranger danger" and the bogeyman is now the stranger. In our present society, stranger danger is an increasingly present threat and education about it is invaluable for the safety of our children. Some children, however, experience intensified fears of kidnapping as a result of the warnings. Adopted children sometimes combine what they know about their adoption with what they know about kidnapping, apply what they believe is logic, and come to the conclusion that their adoptive parents kidnapped them from their birth parents, who would have otherwise kept them. This interpretation can be painful and frustrating for adoptive parents, who know full well that the birth parents' decision was made before they even entered the scene. Talking with children about the sequence of events in their lives, using a time line as a visual aid, can help reinforce the facts of what really happened.

Perfect-parent fantasy. No, children don't fantasize that their parents are perfect, but rather that somewhere, someplace there is such a thing as "perfect parents." In the fantasy, children believe that some children really do have perfect parents. In fact, probably more than half, if not all, the *other* kids on the block do—but they don't. Seven-year-olds, whether adopted or raised by their genetic parents, are fond of the perfect-parent fantasy. Most children raised by their genetic parents at some point or other think there is no way on God's green earth that they could be related to these people who say they are their parents. Even if a child never doubts her relationship to her parents, she is likely to fantasize that another adult— perhaps a relative or the mother of a best friend—would understand her better.

Of course, this fantasy is most likely to arise when a child is angry at her parents. The fantasy is, at least in part, a defense mechanism that protects the child against the fear that her anger will destroy her relationship with her parents. Rather than fear the dissolution, the child convinces herself that the relationship was never right in the first place: her parents aren't doing their job properly, or they were never really related to her anyway. But once the fight is over, a child who is living with her genetic parents in a fairly healthy, functional family will let the fantasy go. She knows she belongs with her parents because she has all the genetic markers to prove it.

Adopted children, on the other hand, know that there *is* someone out there who could have and "should" have parented them. This fact fuels the daydream and reality hooks the fantasy. Children think things like "My birth mom wouldn't make me clean my room." Some will even say it out loud. Consider yourself lucky if your child does; at least you will know where she is at.

Continuing to build object constancy. As mentioned in Chapter 9, the work of developing object constancy is a lifelong task. Throughout middle childhood, children continue to struggle with and, we hope, strengthen their sense of object constancy. Typical fears and fantasies of this age, including the fear of kidnapping and the perfect-parent fantasy, can be triggered by this ongoing struggle with object constancy. Greater awareness of the loss of one set of parents, whether in open or closed adoption, can increase the child's fear of losing his adoptive parents and interfere with the normal strengthening of object constancy that happens in middle childhood.

Dealing with the Dichotomy

The emergence of logical thinking adds a new dimension to the child's understanding of and feelings about adoption. Sometime around ages five to six for girls and six to seven for boys, children realize that in order to be among the "chosen" children, someone must have first chosen not to keep them. Once the dichotomy of the chosen-child message occurs to them, children begin to ask what happened, why, and most of all, whose fault it was. This is also the age at which children first begin to exhibit healthy and toxic shame.

Many parents, placement workers, and therapists oppose discussing the birth parents' decision to place a child for adoption as a "rejection" of the child. Certainly, for most birth parents the decision to place a child is a caring plan, painfully made with the child's best interests at heart. But no matter how caring and painful the decision was for the birth parents, most adopted children, at some point, still feel "rejected." Whatever the reasons for the placement, when a child is not raised by the people who conceived and gave birth to him, it hurts. It is only by recognizing that this is a normal feeling for children to have that parents and others can begin to help them heal the pain they actually feel.

Once the child figures out that there is another side of the adoption coin, and that unlike the chosen-child message, the flip side hurts, her next step is to determine whose fault it was: the child's, the adoptive parents', or the birth parents'. Because the perfect-parent fantasy is usually applied to the birth parents, children commonly conclude that it couldn't be their fault. Sometimes, through immature logic, the blame is turned toward the adoptive parents: "If you hadn't adopted me, my birth parents would have kept me." Some children, however, revert to egocentricism and decide they were to blame because they were bad babies: toxic shame. The excerpt from Ann Fredkove's book *Advice for Adopted Kids* (see box on page 197), which she wrote at age nine, provides a wonderful description of the ways in which many children believe they caused themselves to be placed for adoption.

While we don't want children to *blame* their birth parents, they do need to understand who had the power in the situation. This is where what you know about the birth parents' decision and the circumstances surrounding the placement for adoption helps. In addition to talking about the circumstance, it sometimes helps to ask your child to pick someone she knows who is about the same age her birth parents were and ask how she thinks that person might handle the situation. You can also ask your child what she thinks caused her birth parents not to keep her. If things your child says or does lead you to believe she thinks she either caused her birth parents to place her for adoption or that she could somehow have prevented it, ask her, "How do you think you caused this?" After listening attentively to the answer, gently challenge the magical thinking. You can do this by talking about what babies (or preschoolers, depending on the age at placement) are capable of. Concrete examples, using a baby your child knows and asking your child what that baby could do in a similar situation, help clarify what her own abilities and limitations were.

Above all, children need to hear that their birth parents had feelings, too. Children are often told only what happened and why, without mention of how their birth parents felt. From this, children get a strong message that it is not OK to feel angry or sad about what happened (for example, "My birth mother was poor so I shouldn't be angry"). Talking about the birth parents' feelings—or how they "probably" felt, if you don't know for certain—gives your child permission to have feelings about her birth parents' decision, too. Furthermore, discussing the birth parents' feelings helps bridge the gap between the "chosen" and "rejected" messages by giving the child value on both sides. If the child was someone worth the birth parents' agonizing over losing, then the positive messages of worth from the adoptive parents are reinforced. It is important for parents to teach their children that it is natural to sometimes have more than one feeling about an event or person—that they may simultaneously have two opposite feelings about their adoption (for example, hurt about their birth parents' decision, but happy about being in their adoptive family) and that their birth parents probably had mixed feelings, as well. Children also need to understand that adoption really involves two separate events: the birth parents' decision to place and the adoptive parents' decision to adopt.

From *Advice for Adopted Kids*, written by Ann Fredkove at age nine, distributed by Adoptive Families of America, 1985. Reprinted with permission of the author and her family.

The following is an excerpt from Advice for Adopted Kids, *written by Ann Fredkove at age nine, distributed by Adoptive Families of America, 1985. Reprinted with permission of the author and her family.*

Your Parents Didn't Keep You

Some parents don't keep their kids after they are born. They don't keep them because they used poor judgment taking care of you, or didn't deal with their problems.

They could have been ill. They might not thought they were ill, so they didn't plan for someone to take care of you in the family.

Your parents could have died in a car crash, got run over by a bus, or maybe died in some kind of illness. You never know.

Maybe they thought that they were not making enough money to take care of you. They only had barely enough for themselves. Maybe they didn't have any jobs at all!

It's possible that they were still very young, like in between ten and eighteen. That's very young to have a baby. Still, they used poor judgment because they didn't plan on who would take care of you other than them.

They could also have had drinking problems, drug problems, or some kind of uncurable illness such as cancer or heart attack.

Giving up a child or not planning on the care of a child is a poor judgment because they should be responsible enough to make sure that their child gets good care. They weren't dealing with their problems because we know that there is a way to solve a problem or at least try to solve a problem. Even illness or death isn't a good excuse because they should have had someone else take care of you.

Sometimes some kids think that they did something that made their parents give them up. They might think that they bit people, hit, cried too much, or wet their diapers too much.

I used to think that my parents didn't keep me because I cried too much. Well, babies are supposed to cry!

Thinking that it was your fault that your parents didn't keep you is an incorrect thinking because babies can't do something so bad that their parents wouldn't keep them. Babies are supposed to wet their diapers, hit, bite, and cry because that's how they talk and don't know any better. They don't know right from wrong. Everybody has to learn right from wrong; they don't know automatically.

Even though I used to think that my parents gave me up because I cried too much, I have changed my thoughts. I learned that a baby can't be so bad that their parents would give them up. Babies are supposed to act bad. That's how they learn right from wrong!

Grief and Other Feelings

Throughout middle childhood, from the time the realization of the dichotomy hits, the adopted child will work periodically through grief. For children placed during early infancy, in particular, this is usually the first time adoption-related grief centers on the loss of the birth parents and all the "would have and should have beens." Just as the infant's first relationship is with the mothering figure, turning later to the father, in grief the child's focus is initially on the birth mother (rather than on both parents as a unit or on the father). Children are often curious about their birth fathers, but many will not ask questions or otherwise express their curiosity unless prompted. Children who have no memory of their birth parents rarely grieve for their birth fathers until they have worked through sadness and anger in their grief for their birth mothers. For those who do grieve for the father, this usually doesn't occur until adolescence or even young adulthood. In most cases, grief for the birth father is less intense than that for the mother, in part because the adopted child has learned she can grieve and recover.

A full range of emotions and defense mechanisms commonly accompany grief in middle childhood. Daydreaming, a common pastime of school-age children, is often a means for absenting a child from a situation he would rather not be in at the moment (for example, the classroom). For the grieving child, daydreaming provides an ideal vehicle for yearning and pining, as the child explores through fantasy what life with her birth parents would have been like, what it might be like to be reunited with them, or any number of variations on these themes. Because daydreaming is normal during middle childhood, adopted children are more prone to becoming stuck in yearning and pining. This is especially true for those placed as infants because they haven't experienced actual hurt from past living situations and have no conscious memories that might otherwise challenge the daydreams. Furthermore, without past experiences with and memories of the birth parents, children are more easily engrossed with creating stories to fill the gaps.

Anger—passive aggressive or aggressive—is another defense mechanism common in middle childhood but also common to grief. Children who have conscious memory or subconscious (preverbal) experiences of painful moves or abuse are frequently very angry during these years. Anger acts as a shield against feeling the pain of the loss and against vulnerability to future losses by preventing the child from becoming close to another person. Unless identified and dealt with, anger can also prevent healing from the loss, thus inhibiting bonding and attachment.

Anger in children is one of the most difficult emotions for parents to handle. One reason for this is that anger is often expressed through behaviors that are not socially acceptable and sometimes even frightening (hitting, kicking, stomping, yelling, throwing, etc.). Parents often react to such expressions with anger of their own, especially if they feel they have lost control over their child's behavior. Yet, children need to express strong feelings, including anger, in some fashion. The parents' job is to teach their children acceptable ways of doing so. Encouraging children to verbalize their emotions ("I am so mad that . . . ") is the first step, but anger often requires a physical outlet as well. You need to define which outlets are acceptable in your home. Some choices might be slamming a particular door (not every or any door in the house), throwing foam blocks or Nerf balls at a target or a wall (without pictures or other breakables nearby), punching a punching bag, running around the block, closing the bedroom door and screaming into a pillow, or jumping on a mini trampoline. Once the list of choices is made, your child should be free to determine when she needs a physical outlet; you should not be the one to decide whether her anger warrants a particular expression. Consequences are in order if your child chooses to break things, hurt someone, or otherwise express the anger in an inappropriate way. But she should also be praised when she expresses her anger appropriately (although you may want to wait until after the anger has passed!). Likewise, you need to validate that while feeling angry is OK, not all expressions of anger are acceptable. Keep in mind that your child will also be watching how you react when you are angry; you will have difficulty holding your child to a particular standard if you do not keep the same standard for yourself. Inevitably, however, you will probably make a mistake, doing something you've told your child not to. When this happens, acknowledge your error and apologize.

Grieving children cannot always pinpoint what is bothering them or even exactly what they are feeling. Parents, however, can watch for symptoms of grief, including excessive activity, complaints of stomach pain, frequent outbursts of anger, or signs that the child is experiencing feelings of emptiness. A child may try to fill this latter void through eating, or being consumed with an activity such as playing sports or even watching television. If you notice your child moving beyond moderation in an activity, talk with him about how some adopted children sometimes feel empty and try to fill the emptiness or avoid unpleasant feelings by eating a lot, trying really hard to get better and better at something, or just keeping so busy they don't have time to think about it. Tell your child that it's OK to try to fill the emptiness, but that doing these things doesn't really help. Talking about the feelings can help; so can crying and hugs—hugging either a person or a stuffed animal. Tell your child that even with talk and hugs, the feeling may not go away for good, but excesses will only make him feel worse while still leaving the emptiness. You may also suggest that your child talk things out with the dog, cat, or hamster, if he's uncomfortable telling another person; pets are good nonjudgmental listeners.

A variety of other techniques are available for parents to use in helping their children through grief and other emotions, in both the present and the future. Here are a few:

Permission and validation. The first step in helping children deal with emotions is to give them permission to discuss how they feel about themselves (identity), adoption, their birth parents, and their role and belonging in the adoptive family. One way to do this is using the pebbles technique below. Validation of the child's feelings is crucial not only for helping the child work through the feelings, but also for maintaining open communication. Validation means recognizing and accepting that the child feels a particular way, without judging whether the feelings are justified or trying to explain why the child feels that way. If the child says he is not angry or sad, for example, but is behaving in ways that indicate otherwise, gentle confrontation may be needed to get him to express his feelings (cry or yell) so that he may eventually let them go and move on. An example of gentle confrontation is saying, "Well maybe you aren't sad, but you sure look it. I thought maybe you needed a hug or a good cry."

Pebbles technique. Most children will not talk about negative or painful feelings related to adoption. If attached, they often feel conflicted about raising these issues with their parents, not wanting to hurt them, or feeling they are betraying them by their thoughts and feelings for their birth parents. If not attached, children won't trust their parents enough to feel safe confiding in them. As a parent, you need to take the lead to let your child know it is normal to be curious about birth parents and to have a variety of feelings about adoption, and most of all, that she may talk with you about these things.

One way to do this is by dropping "pebbles" once every few weeks. Pebbles are one-liners, not conversations, that raise an issue and then are allowed to ripple until the child is ready to pick up on it. A pebble might be a comment on a genetic marker: you see your child dancing or scoring a soccer goal, and you say, "I wonder if you got that from your birth mother or your birth father's side of the family. You have a lot of talent in sports and you've worked hard to develop it." A pebble might also be used to comment on feelings: "I was watching you play with your sister and I thought to myself how sad it is that your birth mother missed out on seeing you do that." Some pebbles need to be about sadness and anger, others about birth parents and about the child. They may also be tied to something you've heard or read, for example, "I heard that adopted kids sometimes feel they caused their birth parents to place them for adoption."

One rule to remember about the pebbles technique is not to ask direct questions; just make the comment and leave it to reverberate. If you ask your child direct questions, he will likely try to guess the right answer rather than answer sincerely and risk hurting you or being reprimanded.

Give a well-rounded picture of birth parents. Anger is a normal part of grief. Yet many adoptive parents find it very difficult to allow their children to be angry with their birth mothers in particular. It is normal for children to be angry about their birth parents' decision, but they also need help to move beyond the anger. One way to help mitigate this anger—and nurture a healthy identity for your child—is by providing a well-rounded picture of the birth parents. Children need to know more than that their birth parents had children whom they couldn't take care of. If you do not have information about your child's birth parents, write to the agency (or attorney, if a private placement) to get as much nonidentifying information as possible. Some agencies will look up birth parents to gather more information. Children especially like to know their birth parents' favorite school subjects, colors, sports, and foods, their hobbies, interests and talents, and their physical characteristics in infancy, childhood, and as adults.

Expand your explanation about why your child was placed for adoption. Children who have been told they were placed for adoption because their birth parents couldn't take care of a baby almost always believe those same parents had more babies. Children often worry about these other siblings, even to the point of feeling they must go back to care for the others or rescue them from their birth parents. They may also feel jealous that real or imagined siblings are with the birth parents while they are not. These beliefs and feelings can reinforce a child's hypothesis that she was not kept because she was a bad baby. Find out where your child's magical thinking lies and correct it with accurate information, while validating her feelings.

If you know or believe your child's birth parents are raising other children, find out when their decision not to raise your child was made. Are the other siblings older? If so, did the birth parents decide at the beginning of pregnancy to place your child because they couldn't take care of a second, third, or sixth child? Knowing this can help you explain to your child that her birth parents made their decision before they even knew her; thus, their decision was not a reflection on who she was or how she behaved as a baby. One technique to help a school-aged child understand the challenges her birth parents may have faced is to have her "parent" four or five teddy bears or other stuffed animals for a week. As a parent, she must take all her teddy bear children with her wherever she goes, or arrange for a baby sitter. She has to get them all up in the morning, and dress them; and at night, read them stories, get them dressed, and put them to bed. "Egg parenting" also works well, with the child responsible for the safety and care of four or five uncooked eggs.

If your child was the first born in his birth family, it is possible that circumstances in his birth family changed, enabling his parents to raise subsequent children. But however valid the reasons were for his placement, your child will still need your support for and validation of his feelings over the loss of his siblings. If possible, your child should be allowed to keep in touch with his siblings; if not, talk with him about them.

Supporting Search

Most parents think of search as something they will have to decide to support or not support when their children reach late adolescence. But issues related to search really arise before adolescence. One strong interest of eight-year-olds is to begin looking back at their history and forward to who they will become. At this age, looking back to infancy is different than it was when the child was a preschooler. The preschooler's preoccupation with "when I was a baby (or a little boy or little girl)" is a way for the child to show that he is no longer an infant. The eight-year-old, however, looks back at his past to gain a sense of personal connection to that younger child, as well as to his family and humanity. At this age, interest in the past stems in part from a natural exploration of and search for personal identity and in part from the search aspects of grief.

This is a good age to bring out the family storybook, the child's life storybook, pictures, adoption papers, and facts about the child's personal and genetic history. If you don't have all the information you or your child would like, now is the time to get it; don't wait until adolescence.

Search in domestic and international adoption alike poses fewer problems during middle childhood than during adolescence. The same holds true for visiting the child's previous home or country of origin, or looking up old contacts, such as orphanage workers, foster parents, or siblings. Conducting a search when the child is eight years old allows her time to process what she learns while she is still strongly centered on the family. During adolescence, teens are separating and pulling away from the family on their way toward adulthood. As they pull away, they need a strong sense that their parents still want them. If left until adolescence, visits and searches can stress this separation process. Adolescents frequently misinterpret parent-facilitated searches and visits to previous homes as a sign that the parents would really like them to go back where they came from. Younger children are better able to take in the experience and information offered without misconstruing the message, but they still need to be told that the search is to gather information, not to return them to their birth parents ("We'll help you find your birth mother so you can know who she is, tell her how you feel, and ask her questions. But you may not live with her.")

If your child isn't already asking questions about her past and her genetic history by age eight or nine, raise the issue yourself using the pebbles technique, identifying any ambivalence your child may have about the past, and including your child's cultural heritage into your family system. Keep in mind that race and nationality aren't the only sources of cultural difference. If your child is following patterns from the micro- or macrocultures of her birth family, especially if these patterns don't mesh well with those of the rest of the family, look for ways to show your child that her goals are acceptable and that you value them. One way to do this is by having friends who are from similar backgrounds to your child's birth family, whether ethnically or socioeconomically. Supporting your child's goals does not mean you must support poor choices such as drug use or eventually dropping out of high school.

Sharing Difficult Information

Children fantasize about all sorts of things. When information is missing about the circumstances of their adoption, they usually make up their own theories of what happened. Even when they have the correct information, they often make up alternative scenarios rather than accept the painful reality. When questions are left unanswered about who the birth father was, and what the relationship between the birth mother and birth father was, children make up their own answers. The largest gap in the array of information the child receives about his personal origins often pertains to the birth father's identity and his relationship with the birth mother. When adoptive parents have been told or otherwise are certain that their child was conceived through rape or incest, the natural instinct is not to tell— *ever*—and hope the child never finds out. But odds are that the child will eventually find out or put the pieces together and make his own hypothesis that this was what happened. Because of this, about the only healthy choices the adoptive parents have in this matter are *when* and *how* to tell their child.

When children are given difficult information about their birth families or the circumstances of their conception at about age eight or nine (earlier than this is too young, later is more difficult), the child has time to gradually process the ramifications for their own identity before they begin the normal identity struggles of puberty. Difficult information may include rape, incest, drug use, drug sales, murder, violence, imprisonment, abandonment of one parent by the other, physical abuse of other siblings, or the fact that there are other siblings still in the home.

Among the most difficult information is that the child was conceived by rape or incest. Many adopted people believe or fear this is true even if it isn't, especially if they have no information about their birth fathers. Eight- or nine-year-olds usually won't understand completely what rape or incest means. But they usually will accept that both are acts of aggression and power from people who haven't learned how to handle their feelings and impulses or how to have appropriate adult/child and adult/adult relationships.

Because such facts are very painful and difficult for parents, they should seek professional advice on how to tell their child. Waiting for the child to ask is not an option, since children usually don't ask until much older, when the answers are more traumatic. If the therapist you interview advises you *not* to tell, find another who will tell you *how* to tell. There is no single formula for telling children difficult aspects of their conception or birth family that we could outline here. Furthermore, we strongly feel that parents need professional support and children need a professional to help them talk through what all this means about themselves.

Before telling your child any highly charged information about his genetic past, check to make sure the facts are correct. Sometimes birth parents lie, placement workers make assumptions, or someone along the way arbitrarily fills in missing information to ensure that the records are "complete." The first step in verifying information is to locate the placement worker and ask where the information came from. If you have cause to believe that information in the records is not true, but it has not been deleted or corrected, you still need to tell your child (again, with professional support) what the records say and why you believe it is not true. Of course, if it is true and you would simply prefer not to accept it or that your child not have to deal with it, this approach is not appropriate or healthy.

The goal of telling children difficult facts at this young age is to allow them time to understand that the circumstances of their conception or things their birth parents may have done have no bearing on who they are or will become. Teens, for example, are less able to separate out the sexuality from the violence and power issues inherent in rape and incest. Children also need time to understand that all people have a potential for good and for bad. Though a parent, through choice, environment, or circumstances, followed through on the potential for bad, there is no such thing as "bad blood" or genes that predispose an individual to do wrong. Genetics may play a role in determining impulsiveness, a fast temper, and so on, but these tendencies may be expressed in many ways; how they are expressed is often a choice. Aggression can be used as much to drive a career as it can to dominate others through violence.

Children need to be assured that whatever their birth parents may have done, they are not destined to do the same. They need to hear that it is normal to be upset by this type of information, to worry about it sometimes, and even to feel ashamed of it. The embarrassment and sense of shame (not toxic shame) are for the *actions* and choices of others, but do not define the child. Though such difficult information may not be something the child needs to advertise publicly, the fact remains that what happened is a matter totally separate from the child, who is a good person.

While the child is working through the information, it is more important than ever for parents to reinforce attachment, claiming, and belonging, especially by pointing out ways the child is like the rest of the adoptive family. The less parents and children are able to point out how the children are like the parents, the greater the dysfunction in the family, and the more distressed the family is. If children are unable to identify at least some similarities while in middle childhood, adolescence will be quite a challenge.

Body Image and Sexuality

Freud called the middle childhood years the *latency period* because, having resolved the Oedipus complex, the child's sexuality was essentially dormant and awaiting puberty when it would again emerge. Even so, this period plays an important role in sexuality as a time for establishing a body image and identifying gender roles. An important element in the child's development of a positive body image is that he or she was conceived and born in the normal manner. All too often, the life stories of adopted children are told from the first meeting or the day of placement, not from the day they were born. Without a sense of biological connection to the rest of humanity through birth, many adopted children are left feeling less than human. Some even assume they will grow up and adopt children because they believe they are incapable of procreation.

During this time, children also wonder what they will look like as adults and whether they will be able to attract a spouse. In genetically related families, parents help answer these questions by pointing to their own appearance or that of other family members and to their relationships. Such answers are not generally available to adopted children. Furthermore, adopted children sometimes wonder if they were not attractive enough for their birth parents to keep them, how anyone else will be attracted to them.

Photographs of birth parents are often helpful for adopted children in identifying where their physical features came from and what they might look like as adults. If the photos, however, show the birth parents as unattractive in the child's eyes, you will need to talk with your child about how everyone has a "bad hair day" or takes a bad picture from time to time.

Issues may also arise if the child's build or other features are markedly different from those of the adoptive family, for example, a large child in a petite family or a thin child in an overweight family. Parents can help their children identify what they can change and help them accept what they cannot.

Special Issues for Interracial and International Adoptions

During middle childhood, race and ethnicity can create special issues for adopted children on two fronts: their own identification with a particular ethnic group and their interactions with peers.

Children of color who are raised in predominantly white communities sometimes become confused about their own racial or ethnic identities. As very young children, many believe they, too, are white, even if both their parents are brown skinned. By age six—if not earlier—these children are often rudely awakened to the fact that they are not the same color or of the same ethnic background as their playmates. They may be called a name or told they can no longer play with a friend because the friend's family has decided the children are too old to continue "mixing."

Even when aware of their ethnic background, interracially and internationally adopted children sometimes refer to their ethnic group as "them," as though they were not also part of that group. Siblings in interracial adoptive families often fall into the same trap. For example, children have been known to call other children on the playground racially derogatory names ("nigger," "gook"), not realizing their own sister or brother is also of that race. They may also make exceptions for their sister or brother; for example, "My sister is brown, but she's not really *black* like them." The message is that it is better to be brown with white parents than brown with brown parents. Adults often make the same exceptions.

Parents of interracial or international families (if not all parents!) must challenge these attitudes, making it clear that people are not to be judged by—or ridiculed because of—the color of their skin, their accent, or any other aspect of their ethnicity. They also need to reinforce for the entire family, not just for the child of color, the beauty of diverse cultures and heritages, with particular emphasis on the cultural heritage of the child of color. Again, this is done through reading, attending culture events, and most of all, by having adult friends who share your child's heritage.

The middle childhood years are a good time for exposing your child to many differences, not just their own ethnicity. By third grade, most children can identify the hierarchy of races and ethnic groups in their own community. But they are also open to learning about cultural differences, as well as differences in family structures and lifestyles. Even if your family is not interracial, adopted children do feel different from their peers. Teaching them about cultural diversity and different types of families reinforces that being different is OK.

Peer groups are very important in middle childhood. Though differences are not celebrated in peer groups, during these years peer groups change by function. For example, a child may have one set of friends at school, another in the neighborhood, another at church, and yet another in a club such as scouts. The advantage of this is that a characteristic that causes the child to be rejected or ostracized in one group may be what makes him popular in the next. A bright but physically uncoordinated child may be the last one picked for the baseball team, but the first chosen by the same children for the spelling team. Once children reach adolescence, peer groups tend to be the same, regardless of function. During middle childhood, unless a child has been labeled as the one who is most different, there will be a group in which she will fit and be comfortable. If your child is struggling socially, help her identify a skill she has that will be valued among her current peers or in another setting with a different group of children.

Though school-aged children are more likely than adolescents to forgive and forget, they can also be very rejecting of other children. Boys are often in physical fights; and children of both sexes are big on name-calling. Race and other physical characteristics are used as ammunition in interpersonal conflicts. A child may be angry with a friend because the friend wouldn't sit with her during lunch, but she will tell the friend, "I don't want to play with you because you are (fat, black, stupid, a know-it-all, four-eyes, ugly, a slant-eyes, etc.)." Once the anger subsides, however, even if there is no apology, there is usually behavioral acceptance and the children return to playing together.

Even so, the child who is on the receiving end of name calling will be very hurt. As a parent, your first priority is to validate that the incident hurt, offering comfort and sharing your feelings: "I don't like it when this happens to you." "How do you feel?" "What do you want to do about this?" (Redirect the child if what he wants to do is unacceptable.) The next step is to talk about why kids call names. The place to start may be asking your child why he sometimes does it. Use a specific example, such as "Remember last week when you called Jim a . . . ?" Name-calling usually stems from anger over an interpersonal issue ("You wouldn't play with me or share your new toy") or because the child doing the name-calling needs to build her own self-esteem (the "she's just jealous" syndrome). In either case, children tend to attack the person, not the issue.

If your child is routinely called a particular derogatory name, talk with your child about whether the name is tied to something she can change. If it is, does she want to change or is this something she shouldn't change? If the name is about a physical trait, such as color, size of nose or ears, and so on, change is obviously not an option. If the child is overweight or underweight, change may or may not be possible or desirable. You can ask your child if he'd like you to get him help in making the change (for example, braces for crooked teeth, or help in changing unhealthy eating habits). If the name is tied to a behavior, such as answering all the questions the teacher asks or getting good or bad grades, is this something the child wants to change? Try not to interject your own value judgments, but be sure to help your child to consider the consequences of each choice ("The kids may like you better if you get bad grades, but didn't you say last week you wanted to be a . . . when you grow up?").

While name-calling is never acceptable, you might also need to explore whether your child is provoking the attacks, perhaps by bullying or picking on other children. If asked directly, most children will answer no. Even if you suspect this is the case, gently drop the subject, but bring it up again the next time.

Regardless of the cause of the name-calling, teasing, or bullying, your first priority is to comfort your child and help her develop coping techniques—not to go after the other child or to make phone calls to her parents.

For children of color, parents must also keep in mind that sometimes racial name-calling stems from nothing other than racism. The techniques described in Chapter 10 apply to school-aged children, too. If your child's personality makes using these techniques difficult, teach him to use a gentler, modified approach: Use the same words, only whisper them. Whispering can be equally effective. The child gains control over the situation by forcing the other person to lean forward or to shut up in order to listen. Shy children may need extra help practicing techniques or finding creative approaches to help them cope and take control in such situations. No matter what your child's personality, help her find some technique she *can* use to respond to attacks; don't accept that she can't do anything but walk away or cry.

If Moved During Middle Childhood

In some ways, middle childhood is an easier time to move children. They are verbal, have likely learned something about feelings, and they have memory. What makes moves at this age harder is that the children have history. Any child who is placed during middle childhood (or almost any-time after infancy) comes with family-of-origin issues. Short of a child's having just lost his birth parents through death (which itself is a trauma), if a child is being placed at this age one can safely assume that the child's birth home had some sort of problems. Even in cases where poverty, politi-cal persecution, war, or natural disaster—all elements beyond parents' con-trol—caused the placement, if such a situation was severe enough to warrant the child's removal from the home, the parents' struggle for sur-vival and safety must have taxed and taken energy away from their parent-ing. And though a child may have a very healthy foster home, she will still come with issues from her birth family or from being moved more than once. Each time a child is moved, she learns that:

- big people don't keep little people;
- adults don't keep promises to children;
- she is not valuable and must always move on; and
- it isn't safe to get close to people and trust them, because it hurts when you have to leave.

Furthermore, children in foster homes must pursue individual identity with-out the safe environment of a permanent family.

When a child is moved during middle childhood, counseling should begin before the move. He should be helped to explore his fantasies and expecta-tions of the move, the new family, and the new surroundings (including school, the neighborhood, and friendships he will make). He will also need help clarifying what is happening, why, and how he feels about it. It must be made clear to the child that adults are making the decisions. While this may sound harsh, many children will not address grief and other issues they must work on in order for the rest of their lives to be healthy unless they are freed from feeling responsible for what is happening. Before the placement day, the adoptive parents, the child, and any siblings already part of the family should be counseled that trust, love, and even friendship among the siblings will take time, work, and adjustment on everyone's part.

Social skills often suffer as a result of moves in middle childhood. Parents and professionals may need to help the child learn how to make and main-tain friendships. Because peer groups tend to change by function, if you can help your child find something she does well, she will find a peer group in which she will fit.

Here are some things you and your adoption counselor can do to help your child through the crisis of moving (based on Van Ornum 1987):

- Help your child identify positive relationships she has had in the past as a way of showing her that she is worthy and able to have such friendships.
- Help her identify current positive relationships to which she can turn for support.
- Help her identify coping skills, survival skills, and positive accomplishments in her life. One child we know was abandoned in a cupboard by her birth mother shortly after she was born, but because she cried, she was found and survived. She uses this experience as proof that even as a baby she had good survival skills, and as assurance that she is capable of enduring and overcoming obstacles in her life.
- Search your child's present and past relationships for blessings. An example might be a grandmother who tells the child it is OK to go with and love her adoptive family, and that she is not betraying her birth family. Look also for curses. In one case, court transcripts revealed that during a hearing, the birth mother told her six-year-old that he was no good and would fail no matter where he went. Sometimes, however, children believe they have been cursed when in reality they have misinterpreted what was said or done. For this reason, it is important to investigate any alleged curses. Whether your child is correct or not, do what you can to remove or, at best, counter the curse.
- Before, during, and after the move, help your child to understand the rules, routines, customs, and interaction style of the new family. The adoptive family, as well, may need help in understanding where the child is coming from in these regards.
- Support your child's sense of industry and ability to learn, and reinforce positive self-esteem. Encourage crafts, sports, music, art, household responsibilities, games—anything your child seems interested in, even if she isn't as good at it as you would like her to be.
- Reinforce that no one is perfect. Everyone in the family makes mistakes from time to time, and even this new family has its problems or weaknesses.

If Middle Childhood Does Not Go Well

A child who has had multiple unresolved problems during middle childhood is at greater risk of having a very difficult adolescence. Unresolved issues from earlier years simply carry over into the next developmental stage, becoming increasingly complex. A child who has not had a chance to explore, experience, and express his feelings about his adoption and what it means for his identity will be ill prepared to handle the developmental tasks of adolescence. By dealing with these issues in middle childhood, children develop coping skills that will help them address the same issues as they are revisited on a new level during adolescence.

When an open, accepting environment in which the child can talk about and tackle adoption-related issues is established early on, the child will feel freer to turn to his parents to talk about problems as a teen. If parents deny their child's feelings or sweep them under the rug, then the family—parents and child alike—will have no system for addressing them when they intensify in adolescence.

For Further Reading

• *Steven's Baseball Mitt: A Book About Being Adopted* by Kathy Stinson. Ontario: Annick Press, 1992.

This book gives an accurate look at the feelings and fantasies children have about their adoptions. Reading this book with an adopted child is a wonderful way to get conversations started about those feelings and fantasies. Although the format resembles that of a preschool storybook, the story line and illustrations are good and should be welcomed well by younger school-aged children.

• *Lucy's Feet* by Stephanie Stein. Indianapolis: Perspective Press, 1992.

A delightful look at adoption. Children chuckle, sigh, and keep coming back.

• *Double Dip Feelings: Stories to Help Children Understand Emotions* by Barbara S. Cain, M.S.W. New York: Magination Press, 1990.

Absolutely wonderful book for helping parents and children alike as they struggle with ambivalence.

• *Different and Alike* by Nancy P. McConnell. Colorado Springs: Current, Inc., 1982.

Explores sameness and difference, focusing on physical challenges (i.e., hearing and vision impairments).

• *It's Okay to be Different* by Mitch Golant and Bob Crane. New York: Tor Books, 1988.

Discusses ways parents and teachers can help children accept their unique traits and challenges.

12

❦

Adolescence: Eleven to Eighteen Years

Adolescents are excessively egoistic, regarding themselves as the centre of the universe and the sole object of interest, and yet at no time in later life are they capable of so much self-sacrifice and devotion. They form the most passionate love-relations, only to break them off as abruptly as they began them. On the one hand they throw themselves enthusiastically into the life of the community and, on the other, they have an overpowering longing for solitude. They oscillate between blind submission to some self-chosen leader and defiant rebellion against any and every authority. They are selfish and materially-minded and at the same time full of lofty idealism. They are ascetic but will suddenly plunge into instinctual indulgence of the most primitive character. At times their behaviour to other people is rough and inconsiderate, yet they themselves are extremely touchy. Their moods veer between light-hearted optimism and the blackest pessimism. Sometimes they will work with indefatigable enthusiasm and at other times they are sluggish and apathetic.

—Anna Freud,
The Ego and the Mechanics of Defense

*O*f all the stages of childhood, the most challenging and potentially rocky for parent and child alike has to be adolescence. As the child moves both psychologically and physically toward adulthood, the many changes he or she must undergo can be both exciting and stressful. And the teenager's task of preparing to separate from the family and establish a unique identity means change for the entire family. When the teen is adopted, these tasks are doubly complex because she must not only figure out how she is like and different from the parents who raised her, but also how the genetic package she received from her birth parents fits into the picture.

Anna Freud said essentially that adolescence was redoing childhood in a different way. Others have said that teenagers are really two year olds with hormones and wheels. Though any well-respecting teen would resent this last description, the adolescent's task of separation and individuation parallels the process he first underwent as a toddler in separating from his mother. Whether a teenager or a toddler, separation and individuation involves establishing new roles, patterns of interaction, and levels of independence for both the child and the parent, without altogether forfeiting the relationship established over the years. This process of moving from dependent child to independent adult takes most of the second decade of the child's life.

Adolescence begins at about age eleven. The psychological onset of adolescence does not always move hand-in-hand with the physical changes of puberty. Though some girls begin menstruating and developing breasts as early as age eight or nine, in most cases they are still children psychologically. Likewise, young people who enter physical puberty later than their peers are usually already emotionally and psychologically adolescents. Either scenario—early or late development—can be difficult for the young person, who may be confused by the physical changes, worried by the lack of them, or teased by peers.

Adolescence may be broken down into three stages: early, middle, and late. Early adolescence is usually considered to be from age eleven to somewhere between thirteen and fifteen years old, and is characterized by the young person's first attempts at establishing a more distinct identity and separating emotionally from the family. The classic eleven-year-old is moody, easily embarrassed, and sees parents as highly flawed and a liability to be hidden from peers. During this time, teens try out different roles, often looking for ways to be more popular or better accepted among their peers. Teens turn more to their peer groups for a sense of belonging and identity and less to their families. Early adolescence is a time for practicing being different from the family and being away from the family. Dress, mannerisms, speech, hairstyle, and music all become mediums for exerting independence and proving difference. Young teens also find a variety of ways to be "away" from the family, even without leaving the house, including retreating to their rooms and spending as much time as allowed on the telephone with friends. Being in public with their peers—at the mall, the movie theater, or school sports events—is another way young teens practice being away from family and demonstrate to themselves, their peers, and their parents that they are no longer children.

Early adolescence is a common time for a resurgence of grief for the loss of the birth parents. Though your child may have resolved this grief and come to a point of integration during middle childhood, he is likely to find new meaning in the loss and need to grieve again.

During middle adolescence, ages fifteen to seventeen, teens practice intimacy through both platonic and romantic friendships. A teen, however, will usually spend more time talking with same-sex friends about his or her romance or sexual encounters than with the person he or she is dating. Another task of middle adolescence is to consolidate one's sense of self based on the past, present, and hopes for the future.

This last task continues into late adolescence (ages seventeen to nineteen, and sometimes into the early twenties). Now the young person's thoughts turn to how she will leave home and what she will do with her life. According to Erikson (Hogan 1976 writing about Erikson, 172), college serves as a moratorium on adulthood; young people who go on to college may postpone some of these decisions and often the responsibilities of adulthood until a later age. Though college offers the opportunity for the young person to live away from home, most students continue to rely on parents for financial and other basic support. Of course, some young people do assume an adult level of responsibility for their lives while attending college.

Breaking Away and the Search for Identity

Just as the end of infancy is marked by a consolidation of individuation, from which the child emerges with a sense of self separate from the mother, the end goal of adolescence is for the young person to refine this sense of self into an identity separate from and no longer dependent on the parents—in short, to become an adult.

Defining one's identity and separating from the family physically and emotionally are perhaps the two greatest tasks of adolescence. Neither is accomplished overnight, but for most young people, are achieved through a series of steps—or rites of passage—the nature of which varies according to the teen's micro- and macroculture, personality, and life experiences. Though many cultures have clear-cut rites of passage, in Western industrialized countries, initiating the child into adulthood usually consists of incremental increases in independence, responsibilities, and privilege. Some formal religious rituals such as bar mitzvah or confirmation persist, but most rites of passage are as ordinary as getting a driver's license, a first job, or being allowed to wear makeup, date, or determine one's own curfew or bedtime. Through this gradual increase in responsibility and adult-like privileges, adolescents gain an increasing sense of capability for taking on adult roles and a chance to "practice" at being adults. By enabling, guiding, and supporting their children through these rites of passage, parents help to ensure a healthy transition into adulthood. When a teen is forced or attempts to become an adult overnight, without adequate preparation, or is held back from assuming those adult privileges and responsibilities within his capabilities, the teen is more likely to try to prove himself through unhealthy, pseudo-adult behaviors such as alcohol or other drug abuse, dropping out of school, running away from home, or becoming sexually active without first establishing a healthy intimate relationship.

Individuation and separation are interdependent. The adolescent who has not yet "found herself" won't feel safe to separate from the family. Without an emotional separation from the family and successful assumption of adult responsibilities, the young person will have more difficulty defining herself and her future in a positive way. By emotional separation, we mean the young person no longer feels dependent on or immersed in her family in the way a child is—though the family's emotional support is still important and necessary. Similarly, successful assumption of adult responsibilities means that the young person is not left defeated when things don't go well, but finds a way to work through, resolve, or cope with difficulties.

Before a young person can separate in a healthy way from the family, he must first have synthesized the various aspects of himself from his past, his present, and his dreams for the future—including what he hears other important people in his life saying about him—into a single sense of self. Questions the young person must eventually answer include the following:

Who am I? The answer should provide the young person with a sense of "continuity and sameness" (Erikson 1980, 94) regardless of the setting or role in which he finds himself. In other words, he will not feel he is one person when he is with friends and another when with family, or one person when at work and another when socializing, even though he may express himself differently from one situation to the next. Likewise, other people will recognize a thread of continuity in the young person that carries through regardless of the situation.

Where am I going, what will I do, and how will I get there? Before moving fully and safely into adulthood, the young person must have some sense of what she will do with her life. What work roles will she assume? The answer might be a job or career, caring for family (as parent, or spouse, or looking after an aging or ill adult relative, etc.), or a combination of these.

How and when will I take control of my life? While this question focuses primarily on separation, the answer has direct implications for identity. A young person who feels kicked out or who leaves before he is capable of taking care of himself will be at greater risk of developing a negative self-image because of rejection or failure to make it on his own in a healthy way.

By adolescence, children raised by their genetically related parents already know how they are like their parents; the task during adolescence is to identify how they are different, while maintaining a sense of connection to the family. For adopted teens, this task becomes more complex because they must figure out how they are like and different from both adoptive parents and both birth parents.

Because the actual separation is from the adoptive parents, claiming and belonging remain as important as during earlier years. Though identifying uniqueness is the normal task during this period, adopted teens need to feel they are like their adoptive parents and family in some way if they are to rely on their family and home for a safe base from which to launch into adulthood. Most adopted children can name the ways they are unlike their adoptive parents, but they can't always do the same with their birth parents. Instead of integrating characteristics from all four parents, some adopted adolescents feel they are predestined to be exactly like their birth parents—or their perception of their birth parents. This is particularly a problem for teens who have not resolved the dichotomy of the chosen-child message. Rather than integrating aspects of both birth and adoptive parents and coming up with an identity that is uniquely theirs, these teens often do all they can to move as far as possible from their image of their adoptive parents to become exactly like their image of their birth parents. This, again, is why a multidimensional picture of the birth parents is so critical. Teens need to know that their birth parents were neither perfect nor perfectly horrible.

If all the teen knows, perceives, or focuses on is that her birth parents were fertile, sexually active, irresponsible, and unwilling or unable to take care of children, and if she believes—as almost all children do, even as adults—that the parents who raised her are asexual, then the clearest way to differentiate herself from one set of parents to be like the other is to be irresponsibly sexually active. Teens who have not resolved in a positive way what the chosen-child dichotomy means about them are also at risk for taking on any other negative aspects they know or believe about their birth parents. Though these teens are usually angry with their birth parents, they aim the anger at their adoptive parents because they are available and because anger is an effective way of distancing themselves—which is what teens are normally trying to do with their parents. As an adoptive parent, knowing how teenagers normally act out the frustrations of adolescence can help you keep your cool when he begins behaving in ways you long ago taught him not to.

Even those teens who have resolved the dichotomy and the grief related to adoption often believe they are inescapably slated to be like their birth parents. For many this is a very scary prospect, especially if little is known about the birth parents or if what is known is negative. This belief is intensified if the balance of differences and likenesses between the teen and his adoptive parents is tipped on the side of the differences. The more the young person focuses on these differences, the more likely he is to look to his birth parents or his image of them for shared traits. When he looks he is sure to find likenesses because of the genetically inherited traits: physical features, personality, interests, and talents. The more identity information you have about your child's birth parents, the more ground you will have for pointing out specific ways she is like and unlike them, and thus not necessarily destined to be like the negative aspects.

One way to help reinforce a well-rounded image of your child's birth parents is to expose your teen to other birth parents—mothers and fathers—who have placed children for adoption. Local adoption agencies or other organizations may offer support groups for birth parents. Ask if your teen might sit in on a meeting or encourage your teen's support group to invite one or two birth parents to speak to the group on what it was like for them to place a child and how they have felt about their decision since that time.

Just as the lack of a healthy, well-integrated identity can interfere with separation, separation can interfere with integration of identity for several reasons. First, any separation—especially one as major as that from parents and family—affects one's identity and necessitates a redefinition of self, even if there was healthy identity before the loss. Separation triggers growth in identity formation, but it also makes the task more difficult because previously established definitions of self are no longer enough and new skills and roles may be required to adjust to the change. Leaving home is often more difficult for first children because they must break new ground, while younger siblings have examples of how to—or how not to—leave home from their older siblings. Regardless of birth order, teens can also look to their own past successes in life, as well as to examples set by parents, aunts, uncles, and other relatives, and peers, for reassurance that they have the potential to handle the responsibilities of adulthood.

For adopted teens and others who have experienced significant loss in the past, the impending separation of adulthood can disrupt the identity process. Even if the old losses have been grieved and a healthy resolution achieved, new losses will often resurrect the feelings of previous significant losses. To the degree to which past losses weren't healed, a new loss—

particularly a significant one like separation from parents and family—will bring up the old unresolved losses. Sometimes a person simply learns to *cope* with a loss without really healing from it. An adopted child who has found a way to cope with the losses of adoption without resolving them will likely regress to the developmental and grief stage at which he became stuck.

For example, a child who at age seven asked himself, "Why did this happen to me?" and, applying magical thinking, concluded that he somehow caused his birth parents to place him for adoption, may have decided that if he could just be the best in everything he did—overachieve—he could make himself worthy of his adoptive parents' love and live up to their expectations, thus ensuring that they would not give him up as well. As a teen faced with leaving home within a few years, this old coping technique will likely no longer provide an adequate barrier against old grief, fears, and negative self-image. Without the protection of a coping mechanism, he will be pushed back into the old grief as well as face the impending loss of leaving home. While grieving two losses at once may not be a pleasant scenario, the situation does provide an opportunity for the teen to rework old issues in a healthy way, to resolve the old loss—in this case, the loss of the birth parents—and be better for it.

Because of past losses, especially for children who were placed after infancy, the impending separation from parents can be a great source of anxiety for teens beginning as young as age thirteen. Some adopted teens feel so unsafe and insecure at the prospect of having to leave home that they leave early—sometimes by running away—in order to get it over with. Some go looking for their birth parents because they believe that their time with their adoptive parents is up, but that they still need someone to take care of them. Others search in an attempt to find a missing piece of themselves or because they feel they do not belong where they are, and thus must belong with their birth parents.

Adoptive parents can help relieve these anxieties by clarifying how and when they expect the teen to leave home, what support they will give, and what their relationship will be like after the teen has left home. It helps to talk also about the last time the young person left family (i.e., when he was placed for adoption or moved from a foster or birth family) and how leaving as an adult will be different. When this is not addressed, some young people try to leave home in the same way they left birth or foster homes earlier in life, for example without a goodbye, carrying their possessions in garbage bags. Be very clear, very specific, and very repetitive when talking with your child about leaving home. For example, "After you graduate high school you can choose to go to college or get a job. If you decide on college, we expect that you will live at home during the summers and work. If you decide against college, you will need to get a job, save your money, and pay a small amount in rent here until you can afford to get an apartment of your own. This will probably take a year or two, but that's OK. If you have problems making it on your own we will figure out a way to help. If all else fails, you can always come home." This is a discussion that will need to be repeated multiple times throughout the adolescent years. The more anxious your teen is about leaving home, the more often you will need to talk about how it will happen. Look for natural opportunities for discussing this issue; if you sit your child down for a quarterly when-you-leave-home lecture, he may think you really are trying to get rid of him. The pebbles technique, described in the previous chapter, may be a helpful way of raising the topic, providing reassurance, and uncovering fears your teen may have, without heightening his anxiety.

Other Tasks and Characteristics of Adolescence

In addition to the physical changes of puberty and the psychological tasks of separation and identity formation, adolescence also brings changes in the way children understand and perceive the world around them. These cognitive and perceptual developments, along with impending adulthood, lead teens to explore where they fit into society, their future work roles, and their attitudes and opinions about society. Below are specific characteristics of adolescence:

Abstract thinking. Sometime between ages thirteen and fifteen, teens develop the ability to think abstractly. Abstract thinking is the ability to understand and apply concepts without specific concrete examples. Abstract thinking is also the ability to manipulate and explore ideas. A teen who can follow algebra, identify and understand literary metaphors, or argue philosophy has developed abstract thinking.

This new ability can be both a help and a hindrance when working with young people on issues related to adoption. It is helpful for reframing experiences from younger years, especially to help the teen see where he did and did not have power to affect the placement decision, or to cause or prevent abuse or neglect. When dealing with emotional issues, however, it is often better to stick with concrete terms. For example, *grief* is an abstract concept, but "You lost someone and you hurt" is a concrete translation of grief. Very bright children are often the most difficult to work with effectively because they tend to intellectualize their feelings to avoid actually experiencing them. Experiencing and talking about emotions is a critical element of successful grief and attachment work. Though an intellectual understanding of what happened, and why, is important, without experiencing the emotions of grief, it is very difficult to let go of the pain of a loss.

Idealism. Adolescence is a time when the flaws of the world, society, and parents become all too clear. At the same time that adolescents recognize the imperfections, they believe strongly that the world and its inhabitants can and should be better, and that they perhaps can make a difference. By protesting wrongs and working for change, they gain a sense of personal power, control, and hopefulness. More often, however, teens fight their world battles through heated discussions of the injustices they see. Often, the greater the anger regarding an injustice, the greater the teen's sense of powerlessness to change the situation or to deal with it.

Acquisition of social attitudes and opinions. Related to idealism is the acquisition of social attitudes and opinions. Some teens take stances on politics, religion, society, and mores that are juxtaposed to those of their parents as a way to differentiate themselves. Others adopt their parents' views or modify them slightly. Idealism takes hold when the children take on their parents' values but believe their parents have been hypocritical, have failed to adequately defend their principles, or have given up the struggle prematurely. This scenario has been a major factor in many civil rights movements (and systems of oppression) in the United States and abroad.

Definition of a work role. Choosing an occupation involves matching personal drives and talents to what society offers and allows. "It is the inability to settle on an occupational identity," Erikson writes, "which most disturbs young people" (1968, 132). Expectations from the young person's micro- and macrocultures can have a profound effect on the direction she chooses for her life. As previously mentioned, conflict can arise when the young person feels she cannot meet the expectations of society or her family. But conflict can also arise when the micro- or macroculture restricts opportunities, imposes barriers, or fails to support the young person's efforts to move beyond what those cultures deem appropriate roles.

Such was the case with civil rights leader Malcolm X. In his autobiography he wrote about what he called "the first major turning point" in his life. When asked by a white English teacher if he had considered a career, he said he wanted to become a lawyer.

> Lansing certainly had no Negro lawyers—or doctors either—in those days, to hold up an image I might have aspired to. All I

really knew for certain was that a lawyer didn't wash dishes, as I was doing.

Mr. Ostrowski looked surprised, I remember, and leaned back in his chair and clasped his hands behind his head. . . . "Malcolm, one of life's first needs is for us to be realistic. Don't misunderstand me, now. We all here like you, you know that. But you've got to be realistic about being a nigger. A lawyer—that's no realistic goal for a nigger. You need to think about something you can be. You're good with your hands—making things. Everybody admires your carpentry shop work. Why don't you plan on carpentry? People like you as a person—you'd get all kinds of work."

The more I thought afterwards about what he said, the more uneasy it made me. It just kept treading around in my mind.

What made it really begin to disturb me was Mr. Ostrowski's advice to others in my class—all of them white. Most of them had told him they were planning to become farmers. But those who wanted to strike out on their own, to try something new, he had encouraged. . . . Yet nearly none of them had earned marks equal to mine.

It was a surprising thing that I had never thought of it that way before, but I realized that whatever I wasn't, I was smarter than nearly all of those white kids. But apparently I was still not intelligent enough, in their eyes, to become whatever I wanted to be.

It was then that I began to change—inside. (Haley and Malcolm X 1965, 43–44)

In his study of Malcolm X, Erikson points to this denial of opportunity as a major cause for his striking out against society, as a young adult, through crime (Hogan 1976 writing about Erikson, 175). "Should a young person feel that the environment tries to deprive him too radically of all the forms of expression which permit him to develop and integrate the next step," Erikson writes, "he may resist with the wild strength encountered in animals who are suddenly forced to defend their lives. For, indeed, in the social jungle of human existence there is no feeling of being alive without a sense of identity" (Erikson 1968, 130). But Malcolm X eventually integrated his desire and ability to lead, with his rage at the oppression he felt, into his role as a leader in the Black Muslim community and beyond.

Determination of social role. How a person feels he fits into society is often, but not always, reflective of how he feels he fits into his family. Teens who have felt from a very early age that they did not belong in their family frequently have difficulty finding a *safe* role and group identification in society. In some cases, however, if the young person is the only "healthy" member within a dysfunctional family, he may find he fits better into society at large than he does in his own family.

Parent/Teen Tensions

The adolescent drive to separate from parents and to gain power through autonomy inevitably leads to some degree of conflict between parents and teens. As young as age eleven, teens want to take on greater control of their lives and want their parents not to exert theirs. Billy Joel's 1978 hit song "My Life" has been the theme song of more than a few teenagers with its chorus of:

> I don't need you to worry for me cause I'm alright
> I don't want you to tell me it's time to come home
> I don't care what you say anymore, this is my life
> Go ahead with your own life and leave me alone.

The parents' job is to direct their teenagers to areas where they can safely assume more control. But what a parent believes a teen can handle is not always what the teen believes he can handle. In adoptive families, a common challenge to parental authority during adolescence is "You aren't my real parents." Such statements can be used in four ways:

- to gain power by irritating, hurting, or making the parents angry in retaliation for the teen not getting his way;
- to manipulate the parents into giving in by playing on potential fears;
- to gain power by changing the subject from the original issue, especially if it is something for which the teen was being reprimanded; or
- as a reflection of problems in the parent/child relationship or in the way the teen feels about himself, his adoption, or his membership in the family.

Regardless of the underlying motivation for the statement, the last thing a parent should do in response to this challenge is rattle off a parental curriculum vitae: "I changed your diapers, put clothes on your back, drive you all over town. . . ." Such a defense only proves the child's point by showing that the parent feels he must justify himself. Your first response should be to respond to the issue at hand. For example, "You still cannot have the car keys," "Perhaps another parent would have raised you differently, but I am raising you the best way I know how," or "I don't like your saying that, but let's stick to the issue; why do you think you should be allowed to . . .?"

If you believe your child is saying this because of underlying problems with attachment, claiming and belonging, or lack of information about the birth parents, you can address these issues later. Wait a few days and then bring up the subject of the birth parents again, either directly ("I was thinking about what you said the other day . . .") or indirectly using a more sophisticated version of the pebbles technique described in Chapter 11. Indirect comments work better with adolescents than direct statements or questions. For example: "Sometimes I wonder what you think your birth parents relationship might have been." "You grew out of those jeans so fast. I wonder how tall you'll be?" "I read an article on Korea a few days ago. I wonder if your birth parents still live in Seoul." Don't expect a response right away; simply put the subject out to show that it is not off limits.

Another source of tension between parents and their teenage children is the fact that not only do the children no longer look up to the parents, they often believe their parents are the most flawed people around. This phenomenon is intensified by the adolescent's desire to distinguish herself from her parents, while still trying to figure out what characteristics she has received from them. Some of the flaws teens identify in their parents are actually there; others are their own shortcomings projected onto their parents. For example, many teens act as if their parents are among the stupidest people on the planet, especially when it comes to understanding life as a teen. By believing and acting as if their parents don't know anything, teens guard themselves against feeling stupid because they, of course, know more than—or at least as much as—their parents.

As a parent, you need to avoid getting caught up in self-defense or in proving yourself to your adolescent children, keeping in mind that the issue stems more from teenage insecurities than from your own deficits. A better way to neutralize an adolescent's disdain is to help her feel capable. The more capable she feels, the less she will need to prove herself better than others—including you—by putting them down. Keep in mind that telling your child directly that she is capable and intelligent won't be enough at this age, especially if she's already decided you are an unreliable source (i.e., you don't know anything anyway). You can, however, support and facilitate her in endeavors at school, on the job, or in developing talents and interests.

The most severe clashes between parents and teens arise when adolescents feel alienated from family and society. Alienation is an extreme sense of not belonging that usually starts with the teen not feeling he belongs in the family. But not all adolescents who are struggling with attachment and belonging feel alienated from society, and not all adolescents who feel alienated are unattached. The task of separation itself stresses the attachment between parent and child in even the healthiest of families. Alienation is seldom brought on by a single factor or event in a teen's life. For most young people who feel this way, alienation is a result of a complexity of issues in their lives. Some adopted teens are more vulnerable to alienation. It is easier for a young person to move into the role of an alienated person if he feels disconnected from the human race, feels he is a bad person or causes bad things to happen (shame-based identity), or feels, as one fifteen-year-old adopted male put it, he is "the spawn of fucking, runting garbage."

Conflicts often arise between parents and teens over radical clothing or hairstyles. In some cases, teens don radical styles merely as a fashion statement. Think back to the hippie movement of the late sixties. True hippies were people who felt alienated from society and opted to drop out. But the fashions they chose to reflect their protest against societal norms—long hair, bell bottoms, hip huggers, halter tops, you name it—were taken on in one form or another by the majority of young people in the country. And most of them weren't feeling alienated; they just wanted to be like their peers, be cool, or prove they weren't carbon copies of their parents. Risky behaviors such as living on the streets, prostitution, drug use, and gang or cult involvement are among the most serious and dangerous manifestations of alienation.

If you believe your child is involved in or leaning toward this latter group of activities, it's time to seek professional counseling. Even when alienation is not an issue, many adoptive families find that support groups for adopted teens—and parents—are helpful in dealing with parent/teen conflicts, adoption issues, and other adolescent adjustments. Whenever tensions within the family or the individual become unmanageable or drag out over weeks or months, it is wise to seek counseling for all involved.

Body Image and Sexuality

During early adolescence, much of sexuality is still concerned with body image and gender roles. If physical changes haven't already begun, boys and girls alike worry that maybe they never will. Girls who begin developing breasts at an early age often worry that their breasts will be too large by the time they stop; those who develop more slowly worry that they will be forever flat-chested. Boys are commonly concerned about when their facial hair will come in, whether they will eventually be bald, and about penis size ("Will I be too small or too large for intercourse?").

Young teens are usually concerned about their ability to eventually attract someone of the opposite sex, but they are not usually engulfed in actually trying to do so in the present. Fear of homosexuality can be very strong at this age, whether the young person actually is homosexual or not. Close relationships with same-sex friends, locker-room experiences (looking at and being curious about other naked bodies in the shower), and adult and adolescent derision for homosexuals often trigger these fears.

The definition of what makes a man or a woman also contributes to this fear. As we move away from strict standards of masculinity and femininity in terms of dress, hairstyle, jewelry, occupations, and so on, adolescents have fewer concrete definitions with which to compare themselves. For many adolescents—as well as much of society—a "real" man or woman is determined by whom a person sleeps with sexually. Parents who try to raise their children without sexism often are left defining men and women as male and female adults, respectively. Being a "good" or "real" man or woman is then determined by how well the individual practices his or her humanity. Though we agree that the move toward greater gender equality is a positive one, it can make defining sexuality more difficult for young teens who are only beginning to think abstractly and who are looking for concrete ways to prove their masculinity or femininity to themselves and others without being sexually active.

Adopted adolescents wonder what their birth parents were like as men and women. Again, unless they have been given more information about their birth parents, all they will see is impulsive sexuality. When their own hormones begin to rage, they will look at their adoptive parents, whom they see as asexual, and then at their birth parents, who must have been sexual, and decide they must be like their birth parents. (Of course, the irony of this is that, had they been raised by their birth parents, they would have seen them as asexual also. As someone once put it, each generation believes it discovered and/or invented sex.) The fact that the birth parents are not present and not parenting frees the child to see them as sexual beings. Some use this premise as an excuse for their own sexual activity.

By age thirteen, teens have very strong opinions about their birth parents' sexuality. But not all simply give in to a fate of following in their image of their birth parents' footsteps. Some, in their determination not to make the same mistakes or not to be all the bad things they believe their birth parents were, become so rigid about not being sexually active that, like a diet, their determination is bound to be broken.

Some young teens do date and use their emerging adult body shapes to begin to act sexually. Most eleven- to fifteen-year-olds, however, are not fully comfortable with what they are doing. Others become sexually active in an attempt to fill feelings of emptiness, to escape dysfunctional families, to ease the pain of a loss, or because of past or ongoing sexual abuse. Children who have been sexually abused sometimes become sexually active outside the abusive relationship in order to regain a feeling of control over their own bodies or because they are acting on a negative self-definition ("slut," "whore," "faggot") imposed by the abuser or through self-blame.

By middle adolescence there is much more pairing up and dating. Most teens seem to believe that *everyone* in school has a boyfriend or girlfriend, when really half the kids around them do not. Relationships at this age usually last no more than several weeks. Many teens seem to enjoy the trauma of breaking up, perhaps because the experience provides further proof of their near-adulthood. Often a teen will be more in love with the idea of being in love than he or she is with the other person.

Teens—and adults—sometimes use physical intimacy as a substitute for emotional intimacy. In a rather distorted interpretation of object constancy, the young person believes that if she puts out sexually, he will stay with her and their relationship will be good; if she doesn't, he will leave. Young men often feel that if they don't try for sex, the women they date won't believe they are masculine enough.

Some adopted teens seem to get pregnant to go through the choice of keeping the baby, aborting, or placing the baby for adoption. Some do this to prove they would not make the same choice their birth parents did; others do it to relive their birth parents' script as a way of exploring what their birth parents must have felt and to prove to themselves that their birth parents were pained at giving them up. Still others choose abortion to, in effect, save their babies from the pain they feel they have endured.

Though the decision to keep, place, or abort is usually in the hands of the teenage girl, adopted adolescent boys often become involved in these pregnancies, even if they are not the fathers. For adopted adolescent girls and boys alike, having a baby often offers their first opportunity to see someone who is genetically related to them. When choosing to place their babies for adoption, most adopted adolescents, especially those in closed adoptions, choose open adoption in order to give their babies what they may not have had as adopted children: contact with birth parents, pictures, information.

In late adolescence, most young people move beyond the one-week romances to explore other aspects of their relationships besides just the physical attraction, where they most often start. If a young person still does not feel comfortable or assured in his or her role as a man or woman, that young person will have difficulty developing emotionally intimate relationships during late adolescence and beyond. Of course, even by late adolescence, some teens will not yet be dating—some because they are mature and have chosen to pursue other goals first, others because they are immature and unable to attract a partner or maintain an interaction long enough to get to the first date.

Many adopted people—teens and adults—consciously or subconsciously avoid dating anyone who looks the least bit like themselves for fear of incest. Most teens feel comfortable talking openly about this fear with their parents or in a support group, though a parent or group leader might have to raise the subject. Because of this fear, adopted teens often date people of another race or nationality. Teens who have been adopted interracially often choose to date people of a third race; for example, an African-American teen adopted by white parents is more likely to date Native Americans, Asians, or Hispanics than people of their own race or that of their parents.

If your child begins dating interracially, keep in mind that parents of color may be just as upset as white parents by interracial dating and marriage. There is nothing inherently unhealthy about an interracial relationship unless it is motivated by an unhealthy need or belief. Choosing a partner solely to irritate one's parents is not a healthy basis for a relationship. While it may be fine for the young person to make a statement, such a relationship is not fair to the other person involved—after all, no one likes to be used. Some people, regardless of adoption, restrict their choice of dating partners to specific races or ethnic groups other than their own (for example, a white woman who will only date black men). Such situations should raise concern about unhealthy underlying beliefs or motivations (negative racial or ethnic self-image, stereotypes, challenging parents' values, etc.).

Talking About Sexuality

Surveys show that a large majority of kids today are becoming sexually active before the age of eighteen (Fishel 1992). This means that parents need to talk with their children about sexuality before they have the opportunity to become sexually active. A good time to begin these discussions is between the ages of nine and eleven, before your credibility is diminished as a result of your child's urges to separate and individuate.

Among the most important facts of life teens need to know include:

- Everyone has sexual urges.
- Everyone has control over what they do with those urges (even if your date says he doesn't).
- Everyone is responsible for their own actions and urges (in other words, just because someone says you led them on, you are not obligated to any sexual activity you don't wish to partake in).
- No means *no*. Even if a date is playing games (saying no but really meaning yes), you must respect what the person actually says. If this

causes conflict, tell the person you are dating to say what he or she means.

- Everyone has the right to say no to sexual activities they do not wish to engage in. Celibacy is an acceptable choice.
- Teens need to know how to exercise control over sexual situations not only when it doesn't feel good, but also when it does but they do not want to go further. Sol Gordon, Ph.D., has several very good resources for teaching teens how to control sexual situations, including a video entitled *How Can I Tell if I'm in Love?* (1987, with Justine Bateman and Ted Danson) and a book written with Judith Gordon, M.S.W., *Raising a Child Conservatively in a Sexually Permissive World* (1989). *Seduction Lines Heard 'Round the World and Answers You Can Give* (1987), also by Gordon, is packed full of witty and effective one-liners from around the world that young people can use to respond to unwanted sexual advances.
- Each person bears a responsibility to exercise control to protect himself or herself from unplanned pregnancy, unhealthy intimacy, sexually transmitted diseases, including AIDS, and from interfering with his or her personal goals.

Adoptive parents need to do more than just set down rules about dating. Unless parents are able to talk with their teens—or find someone else who can—regarding their image of and attitudes about their birth parents' sexual behavior, teens are left interpreting their own sexual responses in terms of how they are like or unlike their birth parents.

Parents, too, need to get in touch with their own image of their child's birth parents' sexuality. If you are feeling judgmental of the birth parents, it is bound to come across eventually in your attitude. One adoptive father we know struggled with judging his child's birth parents for being promiscuous. When he went to his pastor for advice on how to overcome these feelings, his pastor pointed out that "there but for the grace of God go we." One step further, one time, makes a baby. It's possible that your child's birth parents were not as sexually active as you at the same age, but they were fertile or the timing one time just happened to be right for conception. If you practiced celibacy as a young person, was it because you were being true to your values, or because you were afraid or lacked the right opportunity? How many of us as young people found ourselves in unsafe situations where the only thing that kept us from a date rape was fast thinking or mere luck that the other person stopped? The point is that in most cases, it is impossible to know all the dynamics leading up to your child's conception. You must come to grips with how you feel about your child's birth parents and, if those feelings are negative, to find a way to let them go because inevitably your child will sense that you feel the same way toward him or her, whether it is true or not.

Finally, even though studies in recent years indicate that young people are becoming sexually active at younger and younger ages, there is a common misconception that, as one parent put it, "once the barn door is open, there's no closing it." The fact is that many young people have intercourse once and then don't have it again for some time to come—even for a number years. Even teens who have had an ongoing sexual relationship with one boyfriend or girlfriend do not necessarily have intercourse with everyone they date thereafter. We have known quite a number of teens (girls in particular) whose parents were convinced they were promiscuously sexually active, only to find out later, upon medical examination, that they were still virgins. Adoptive parents often become particularly fearful about their daughters if they know or believe the birth mother was a prostitute. According to Thomas Bouchard, Ph.D. (in a lecture to Resources for Adoptive Parents, Golden Valley, Minnesota, December 1992), lead researcher in the University of Minnesota twins studies, daughters of prostitutes usually do not become prostitutes themselves. Adoptive parents, like their children, need to remember that their children are not genetically destined to be promiscuous!

Supporting Search and Reunion

By late adolescence, identity issues and curiosity lead some adopted teens to search for their birth parents. Search can be scary and frustrating for everyone involved—the child, the adoptive parents, and the birth parents, once found. Despite the many fears, adoptive parents need to support their children's choice to search for their birth parents. But no matter what your child's age, you need to give clear behavioral and verbal messages that he or she is and always will be your son or daughter and part of your family.

Not all adopted people feel a need to search in adolescence, as an adult, or ever. For those who do, search and reunion may aid in their healing from the losses of adoption; but this isn't true for everyone. An adopted person can heal *without* searching or finding, can search and find and still *not* heal, or can search and find *and* heal. No matter what the young person decides now or later about searching, the overriding objective must be to heal: to grieve the loss, find resolution, and come out of it all with a positive sense of self.

The frustration of searching comes from the powerlessness the adopted person often feels in gaining access to information about herself—information nonadopted people have access to as a birthright. We hope that adopted people will eventually have free access to their birth certificates, at least by the age of majority. England (1976), Finland (1926), Scotland (1930), Holland (1956), Israel (1960), New Zealand (1985), Australia N.S.W. (1991), and the state of Hawaii (1991) already allow for such access, but not every adopted person chooses to pursue it (Griffith 1991). Simply knowing that it is available is often enough.

As we explained earlier, an adopted child's need to search is not a reflection on the adoptive family or the child's feelings for them. Even if you know this is true, as a parent you are bound to have strong mixed emotions, ranging from a desire to be supportive and helpful, to fear that your child will be hurt or will leave you to rejoin his birth parents, to anger and pain.

Though adoptive parents need to give clear consistent messages of support and approval for the search and reunion, they also need to address their own mixed feelings about it. While you can tell your child that you are scared of losing him once he finds his birth parents, you also need to be clear that it is your responsibility—not his—to work through these fears. Before you can help your child, you must help yourself. Support groups or individual counseling can help you identify and understand your feelings, and find ways to be supportive without denying how you feel. You will also need to learn when to give support and when to back off and let your child go it alone. If you have more than one child in your family, your other children may share many of your fears and feelings and need the same type of support and counseling you do.

In an effort to be supportive, adoptive parents sometimes try to push the search along faster than what the adopted child is ready to handle. Many young people spend long periods in an inactive search, contemplating what it might be like to find their birth parents. During this phase of search, you can help your child by talking with her about what she expects to find, how she thinks she will feel, and what she believes she will gain from the reunion. This is another good time to pull up old information you may have about the birth parents, and if your child desires, help her to get more.

As a parent, however, you need to remember that your teenager must retain control over how fast the search proceeds. She may vacillate between insatiable curiosity and excitement at what she might find, and fear that, once found, her birth parents will reject her or that she will lose her relationship with you in the process. Search may also raise old fantasies about the birth parents, as well as pain. Your child may benefit from professional counseling periodically throughout the search to help her understand her fears and expectations, and to deal with any painful pieces she may find along the way.

The actual reunion can raise intense feelings for both the young person and the birth parent. Either may decide that meeting once is enough to satisfy their curiosity. The child or the birth parent may also alternate between approach and avoidance. Your child may get a letter and not respond, or send one and not hear back from the birth parent. Each may need time between contacts to work through old and new feelings.

The first meeting may create an intense euphoria for both child and birth parent, as they find similarities and differences and revel in finally meeting again. If both desire to establish a relationship, there will be a time of fog, symbiosis, and finally differentiation. Some adopted people and their birth parents never develop a deep relationship, but even so they will follow this same basic pattern. (Actually, the pattern of relationship formation established between mother and child in infancy carries through to some degree to all intimate relationships.)

It is not uncommon during these early stages of relationship building for birth parents or adopted young people to experience physical sensations similar to those of sexual attraction. Some have called this "genetic sexual attraction." Parents often experience similar feelings with their infants during fog and symbiosis stages, but in either instance, these feelings usually subside as the relationship builds. Birth parents and adopted children who are pursuing a reunion should be told in advance that this might happen and that it is natural, though not something to act on. People who are not told ahead of time about this phenomenon often feel guilty and "dirty" at the experience.

Until the relationship between the young person and birth parent moves beyond fog and symbiosis, it can be very painful and threatening for the adoptive parent to watch, in part because the young person, engulfed in the new relationship, often tunes out the adoptive family. It is OK for adoptive parents to draw the line if they are feeling they are being taken advantage of. Often adoptive parents need to set boundaries because their teenagers may not be able to do it themselves. For example, one adoptive parent we know was very upset that her son's birth mother had invited him to spend Thanksgiving with her. The birth mother defended her invitation, saying that the adoptive parents had had years of holidays to spend with the young man, so she was entitled to have this one. The adoptive mother thought she *had* to let him go without complaint, so she lied and told her son she didn't mind. Later, after giving the situation some thought, she told her son how she really felt. He told her that when she said he could go, he thought she no longer cared whether he was around or not.

In addition to situations like this, adopted children often will take out their anger at their birth parents on their adoptive parents. As your child's parent, you have the right to refuse to be dumped on and to draw family boundary lines, just as you would if any other of your child's friendships was disrupting the family.

Special Issues for Interracial and International Adoptions

Peer acceptance is one of the most difficult aspects of adolescence for the child who is a racial or ethnic minority within the community. In middle childhood such children often face verbal rejection and teasing because of their ethnicity, but they are still included in play. The dynamics, however, change in adolescence to match the adult model of behavior: verbal acceptance, but behavioral rejection. This can be very confusing for the child of color, especially if his adoptive parents are white and he has never before experienced this type of covert racism. The problem is often further complicated if the parents tend to deny or are unable to recognize the subtle prejudices their children experience.

As adolescents work on separating from parents and turn increasingly to peers for identification, similarities and differences with peers become very important. The child of color raised by white parents is often rejected and stereotyped by peers of color. These teens are likely to hear comments such as "You don't act your color." They may also be called a "wannabe," because they "want to be" a different race than they are. Wannabe is the latest equivalent of "Oreo" (black on the outside, white on the inside). In integrated communities, wannabe may be applied to a white teen who hangs with kids of color or a teen of color whom the group feels is not acting his race. Pressure to "act one's color" serves to restrict individuation.

Teens of mixed heritage or whose ethnicity is rare in the community in which they live (even if raised by same-race parents) may face even greater difficulty finding comfortable peer groups because they are often rejected by the groups with which they identify. For example, an East Indian teen may identify with the African-American kids because of similar skin tone, but the African-American teens may reject him because his hair is too straight or because his mannerisms are different from theirs. The same may occur for biracial children whose physical features are not easily categorized by stereotypic racial groupings. Even if her peers recognize and accept her dual ethnic heritage (in this example, African-American and Caucasian), under the "one-drop theory" (one drop of black blood makes you black), the larger white society may react to the teen in a way that clearly tells her she is not white and that it will not recognize that part of her heritage.

When living in an ethnically diverse community, these teens often find themselves pushed into a peer group in which everyone is of mixed heritage, though not necessarily the same mix. This is not necessarily negative, but it is one more instance in which the larger society imposes definitions without regard to how the teens see themselves. Some teens will be able to find a multiracial peer group in which the members have some common denominator other than race, perhaps a belief in multiculturalism or an extracurricular activity. Others, feeling alienated, may turn to the most radical group on campus, the common denominator of which is that they all reject or feel rejected by everyone else.

Even the most savvy adoptive parents often fall into the trap of telling their teens that there is no such thing as "acting your color." While this is a wonderful moral ideal, the reality for the young person is that her peers believe there is and reject her on those grounds. A better approach to helping your teenager is to do the following:

- Validate and discuss your teen's feelings.
- Ask if she knows what they mean by "acting your color." The definition will change from group to group. If she isn't clear what her peers mean, tell her to ask them the next time they say it. Most teens will have something very specific in mind.
- Ask: "What is your color or ethnic group? Is your heritage truly the same as those who are criticizing you?" Perhaps one of the reasons the teen isn't "acting" Puerto Rican is because he is biracial African- and European-American, and just looks Puerto Rican.
- Once she understands what her peers consider "acting her color," ask her if she wants to act in any of those ways. Is there a way she can be a blend of both who she is and who they expect and still be accepted and feel good about herself? Leave the decision to your teenager. If the mannerisms she adopts don't fit with her personality or her values, she will probably return shortly to a style that is more natural for her.

For many teens of color, it is easier to find an appropriate retort when a white kid insults their ethnicity (or perceived lack thereof) than it is when another teen of color does the same. Of course, no matter who makes the remark, the prejudice is equally bad; but an insult from people with whom you are trying to identify carries a greater sting. True racial freedom will come when everyone can express themselves in their own way—but we are still a long way from that.

Another way to help your child work through these peer problems is to find a support group with other adopted teens. Ideally, such a group would include teens from interracial, international, and same-race adoptions. This mix will help teens identify what issues are a normal part of adoption—and commiserate about those problems—and what issues are specifically related to race or ethnicity. By separating the issues in this way, the task of overcoming the race-related problems may be less overwhelming. White teens raised by white parents can benefit from such support groups, too. Cultural identity is important for everyone, yet many white Americans— especially those whose families have been in the United States for several generations—don't feel they have a rich cultural heritage. They need to know that culture is that which is common and customary for a group of people; a culture only becomes exotic when it is taken from its original setting and moved into another cultural setting. Thus McDonald's, rock and roll, jazz, baseball games, and blue jeans all have the potential to take on a richer feel for Americans living abroad than they do at home.

Often teens raised in international adoptive families may find it easier to relate to second-generation immigrants (children of immigrants) than to the group as a whole. Many second-generation immigrants assimilate some of the culture of their new country, while maintaining strong emotional ties to their parents' country of origin. The struggle of ethnic identity is much the same for these young people as it is for children who are raised in "American" families, though they were born in another land and still bear the appearance of people in that country. In response to "You don't act your ethnicity," young people who are adopted internationally can respond saying, "I was born in . . . ; I was raised American." If they choose, they can go on to explain what parts of their cultural heritage they celebrate.

Struggles with peer-group issues may also be used as an opportunity to talk about birth parents, while still addressing the problem at hand. You can ask, "How do you think your birth mother handled this sort of situation?" or "Do you think it would be easier if you were raised in your country of origin or by parents who shared your ethnicity?" If your child answers yes to the last question, don't take it personally; in this context especially, her answer is a statement on society, not on your home.

Peer-group identification is usually more difficult than race-related dating issues. First, teens are faced with the task of finding a peer group at a much younger age than they normally begin dating. Second, once peer groups are established there is little dating across group lines: athletes and kids in the band usually don't date one another. Though dating can raise some issues for interracially or internationally adopted teens, most interracially and internationally adopted teens *do* date. Most date across racial and ethnic lines, in part following a natural instinct to avoid dating someone with features similar to their own for fear of incest. Interracial dating may pose a particular challenge for parents who chose to adopt Asian or South American children because they felt they and their families wouldn't be able to aid an African-American or Native American child. Suddenly, they find their children dating and even marrying young people from these groups and they must now deal with their own biases. Interracially adopted teens may also use interracial dating to test their parents: "If you accept *my* difference, do you accept all differences? If not, how long will you continue to accept mine?"

In addition to dating and peer-group identification, interracially and internationally adopted teens will also have to balance their hopes, dreams, and self-images with what the larger adult society offers for their future. At home, you may have taught and prepared your child to be anything he wanted; but because of his ethnicity, the macroculture may attempt to redirect him to a more "socially acceptable" role, or place obstacles in his way for which he is not prepared. Role models are important for children of color at all ages, but by adolescence, kids need more personal, mentoring relationships with adults of their own race or ethnicity who have already achieved some of the goals to which they are aspiring. "The Cosby Show" is not adequate evidence that an African-American child can grow up to be a doctor or a lawyer. Studying about famous black physicians or lawyers provides better support; but the best support comes from real people your child can talk with and get advice from on how to make her dreams a reality.

If a trip to the teen's country of origin is planned during adolescence, it is often made emotionally easier if the teen travels with an organized group, rather than with his adoptive family. Family trips work better during middle childhood or young adulthood; when taken during adolescence, teens often feel—consciously or not—that their adoptive parents are trying to, or would like to, send them back. This is especially true if the parents and teen are struggling in their own relationship. No matter how strongly parents emphasize that the purpose of such a visit is to see the country, most adopted teens will find themselves throughout the trip searching women's faces, wondering (like a four-year-old) if any of them might be their birth mothers. If you decide that this is the only opportunity to travel back, then plan far in advance and spend much time talking openly with your teen about the purpose, what will happen, possible feelings, and most of all, that you will *all* come home *together*.

Family Life Cycle

In addition to the many struggles and changes your child will face, by the time he reaches late adolescence you will probably have a few of your own. Many marriages go through crisis at about the time children are leaving home. When the first child joined the family, your relationship with your spouse underwent a change from a dyad to a triad, making room for the child and for your new roles as parents. When the job of parenting is no longer as big as it once was, the couple is left to renegotiate their relationship, moving it from a partnership in parenting back to a dyad.

This empty-nest transition may also coincide with the midlife crises of either or both parents. For some parents, watching their children gain in power as they approach adulthood heightens their own sense of declining power and potential despair if they see they will probably not achieve their life goals. For infertile parents, watching their children become sexual can raise old grief about their own infertility.

Finally, parents often find it difficult to accept that their children are becoming adults, even if they are doing it in a healthy way. For adoptive parents, this transition can be even more difficult because it highlights all the ways in which their children are different from them. A parent who has hoped or needed all along to "mold" a child will undoubtedly face a greater degree of pain and conflict with his or her teen during this time.

If Moved During Adolescence

Permanent placements are very different when children have already begun adolescence than they are for younger children. Anyone considering adopting a teen needs to be aware that the quality of the relationship with that teen will be very different from the traditional parent/child relationship. At best, you should expect to have a friendship with the teen, in which you are an authority figure and mentor.

Forming parent/child attachments during adolescence can be very difficult because the natural task at this age is to separate from parents. The goal of parenting a teen who joins the family during adolescence is to nurture a sense of membership in the family. Even sibling relationships will be different under these circumstances than if the placement had been made at a younger age.

Before any placement decisions are made, a relationship should first be established between the prospective parent(s) and teen, and the teen should be involved in the decision making. The placement process should move at a slower pace than customary when placing younger children. The prospective parents and teen should have a chance to get to know each other first, and then move to a foster parent/child relationship, with the option or goal of becoming a permanent adoptive family (similar to living together before getting married).

Throughout the process, the prospective parents and the teen should receive individual and family counseling to help each explore his or her needs and expectations of a permanent family relationship, as well as any hidden agendas or fantasies on either side. For example, the teen may believe that if only he were adopted all of his problems would be solved and his life would be like the Waltons' or the Cosbys'. Prospective parents may be wanting to "rescue" a young life; whether this is possible or not depends on the teen, but chances are the teen will not always be giving 100 percent to the parent/child relationship because he is trying to become an adult. Some teens will be ready to truly belong to a family; others may want a safe haven with some sense of family, but continued autonomy.

Expectations of one another should be clearly laid on the line so both parents and teen can decide if they are willing and capable of meeting those of the other. Household rules and rules of the relationship need to be clearly defined—even put in writing—so the teen understands what behaviors and responsibilities are expected of him.

Prospective parents should have a fairly clear picture of the adolescent's past to help them realistically decide whether they are capable of parenting the teen, and also to help them recognize early on problems related to the past, should they arise. This may mean digging around in placement records and talking with her about her childhood—good and bad. Advocate for a complete history of moves, reasons for each, and any traumas known or believed to have occurred.

Often children adopted as teens establish closer relationships with adoptive grandparents and other extended family members than they do with their adoptive parents. Again this is normal given their task to separate.

Once your new son or daughter is living with you, it is important to include his or her history, favorite foods, and traditions into those of your family. Ask the teen to choose which foods and traditions she would like to add to the family, but be aware that even though she selected them, they may trigger grief or bad memories. If you notice the young person acting out or becoming upset or uncomfortable, bring the behavior to the teen's attention. A solution may be to select a different tradition or to choose a different day for celebrating it. For example, if the teen has a favorite Christmas tradition, you may want to recognize that tradition sometime during the holiday season, but not at the traditional time. If changing the day or modifying the tradition still brings distress, have a candle-lighting ceremony in memory of that tradition and past times; then work together to create entirely new traditions.

Newly adopted teens—and sometimes younger children who have been exposed to sexuality through abuse—often worry when they are romantically or sexually attracted to other members of their adoptive family. Perhaps Mom is really cute and sexy, or Dad is handsome and caring, or a sibling is just the type of person he or she would like to date. Teens need to know that it is normal for people who are forming emotional relationships to be physically attracted to one another or to have sexual thoughts about other members of their new families—but that these thoughts and feelings are not something to act on.

Before the young person even moves into the home, this issue should be openly discussed and the teen given suggestions for how to change or deal with these feelings should they occur. One way to change the feelings is to change the thoughts. One young man who found himself becoming physically aroused when his adopted mother was near discovered that by telling himself, "She's a mother; mother's aren't sexy," each time the feelings began, he eventually was able to stop them from happening. (Of course, someday when he is married and has children, he will have to erase this thought track!)

Parents can also watch for signs that this is happening. Romantic gazes, flirtatious looks, avoidance of or overenthusiasm for hugs, kisses, or other physical contact, and inappropriate touch are all signs that a teen is seeing the parent in a sexual light. One father who noticed his recently adopted daughter watching him (primarily his behind) as he walked across the room, turned to her and said, "I know it's cute, but I'm you're father." Parents need to be ready to discuss sexual feelings and to correct their teens when behavior is inappropriate. If you cannot talk frankly about these feelings, don't adopt an adolescent.

Also, be aware that your teenager may be attracted to you or have sexual thoughts regardless of how sexually "unattractive" you may believe yourself to be. One woman who adopted a teenage boy thought she was the safest person around to adopt a teen boy because there was no chance he would ever be bothered with sexual thoughts about her. The woman assumed that her rather round, heavy-set figure would be the last thing to arouse a teenage male. What she didn't realize was that every time she hugged her adopted son, his head unavoidably landed between her rather large breasts. Even if she wasn't swimsuit-model material, this situation was bound to trigger sexual thoughts in a teenage boy! After this was brought to her attention and her son said that he had found the hugs unnerving, they worked out a different way to hug: they found they could hug sideways, each putting an arm over the other's shoulder and squeezing.

Touch can reinforce and help build emotional intimacy among family members. But if the physical contact, no matter how innocuous, causes sexual feelings in your teen, it's better to modify or stop that particular interaction, replacing it with something else (a pat on the back, squeeze of the hand, or silly look or greeting) that will reinforce for the teen that you love and care about him or her without causing undo discomfort or encouraging inappropriate behavior.

Issues That May Arise

Adolescence can be a rough time for young people and their parents. If the earlier childhood years did not go well—that is, the child's basic physical, emotional, and developmental needs were not met—adolescence can be particularly rocky. Parent/teen conflicts are natural, as is some degree of rebellion, but for some teens these years are complicated by serious psychosocial issues. Behaviors that fall outside the bounds of normal adolescent rebellion and that should trigger particular concern include the following:

- extreme truancy;
- delinquent behavior;
- running away from home;
- extreme lack of discretion in choosing friends, and in dealing with strangers;
- alcohol or other drug use problems;
- verbal, physical, or emotional abuse of family members or others (more than arguments, which are normal);
- talking, thinking about, or attempting suicide;
- self-mutilation (though parents may feel otherwise, this does not include tattoos or having one's nose pierced for jewelry); and
- behaviors that threaten the young person's personal safety, including prostitution, gang, cult, or occult involvement, or living on the streets.

Whether or not your child's behavior is as deleterious as you believe it to be, it can never hurt to get another opinion from a professional therapist. If your teen is acting out in any of the above ways, the entire family is likely to be affected. In addition to seeking help for the teen, parents need support and help in identifying parenting techniques to help them better manage the situation. Other children in the family may also need help understanding what is happening with their brother or sister, and coping with the effects the situation may be having on the entire family.

Whenever an adopted teen is acting out in severe ways, assume that adoption issues are involved, and then rule out adoption if it proves not to be a factor. It is better to be wrong than to have overlooked the cause.

For Further Reading

• *Filling in the Blanks: A Guided Look at Growing Up Adopted* by Susan Gabel. Fort Wayne, IN: Perspectives Press, 1988.

A rather lengthy, but helpful, workbook for parents and young teens designed to facilitate discussion of adoption issues.

• *How It Feels to be Adopted* by Jill Kremetz. New York: Alfred A. Knopf, 1983.

Nineteen boys and girls, aged eight to sixteen, share their feelings, memories, and experiences of adoption. Especially good for preteens.
* *I'm Still Me* by Betty Jean Lifton. New York: Alfred A. Knopf, 1981.
  The story of a teenager's search for birth family.
* *Birthmark* by Lorraine Dusky. New York: M. Evans, 1979.
  A birth mother shares her story.

13

❧

School and the Adopted Child

*I*n most respects, adopted children have the same kind of school experiences as nonadopted children. But any time children struggle with personal issues, their school performance is bound to be affected. Grief, unrealistically high or low expectations of the child on the part of parents, and simply feeling different from other children are all potential obstacles to learning. Furthermore, the incidence of attention-deficit disorder (ADD) and attention-deficit hyperactivity disorder (ADHD), as well as other learning disabilities, appears to be higher among adopted children than among children raised with their genetic parents.

The first step to ensuring the best possible education for your child is choosing a school (if this is an option in your local school system). One quality to look for in a school is diversity among both students and faculty. This is especially important for children of color. But it is also highly beneficial for white children because a culturally diverse setting teaches children that it is OK to be different. Even if, for example, you are African-American, your adopted child is African-American, and you live in a predominantly African-American neighborhood with a predominantly black school, you should still ask how the school handles and teaches about differences. This is because the child who is most different is likely to face the greatest problems with peers and even sometimes with teachers; and adoption can sometimes be the difference that sets a child apart from his peers.

If you are unable to choose your child's school, or if all the schools in your district are equally homogeneous, when your child is still young (preschool through early elementary), invest in age-appropriate multicultural books and books on prejudice, different kinds of families, and adoption.

Before the school year begins, meet with your child's teacher and explain that your family is different and that other children may be both curious and concerned about adoption. Ask the teacher if he or she would work into the class's curriculum some of the books you've collected, then donate the books to the teacher or the school. By donating the books you will demonstrate that your concern goes beyond just *your* child's welfare. The more you can do to encourage and support a multicultural approach in the classroom the better, because it turns the focus from just your child to different cultures in general and prevents your child from feeling as though she is on display in a zoo. A multicultural curriculum or teaching approach should include discussion not only of cultures, but also of adoption and other ways families are formed.

Teachers generally like to have outside guests come to give special presentations. Offer to arrange for an expert to come in to talk about adoption (and other family structures) or your child's particular ethnic heritage—or volunteer to speak to the class yourself. Before volunteering, however, run the idea by your child. You don't have to allow him final say on whether or not you do it, but at least check in to make sure it will not create undo havoc at home. You might give your child the option of choosing which parent will come in, or perhaps he would prefer a family friend who is also knowledgeable on the subject. When someone other than a family member speaks to the child's class, the focus is turned from that child personally to the issues and people as a group.

This last point brings us to two common questions of adoptive parents: Should you tell the teacher or school your child is adopted? Should the child be encouraged to tell not only the teacher but her classmates? We hear many parents saying things like "We think he shouldn't be sharing this piece of information because it is private and personal. We are afraid he will be teased." While both points are valid, telling your child that his adoption is something he should keep secret is potentially more damaging than any mistreatment he might endure at the hands of other children.

It is good to share this information in an appropriate manner with the school. One way to do this is to simply include on the registration form that your child joined the family through adoption. This way the information will be available to your child's teachers and the school administration, without you or your child needing to *tell* them. You might also meet with the teacher or administration to talk about special concerns for adopted children and ask if they are open to learning more on the subject. If they aren't, you may wish to choose another school, if possible, or see if your child might be placed in a class with a different teacher. Should your child begin to have problems academically, behaviorally, or with other children, talk with the teacher about potential causes and what might be done both at home and at school to help resolve the problem—this is good advice for all parents.

Modifying Common Elementary School Projects

Two common elementary school projects that can create problems for adopted children are being asked to bring in baby pictures and drawing family trees. The purpose of the first project is to show children that they grow and change. Because not all adopted children have baby pictures, one parent and teacher we know suggests that parents ask the teacher to refocus the project by having the children bring in pictures of themselves when they were younger than they are now. Children should also be given the option of drawing pictures of themselves as babies so those who do not have photos aren't made to explain why they don't. Of course, adopted children aren't the only ones who might not have baby pictures. An adult we know was faced with a similar situation at work when his department decided to have a holiday contest of matching baby pictures to coworkers. His family did not own a camera when he was little, so not having a picture of himself, he brought in one of Buckwheat from the Our Gang movies and pinned it on the bulletin board instead.

The second activity, drawing family trees, can also be stressful for adopted children because their family structures often do not fit the tree model and the children are often missing information. In early school years, the primary purpose of the exercise is to teach children about extended family relationships—for example, that your aunt is your mother's sister. From preschool to third grade, allow your child to fill out the work sheet using information from the adoptive family. Don't worry about genetic correctness. There will be time enough later to clarify the details, but during these early years it is more important that the child feel that his adoptive family and relatives are his "real" family. To acknowledge the genetic differences, you can have your child write the date he joined your family next to his birth date. The older your child gets, the more details you can help him add, for example racial or ethnic heritage.

Sometime between fourth and sixth grade, the focus of the family-tree exercise shifts from kinship to basic genetics. This is the time to add greater detail to clarify how race, ethnicity, and physical features are passed along from one generation to the next. Presumably, you have already been talking with your child for a number of years about the fact that he inherited his physical features, as well as other characteristics, from his birth parents. Fitting birth parents, genetically related siblings, and other known relatives from the birth family into the family tree will simply build on what he

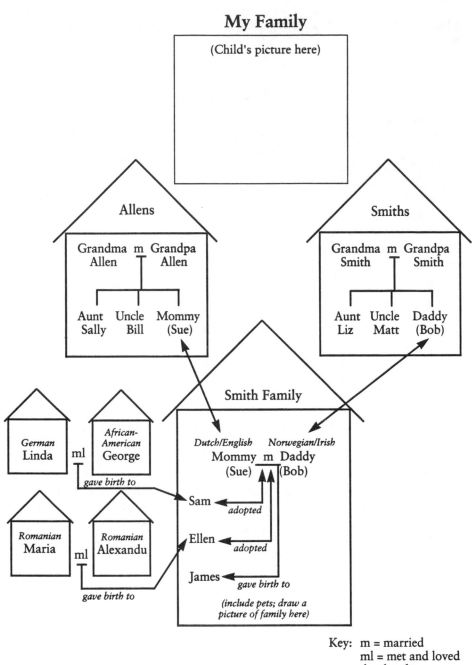

My Family

(Child's picture here)

Allens

Grandma m Grandpa
Allen   Allen

Aunt   Uncle   Mommy
Sally Bill   (Sue)

Smiths

Grandma m Grandpa
Smith   Smith

Aunt   Uncle   Daddy
Liz   Matt   (Bob)

Smith Family

German
Linda

*African-
American*
George

ml

gave birth to

Romanian
Maria

Romanian
Alexandu

ml

gave birth to

Dutch/English   *Norwegian/Irish*
Mommy m Daddy
(Sue)   (Bob)

Sam
adopted

Ellen
adopted

James *gave birth to*

*(include pets; draw a
picture of family here)*

Key: m = married
ml = met and loved
d = dated

Figure 13.1

already knows. The challenge lies in making the tree model work within the adoptive family.

One way to make genetic lines easier to comprehend and represent graphically is to use houses instead of a tree (see Figure 13.1). By using houses, you also show that other family members, such as parents, have left one home to start a new home with new members. Before your child hands in a family "tree" drawn out with houses, however, you should first contact the teacher to explain why your child is taking a different approach to the exercise. Should the teacher insist that your child complete the assignment as assigned (though we expect that most teachers will have no objections), help him as best you can to do so. When he is done and you have a little more time, sit down with him and repeat the exercise using houses to ensure that he understands how his own genetic lines and family relationships fit together.

Academic Considerations

Parent and teacher expectations can influence how well or how poorly a child does in school. When expectations are beyond the child's capabilities, she will become discouraged, frustrated, and feel incapable; these feelings will inevitably lower her performance further or lead her to give up altogether. Inappropriately low expectations can be equally detrimental in limiting the child's ultimate achievement. Adoptive parents sometimes fall into the trap of setting lower expectations for their adopted children than for their genetically related children. Often this is based on assumptions about the genetic package passed on from the birth parents, or on racial or ethnic stereotypes.

Expectations should be based on the child's demonstrated aptitudes. Each child should be expected to do the best he or she realistically can. Parents must remember that each child's interests and talents will be different. Avoid pushing your child to achieve in a certain area simply because that is where *your* interests or talents lie. This can be difficult and even painful for any parent, but especially for infertile parents and those who have only one child, because of the loss that their interests will not be passed on. Even if not infertile, adoptive parents may have a greater struggle with this issue if they feel their child's lack of aptitude or interest in a certain area is a reflection on their ability to mold the child or a sign of rejection on the child's part.

Get to know your child and accept what you discover. Nurture her abilities and accept her difficulties. In many cases, lack of talent in a particular area is not all that important. A child who is tone deaf may never be a musician, but does she really need to be? If your child has a learning disability, however, seek appropriate help to ensure that the disability doesn't stand in the way of her ability to achieve to her full potential and feel good about herself. Learning disabilities have no bearing on intelligence; many very gifted people have been learning disabled.

You will learn what your child's interests are just by living with her. But knowledge of her birth parents' abilities and talents will help you validate your child, as well as help you put her abilities and struggles into perspective. Share with your children your own childhood scholastic struggles and achievements. In your sharing, keep a balance between achievements and struggles so your children will not feel they are unable to live up to your example.

The start of kindergarten and first grade can raise big separation issues for both children and parents, especially for children who have been cared for primarily at home, as opposed to day care. Even if a child has already attended kindergarten, the transition to full-day school in first grade—and being away from home and family all day—can be difficult. First grade can be particularly stressful for children. No longer is the school day filled primarily with play, as it was in kindergarten and preschool. Compounding the usual separation issues is the fact that these transitions into school occur at about the same time adopted children are discovering the loss of their birth parents and struggling with the dichotomy of the chosen-child message. If your child is finding the all-day separation from you and home difficult and if she is struggling with the dichotomy, she may also begin to question whether she really belongs in the family. Some children—adopted and raised in birth families—feel "kicked out" when they have to start school. Of course, keeping children home is not generally a realistic option (though some parents do opt for home school), so reinforcing claiming and belonging at home and talking about school anxieties and adoption issues become all the more important.

Children who have conscious or subconscious memories of losing their parents may feel particularly vulnerable during this transition, losing some of their newly formed object constancy. Parents and teachers can help children feel safer by offering support periodically throughout the day—similar to the "refueling" behaviors of younger children. Parents might leave notes in the child's lunch bag or pockets. Teachers can offer reassurance through a special look or pat on the back.

Learning Disabilities and Adopted Children

The incidence of ADD, ADHD, and other learning disabilities appears to be unusually high among adopted children. At present, no one knows for certain why this is so, but a number of theories do exist. Some learning disabilities, such as dyslexia, have been shown to be genetically inherited. Based on this information, some experts believe adopted children with learning disabilities inherit the trait from their birth parents. Three of the most serious long-term effects of learning disabilities are low self-esteem, poor self-control, and low tolerance of frustration. As a result of these long-term effects, the theory states, young people with these traits are more likely than the general population to be faced with unplanned pregnancies that result in adoption placement, thus explaining the higher incidence of learning disabilities among adopted individuals (Bordwell 1992).

Other factors that may contribute to the high incidence of learning disabilities among children and adults who joined their families through adoption include the following:

- poor parent/child fit, abuse, neglect, or other problems during the first two years of life which may interfere with attachment, and thus with the child's ability to learn cause and effect and to learn *how to learn* (Fahlberg, *Attachment and Separation*, 1979, 46–47, and Minsky 1985);
- prenatal exposure to alcohol or other drugs, resulting in fetal alcohol effect (FAE), fetal alcohol syndrome (FAS), or drug addiction at birth;
- prenatal or early childhood malnutrition—either not enough food or an imbalance in the diet;
- exposure to foreign substances, such as through lead poisoning.

If your child is struggling inordinately in school, ask that he be tested for learning disabilities as young as possible. Learning disabilities affect the way in which the brain processes and retains information. Though these disabilities cannot be "cured," the child will still be capable of learning provided the educational environment is geared to address his specific challenges. For most children, this means conveying information in nontraditional ways, using as many of the child's senses as possible. Traditional teaching relies primarily on the child's visual (sight) and auditory (hearing) senses; for example, the teacher teaches phonics by showing each letter or combination of letters and saying the sound. To reinforce what he sees and hears, a learning-disabled person might also trace the letters in a tray of sand, while hearing and repeating the sounds they make, to help the brain absorb and remember the patterns by including tactile (touch) and kinesthetic (large-muscle movement) senses, along with sight and hearing.

Attention-deficit disorder and attention-deficit hyperactivity disorder are often discussed separately from other learning disabilities because they affect behavior as well as learning. Diagnosis of ADD/ADHD is based on a collection of behaviors which can also appear for reasons other than genetically inherited ADD/ADHD. According to the diagnostic criteria, at least eight of the following fourteen symptoms must be present for a minimum of six months for the child to be considered to have ADD/ADHD. These behaviors must also begin before age seven and be considerably more frequent than is normal for children of the same developmental age. The American Psychiatric Association lists the following behaviors as symptoms of ADHD:

- often fidgets with hands or feet or squirms in seat (in adolescents, may be limited to subjective feelings of restlessness);
- has difficulty remaining seated when required to do so;
- is easily distracted by extraneous stimuli;
- has difficulty awaiting turn in games or group situations;
- often blurts out answers to questions before they have been completed;
- has difficulty following through on instructions from others (not due to oppositional behavior or failure of comprehension), e.g., fails to finish chores;
- has difficulty sustaining attention in tasks or play activities;
- often shifts from one uncompleted activity to another;
- has difficulty playing quietly;
- often talks excessively;
- often interrupts or intrudes on others, e.g., butts into other children's games;
- often does not seem to listen to what is being said to him or her;
- often loses things necessary for tasks or activities at school or at home (e.g., toys, pencils, books, assignments);
- often engages in physically dangerous activities without considering possible consequences (not for the purpose of thrill-seeking), e.g., runs into street without looking. (DSM-III[R] 1987, 52–53)

The most effective treatment for ADD/ADHD is a three-pronged approach of medication, academic planning geared specifically to assist the child, and behavior management techniques that parents can use to help the child learn to manage his condition, as well as to effectively discipline the child and support his growth (Taylor 1990). Treatment with medication alone has been shown to have a lower success rate than when it is used in conjunction with the other two approaches. Academic planning and behavior management, without the use of medication, has proven effective for some children.

While genetics may be one factor in the high incidence of ADD/ADHD among adopted children, other situations related to adoption may lead to similar symptoms, and thus a misdiagnosis in some cases. Such situations are as follows:

Unresolved grief. Grieving children may exhibit symptoms similar to those of ADD/ADHD as a result of anxiety or attempts to stop intrusive or unpleasant feelings of grief.

Poor attachment or anxious attachment may appear to be ADD/ADHD because the child does not feel safe enough to relax or sit still (because the world is too unsafe), or as a result of failure to learn or continue to learn cause-and-effect reasoning or how to mitigate anxiety and frustration.

Post-traumatic stress disorder (PTSD). Symptoms of PTSD include anxiousness and vulnerability, which usually manifest in part as an inability to concentrate. Past abuse, witnessing the abuse of a loved one, or the trauma of being removed from the home may all lead to PTSD in adopted children.

Underachievement. Symptoms of underachievers in school and life are similar to those of ADD/ADHD. Poor self-image, which may result from attachment and grief issues or dysfunction in the family environment, is often a major factor leading to underachievement. Other learning disabilities, too, can cause underachievement, and thus behaviors similar to those of ADD/ADHD.

Even if your child has been misdiagnosed as having ADD/ADHD, medication is usually not harmful and can be helpful if the other issues are addressed as well. Issues such as unresolved grief may appear in conjunction with true ADD/ADHD, intensifying the symptoms of both. If other issues are involved, use of medication without addressing the other issues will in the long run leave the child with the same symptoms as before. Because grief is a common issue, grief work should be added as a fourth treatment modality for adopted children with symptoms of ADD/ADHD.

One key difference between attention deficits caused by grief and those caused by true ADD/ADHD is that the child with unresolved grief will have times when he can sit still, concentrate, and pay attention for extended periods without being easily distracted; most children with ADD/ADHD will not be able to do this without medication. Adoptive parents should ask that the school psychologist observe their child at different times during the day and week, as well as in a variety of situations. The ability to concentrate often follows a pattern when unresolved grief is involved.

Fetal Alcohol Syndrome and Fetal Alcohol Effect

Prenatal exposure to alcohol or other drugs can cause lifelong neuropsychological impairments. Fetal alcohol syndrome (FAS) is often diagnosed at birth by characteristic facial abnormalities, known or suspected chemical use by the mother, and neuropsychological impairment. Depending on the degree of exposure, children whose mothers used alcohol or drugs during pregnancy may suffer permanent neuropsychological impairments without the physical abnormalities present in FAS; some refer to this condition as fetal alcohol effect (FAE). The neuropsychological impairments involved in FAS and FAE include problems with memory, abstract thinking, attention, judgment (cause-and-effect reasoning), and impulse control, but normal or near-normal verbal skills, verbal memory, and intelligence (Rathbun 1991). Impairments in only a few of these areas is usually not indicative of FAS/FAE.

As an adoptive parent, you may never know for certain whether your child was exposed prenatally to alcohol or other drugs. If you believe your child has FAS/FAE, consult a pediatrician or a pediatric neurologist for testing to determine the type and extent of impairment, if any. Once impairments are identified, you can begin to look for ways to overcome, work around, and cope with the impairments at home and at school. For more information on FAS/FAE, we recommend reading Michael Dorris's book, *The Broken Cord* (see reading list below) and talking with your child's doctor.

For Further Reading

• *The Broken Cord* by Michael Dorris. New York: Harper Perennial, 1989.

A sensitive telling of an adoptive father's struggle to understand and meet the needs of his son, who was born with FAE.

• *Helping Your Hyperactive Child* by John F. Taylor, Ph.D. Rocklin, CA: Prima Publishing, 1990.

A comprehensive resource for parents, teachers, and professionals, with practical techniques for helping the child who has ADD/ADHD.

• *Learning Disabilities: A Family Affair* by Betty B. Osman. New York: Random House, 1979.

A practical guide for parents and teachers to helping children with learning disabilities at home, at school, and in dealing with social situations.

• *The Hidden Handicap* by Judith Ehre Kranes, Ph.D. New York: Simon & Schuster, 1980.

With a focus on children with mild learning disabilities, Kranes offers advice for professionals and parents for closing the gaps through which these children fall.

• *Children with Fetal Alcohol Syndrome: A Handbook for Caregivers* by Lisa Gerring, M.S.W., L.C.S.W. St. Paul, MN: Human Service Associates, 1993.

A welcome monograph on understanding and meeting the needs of FAS/FAE children. Topics covered include discipline, emotional issues, classroom strategies, and how to find professional help.

14

Adoption Issues in Adulthood

*T*hough we become adults, we never truly leave behind who we were as children. We may change, choose to take our lives in new directions, and even overcome deficits we began with, but our childhood experiences remain in some way a part of us forever. The love we felt, the fears we had, the traumas we faced, and the triumphs we took pride in become part of who we are.

For the adopted person, childhood experiences and interpretations of, as well as questions and answers about, what it means to be placed for adoption and then adopted also carry through into adulthood. Unanswered questions about adoption and birth parents may lie dormant after adolescence, but they are likely to pop up again, especially at times of major transition. Holidays, marriage, the birth or adoption of one's own children, loss of a loved one, and the death of a parent are some of the life events that often raise new or old questions for the adopted person. Just as in childhood, each transition into a new life stage has the potential for bringing new meaning and new questions about adoption for the adult, and a decision whether or not to search for the birth parents. Even if the adopted person had contact with his birth parents right along or had searched and found one or both, at each new life stage, he may still find questions he'd never before asked.

According to Erikson, adulthood is comprised of three stages of psychosocial development, each with its own theme and task. The first of these stages is young adulthood, which Erikson describes as a time of intimacy versus isolation. Having resolved the identity crisis of adolescence and separated from the parents to become an adult, one of the tasks for the young person is to form healthy intimate relationships—platonic as well as romantic or sexual. "Freud was once asked what he thought a normal person should be able to do well. . . . Freud simply said, '. . . to love and to work'" (Erikson 1968, 136).

The ability to achieve emotional intimacy (not merely sexual intimacy, though this may also be affected) depends on successful resolution of earlier life stages. Hogan, writing on Erikson, puts it this way: "Intimacy is possible only when based on a firm sense of identity; one must know clearly who he is before he can risk losing himself in another person" (1976, 175). Unmet emotional needs from childhood will also carry over into intimate relationships, sometimes leading the adult to seek fulfillment of these needs from another person. In most cases, this leads to difficult, if not unhealthy, relationships because the level of dependence involved can lead to severe vulnerability should the relationship falter.

Couples are often referred to as two halves of a whole. A better metaphor for healthy intimate relationships is two overlapping circles; each circle maintains its own integrity, while sharing a common area of intersection, just as two people each maintain their own identities while sharing a portion of their lives with one another. As Hogan writes, "People who fail to develop a capacity for intimacy come to avoid intimate contacts; they withdraw into themselves, feel isolated, and become self-absorbed" (1976, 176). Failure to develop a capacity for intimacy may also lead to a lack of ethics: "an ethical sense evolves as one recognizes the areas of adult duty, as one learns with whom he must and must not compete" (Hogan 1976, 176).

The adopted person who has tried but continues to have difficulty developing and maintaining healthy intimate relationships should look at whether unresolved adoption issues may be contributing to the problem. Some people sabotage relationships with those they love or prevent themselves from becoming intimately involved because such intimacy makes them feel vulnerable. If they let themselves get too close, they risk the pain of being rejected. Those who do have problems in this area—and want to resolve them—should seek professional help to look at how they form trust and a sense of belonging, how they fit into their adoptive families, how they left home, how they feel about their adoption, and how they define themselves.

Though children become adults, parents never stop being parents; their roles and relationships with their children simply change. According to Erikson (cited by Hogan 1976, 175), early adulthood is the time when generation gaps, if any, occur. Watching their children make "mistakes" as adults can be difficult for parents. This is often especially true when the "mistakes" involve the adult son's or daughter's choice of partner and lifestyle. As a parent, you may watch your son or daughter reject good partners, choose bad ones, or move in and out of relationships. Some of this is a normal part of searching for a compatible partner—in other words, of dating. As a parent, you may voice your concerns about relationships and lifestyles to your child, but you must remember that your approval is no longer required. If you wish to maintain a good relationship with your grown child, you may have to learn to accept the person she chooses to love or the lifestyle she chooses to lead. Keep in mind that virtually everyone has positive characteristics and potentials; focus on these, rather than on what you believe to be your child's or your child's partner's faults.

Even for adults, a positive, supportive relationship with one's parents provides a sense of security necessary to tackle life's challenges. This is particularly true for the adopted person, whose past loss of birth parents may create added vulnerability. Still, grown children—adopted or not—sometimes slam the door on their parents. Should this happen, you need to let your son or daughter know he or she is free to come back and work with you to heal the relationship. In doing so, however, you also need to be clear about what you will and will not do for your grown child, so that your relationship with your son or daughter is not held for ransom.

The second stage of adulthood, according to Erikson, is generativity versus stagnation. This brings us full circle to where this book began: finding a way as adults to leave a mark on the world that will live beyond our own mortal lives. For some, this means having and raising children. But, as Hogan points out: "Merely to want or to have children is not evidence of generativity. On the contrary, many people who are parents have not reached this stage, because of failures at any of the preceding stages" (1976, 176). Generativity refers to expressions of creativity and productivity: to generate something beyond oneself. Without generativity, adults stagnate, often "indulging themselves as if they were their own—or one another's—one and only child" (Erikson 1968, 138).

Still, this stage of life often does correspond with the time when adults are building families. The adopted person may be concerned about what kind of parent he or she will be, wondering again what she learned from her adoptive parents and inherited from her birth parents. For the adopted person, an added drive to have children may also be a need to see someone who is genetically related to him or her. If not kept in check, however, this drive can become consuming, having a negative effect on one's parenting if the person is unable to let go and let the child be himself and not a reproduction of the parent. There is also the very real chance that the baby will look and act like the other parent, and nothing at all like the adopted person.

For the adoptive parent, the joy of watching a grown child form family and prepare to parent may also recall old grief over infertility or over the differences between the adoptive parent and child. At the same time, parents can get pushy and upset if their children show no desire to produce grand-children.

The third stage of adulthood, according to Erikson, is integrity versus despair. This stage corresponds with what is more commonly called midlife crisis. It is basically the flip side of the identity crisis of adolescence. Now the adult must look at his or her life to this point and come to grips with both the successes and failures in order to enter old age and prepare for death with a sense of contentment with the life he or she has led. Hogan, writing on Erikson, states: "Integrity is characterized by the feeling that subsequent crises in living can be managed, a feeling that life is somehow worthwhile in spite of the suffering it contains, and a sense that one's life was as it had to be" (1976, 177). If in reviewing his or her life, the adult cannot find contentment, he or she will experience despair and a fear of death. Hogan describes this, saying, "Despair reflects the person's feeling that there is no time to begin another life, to seek a better path" (1976, 177).

While Erikson speaks of this stage as a single phase representing midlife to old age and finally death, we believe that most people in our society go through two cycles of integrity crises: the first during middle age and the second at about the time of retirement or sometime thereafter, depending on the individual. This second cycle involves redefining one's work role and function in society and family. Even though disability or death may be ten to twenty years—or more—down the road, it is felt as an impending reality. For most people, the realization of one's mortality, which occurs during the first integrity crisis, produces a sense that time has almost run out to accomplish one's life goals. The task of the second integrity crisis is to come to peace with life; this process often leads the individual to begin to wrap up his or her life in preparation for death. If a person is unable to achieve a sense of integrity, he is likely to wish for and dwell on death (though not necessarily in the same way as someone who is suicidal), feeling there is no meaning to his life and that he has nothing further to offer the world or those around him.

For the adopted person, the first cycle of integrity crisis again raises questions of search or reestablishing contact with birth parents. Questions regarding family medical history, longevity, chronic illnesses, and even gray-ing may be practical reasons behind the desire to search for or talk again with genetically related family. But even more, the identity crisis of middle age and facing the reality of one's mortality can bring new impetus to the adopted person's desire to know more about his or her genetic past. Furthermore, facing the reality of his or her own mortality often leads the adopted person to feel that the clock is ticking away the opportunity to find the birth parents before they die (if they haven't already) and the answers are lost forever. Death of the adoptive parents may free the adopted person to search without guilt and without fear of hurting them. Other adopted people initiate a search in middle age to answer their children's questions about their genetic heritage.

As an older adult, the loss of friends and loved ones may bring more intense struggles with grief if the adopted person has still not resolved the earliest of losses: that of the birth parents. Even into old age, if the adopted person has never found a way to feel good about herself despite her birth parent's choice, or their inability to parent, she is likely to live her latter years in bitterness and despair. Fortunately, there is a lifetime of opportunity to bring healing for the loss of the birth parents and positive resolution to what it means to be an adopted person, and thus ample opportunity for living a meaningful and productive life filled with loving relationships and culminating in peace.

For Further Reading

- *Lost and Found* by Betty Jean Lifton. New York: Dial Press, 1979.
  An adult's careful retrospective look at growing up adopted.
- *Twice Born* by Betty Jean Lifton. New York: Dial Press, 1979.
  Memoirs of growing up adopted.

15

On Being Family

Adoption can raise many issues for parent and child alike, but most of all, it can create many blessings for the entire family. We are always overjoyed to discover just how many adoptions work well for both parent and child, despite or perhaps because of the potential challenges. Sharing and validating feelings and supporting others in grief brings people closer together.

Successful, happy families, however, don't happen by accident. Several studies have identified factors that contribute to families working well together; they include the following:

- strength and quality of the parent/child relationship;
- parents' acceptance of who their child is;
- parents' acceptance of how the child became theirs;
- flexibility;
- realistic expectations of parent and child;
- parents' self-esteem and individuality;
- verbal and behavioral acceptance of differences;
- open communication about feelings and the parent/child relationship; and
- parent/child fit.

All of these are factors parents can actively enhance or create within their families. Even when parent/child fit isn't going well, parents can improve the situation by learning to understand, work with, and accept the traits that make their child different from themselves. For adoptive parents, knowledge of adoption issues and child development, and support from other adoptive parents (friends or an organized support group) can further enhance how well the family works.

Most adopted children will not struggle with every issue discussed in this book; even for those who do, there is much parents can do to help their children through the rougher times. Some adopted children do quite well until about age eleven or twelve, and then parents notice adolescence is more difficult for them than it is for the kid and family next door. If your child has done well during the early years, chances are your relationship with him—as well as his own life—will return to a smooth state once adolescence is over. As it says in the Bible: "Train up a child in the way he should go, and when he is old he will not depart from it" (Proverbs 22:6, RSV). Adolescence may be rocky, but hope is not lost!

Choosing Your Child

In the early chapters, we discussed the need for introspection before deciding to adopt. The next step in making an adoptive family work lies in choosing a child. We tell our children we chose to adopt them and they are very special to us; and this is true—adoptive parents have some choices on who will become their children. But as we've said, no child is a blank slate; each comes with his or her own personality and potential. Adopted children also come with a genetic and, in the case of older children, experiential past. Part of the control adoptive parents have lies in choosing a child they feel they can successfully parent and in exercising their choice not to adopt children they feel they cannot parent. Though all children awaiting adoption are *adoptable*, this doesn't mean any adult can adopt any child and make it work. In addition to issues of parent/child fit, some children awaiting adoption are not psychologically or emotionally ready to join a family, even though adoptive homes are actively being sought for them.

The field of child placement has come a long way over the years in the area of openness. Open adoption has its pros and cons, but whether contact with the birth parents is maintained or not, information about the child's genetic and experiential past is very important. It is time child placement laws and practices follow the example of the medical community. A few decades ago, doctors could filter information to patients based on what they believed their patients should know or could comprehend, and to protect them from undo concern. Patients were not regularly informed of risks of procedures they were about to undergo or of all the possible outcomes of conditions they had. Since then, the concept of informed consent has evolved such that physicians are required to inform their patients not only of the benefits of recommended treatments, but also of the risks. It is no longer considered appropriate to "protect" a patient by withholding information, for example, by not telling the patient that the condition he has is fatal. We believe it is time to apply the concept of informed consent to the placement of children. Prospective parents need to know all that is available about a child's past and genetic endowment if they are to make a wise decision about whether they are able to provide for that child's needs.

Among children awaiting adoption there are many who have special needs. For the child's sake and their own, prospective parents should fully understand what these are before agreeing to adopt a child who has a special need. We have not fully discussed how to parent adopted children with special needs because that issue is a book in itself. One special need, however, that is unfortunately too common among children who have been in transitional care (foster home placement or institutional settings) is past sexual abuse. Though the thought that children are sometimes sexually abused is not a very empowering one for prospective or adoptive parents, we would be remiss if we did not say something about it. The fact is that a large percentage of children who have been in transitional care have been sexually abused, before or after removal from their birth homes (McNamera and McNamera, 1990). (We want to emphasize, however, that we are not implying that foster parents are not good people; many foster families provide very good homes for children in transition, providing safe, nurturing environments.)

Adoption laws currently on the books in most states were designed in part to wipe the slate clean, preventing children from being stigmatized by their past and protecting prospective parents from preconceived notions about the children they were adopting. Today, prospective parents are usually told about known or suspected physical and emotional abuse, but sexual abuse is still often left unmentioned unless the evidence is unequivocal. Prospective parents need to be told of known or suspected sexual abuse if they are to get help for the child. Without clinical intervention, a child who has been sexually abused or a witness to sexual abuse will almost always act out that behavior, often on a younger child. Unless the child receives appropriate help, dysfunctional behaviors stemming from past sexual abuse can damage the entire family—and especially the child who was abused. When sexual abuse is known or suspected, consider carefully whether you can provide a safe environment for that child and other children in your family. Often it is best that abused children be adopted into families where they will be the youngest. The youngest child in the family usually receives more nurturing, which abused children need. This position in the family also removes the opportunity for the abused child to reenact his or her own abuse on younger siblings—a situation that is as harmful to the abused child as it is to the sibling victim. If you are considering adopting a child who has been abused, we suggest reading *Adoption and the Sexually Abused Child*, edited by Joan and Bernard McNamera.

Prospective parents often feel themselves at the mercy of the placement agency or other facilitator: to get a child, they feel they must go with the flow. But parents need and have a right to complete information about their children. Before agreeing to adopt a child, ask the placement agency or other facilitator to sign a statement saying they have disclosed all information available to them about the child and that they have done all they reasonably can within the confines of applicable state or foreign laws to get nonidentifying information about the child's genetic past and life history, including any known or suspected physical, emotional, or sexual abuse. If they say they don't have the information you have requested, ask why not. Specific information and services parents should ask for include the following:

Moves. Get a history of all moves, ages at time of moves, and how each move was made. Was the child allowed to say goodbye? Were blessings or curses given? Are there people from the child's past who have wanted to remain in the child's life, who could bless the placement and provide continuity for the child?

Assessment of attachment. Insist that the agency provide an assessment of the child's current attachment to the present caretaker and whether she was attached in the past to other caretakers. The most challenging children to parent are those who have never shown trust in any adult (no bonding or attachment). These children may be *adoptable*, but without early and extensive specialized therapeutic intervention, they are often difficult, if not impossible, to parent.

Past therapy. Ask for a history of any attempts at therapy, and what the diagnosis, prognosis, and outcome were at that time.

Postplacement support and counseling. If the agency or other facilitator does not provide postplacement support services, look for someone who can objectively monitor the progress of attachment between you and your child. Most pediatricians are skilled at recognizing attachment behaviors and discerning when a parent/child relationship is as it should be. If working with an agency, ask that postplacement follow-up provide more than simply a friendly assessment of your home and the child's progress; ask also for family counseling to help move through the relationship-building stages that parallel the fog to object constancy phases of infancy.

In addition to these, adoptive parents and those working in adoption need to advocate for state legislative and agency internal policy to provide access to, at minimum, complete disclosure of the children's genetic ancestry (with or without last names), personal and family medical history (including mental illness), and occupations and interests of birth parents. Adoption agencies and support organizations should also be encouraged— if not pushed—to have professionals and paraprofessionals on staff or readily available who are trained in adoption issues and child development.

Where to Turn for Help

You are the best expert on your child. You will be able to handle most of the adoption issues that will arise in your child's life yourself, especially now that you know what to look for and how to help. But there still may be times when outside help will be necessary. Finding a therapist who specializes in working with adoptive families is ideal; unfortunately, there aren't many around. Whether you know of a specialist or not, here are some things you should do and questions you should ask when seeking a therapist:

Get references from other adoptive parents, step-parents, or foster parents—all face similar issues.

Shop around. If possible, have at least one session with several different therapists so you can compare approaches and their assessments of the problem.

Ask about experience and expertise. Find out what training or knowledge the therapist has in adoption, bonding and attachment, grief counseling, family life cycle, and family systems. If your family is interracial, international, or a family of color, ask also about the therapist's experience working with people of color, interracial families, and issues related to culture. If a therapist you are considering lacks expertise in these areas, ask if he or she is willing to learn. Choose someone else if he or she is not or if the therapist says there are no special issues related to adoption.

Ask about therapeutic approach. Look for someone who uses a variety of clinical modalities, beginning with education—which may be all you need. Support groups, play therapy, and family therapy are among the most important and effective modalities. Any therapist you choose should not only be nonjudgmental and empathetic, but also willing to state his or her honest opinion, even if it might be unpleasant to hear or you disagree with it.

Avoid any therapist who does not validate that you are your child's parent; even if you have made mistakes in your parenting, you should not be excluded from your child's therapy. Individual therapy—either parents or child alone—is generally not recommended by itself because any problem affecting one family member affects the entire family.

A Final Word

Raising children is one of the most demanding and vital jobs in the world. Though it seems to come more easily for some people than for others, we all do the best we can. If you've read this far, we would guess you are trying harder than many to be the best parent you can possibly be. Though none of us will get it all right, be assured that you are probably doing better than you know.

One adoptive mother spent three years dropping pebbles to her son about his adoption and birth parents. Each time she did, he would pause momentarily, but in three years he never once picked up on a pebble. His mother was often convinced her messages weren't sinking in.

Then one day, at age eleven, the boy said to his mother, "You know all those things you've been saying about my birth parents? Well, I've come to the conclusion that those poor suckers lost a good thing."

We hope you and your child come to feel the same way!

Bibliography

Balaban, N. 1985. *Learning to Say Goodbye: Starting School and Other Early Childhood Separation.* New York: Signet.

Berry, B. 1963. *Almost White.* London: Collier Books.

Bordwell, M. 1992. The link between adoption and learning disabilities. *OURS Magazine* 25(5):16–19.

Bourguignon, J.P. and Watson, K. 1987. *After Adoption: A Manual for Professionals Working with Adoptive Families.* Illinois: Illinois Department of Children and Family Services, Fed. Grant #90-CO-0287.

————. 1987. *Training Guide—After Adoption.* Illinois: Illinois Department of Children and Family Services, 1987.

Bowlby, J. 1968. *Child Care and the Growth of Love.* Middlesex, England: Penguin Books.

————. 1969. *Attachment: Attachment and Loss (Vol. 1).* New York: Basic Books, Inc.

————. 1973. *Separation: Anxiety and Anger (Vol II).* New York: Basic Books.

————. 1980. *Loss: Sadness and Depression (Vol III).* New York: Basic Books.

Bradshaw, J. 1988. *Healing the Shame That Binds You.* Deerfield Beach, FL: Health Communications, Inc.

Bouchard, J.T., Jr. 1984. "Twins Reared Together and Apart: What They Tell Us About Human Diversity." In *The Chemical and Biological Bases of Individuality,* ed. S.W. Fox, 147–178. New York: Plenum Press.

Bouchard, J.T., Jr., et al. 1981. "The Minnesota Study of Twins Reared Apart: Project Description and Sample Results in the Development Domain." In *Twin Research 3: Part B. Intelligence, Personality and Development,* eds. L. Gedda, P. Parisi, and W. Nance, 227–233. New York: Alan R. Liss, Inc.

Brazelton, T.B. 1982. *On Becoming a Family: The Growth of Attachment.* New York: Dell.

Brazelton, T.B., Nugent, K.J., and Lester B.M. 1987. Neonatal behavioral assessment scale. In *Handbook of Infant Development,* ed. J. Doniger. New York: Wiley Interscience Publication.

Children's Television Workshop. 1992. "3–2-1 CONTACT Extra: What Kids Want to Know About Sex and Growing Up." New York: Children's Television Workshop.

Cline, F. *Post Placement Services for Adoptive Families—An Overview.* Fort Worth, TX: Psychiatric Institute of Fort Worth.

Curran, D. 1983. *Traits of a Healthy Family.* New York: Ballantine.

DiGiulio, J.F. 1987. Assuming the adoptive parent role. *Social Casework* 68(9):561–566.

Dorris, M. 1989. *The Broken Cord.* New York: Harper Perennial.

Eagan, A.B. 1985. *The Newborn Mother: Stages of Her Growth.* New York: Henry Holt & Co.

Edward, J., Ruskin, N., and Turrini, P. 1981. *Separation-Individuation Theory and Application.* New York: Gardner Press.

Erichsen, J.N., and Erichsen, H.R. 1992. *Butterflies in the Wind: Spanish/Indian Children with White Parents.* The Woodlands, TX: Los Niños International Adoption Center.

Erikson, E.H. 1963. *Childhood and Society.* 2nd ed. New York: W. W. Norton & Co.

———. 1968. *Identity, Youth and Crisis.* New York: W. W. Norton & Co.

———. 1980. *Identity and the Life Cycle: A Reissue.* New York: W.W. Norton & Co.

Fahlberg, V. 1979. *Attachment and Separation: Putting the Pieces Together.* Evergreen, CO: Michigan Department of Social Services.

———. 1979. *Helping Children When They Must Move: Putting the Pieces Together.* Evergreen, CO: Michigan Department of Social Services.

———. 1982. *Child Development: Putting the Pieces Together.* Evergreen, CO: Michigan Department of Social Services and The National Resource Center for Special Needs Adoption.

———. 1982. *The Child in Placement: Common Behavior Problems—Putting the Pieces Together.* Evergreen, CO: Michigan Department of Social Services and The National Resource Center for Special Needs Adoption.

FAS and FAE children at risk—another look. *Roots and Wings* (Winter):20(1991).

Fetal Alcohol Syndrome/Effects Conference Proceedings. Nov. 20, 1985, Saskatoo, Saskatchewan. Cosponsored by Saskatchewan Alcohol and Drug Abuse Commission and Saskatchewan Institute on Prevention of Handicaps.

Fishel, E. 1992. Raising sexually healthy kids. *Parents Magazine* 67(11):110–116.

Fraiberg, S.H. 1959. *The Magic Years: Understanding and Handling the Problems of Early Childhood.* New York: Charles Scribner's Sons.

Frank, E., and Rowe, D. 1990. Preventive-intervention groups with adoptive parents and their babies: minimizing the risks to emotional development in the first three years. *Zero to Three* (June):19–25.

Freud, A. (trans. Baines, C.). 1946. *The Ego and the Mechanics of Defense.* New York: International Universities Press.

Gale, J. *A Parent's Guide to Teenage Sexuality.* New York: Henry Holt & Co.

Ginsberg, H., and Opper, S. 1969. *Piaget's Theory of Intellectual Development: An Introduction.* Englewood Cliffs, NJ: Prentice-Hall.

Goodman, M.E. 1952. *Race Awareness in Young Children.* New York: Collier.

Gordon, S., and Gordon, J. 1989. *Raising a Child Conservatively in a Sexually Permissive World.* New York: Simon & Schuster.

Greenspan, S., and Greenspan, N.T. 1985. *First Feelings: Milestones in the Emotional Development of Your Baby and Child.* New York: Penguin.

————. 1989. *The Essential Partnership: How Parents and Children Can Meet the Emotional Challenges of Infancy and Childhood.* New York: Penguin, 1989.

Griffith, K.C. 1991. *The Right to Know Who You Are: Reform of Adoption Law with Honesty, Openness, and Integrity.* Ottawa, Ontario: Katherine W. Kimball.

Haley, A. 1965. *The Autobiography of Malcolm X.* New York: Ballantine.

Harley, W.F., Jr. 1986. *His Needs, Her Needs: Building an Affair-Proof Marriage.* Old Tappan, NJ: Fleming H. Revell Co.

Helfner, R.E., and Kempe, H.C., eds. 1976. *Child Abuse and Neglect: The Family and the Community.* Cambridge, MA: Ballinger.

Hogan, R. 1976. *Personality Theory: The Personological Tradition.* Englewood Cliffs, NJ: Prentice-Hall.

Ilg, F.L., and Ames, L.B. 1955. *Child Behavior From Birth to Ten.* New York: Harper & Row.

Ilg, F.L., Ames, L.B., and Baker, S.M. 1981. *Child Behavior: Specific Advice on Problems of Child Behavior.* New York: Harper Perennial.

James, J.W. 1986. *The Grief Recovery Handbook.* Beverly Hills, CA: Grief Recovery Institute.

Jewett, C. 1982. *Helping Children Cope with Separation and Loss.* Cambridge, MA: Harvard Common Press.

Kagan, J. 1981. *The Second Year: The Emergence of Self-Awareness.* Cambridge, MA: Harvard University Press.

————. 1984. *The Nature of the Child.* New York: Basic Books.

Kagan, J., and Lamb, S., eds. 1987. *The Emergence of Morality in Young Children.* Chicago: University of Chicago Press.

Kendrick, M.S. 1991. The journey to become "real." *Roots and Wings* 2(3):3–7.

Kennell, J., Foos, D., and Klaus, M. 1976. "Parent-Infant Bonding." In *Child Abuse and Neglect: The Family and the Community,* eds. R.E. Helfner and H.C. Kempe.

Kirk, D.H. 1984. *Shared Fate: A Theory and Method of Adoptive Relationships.* Port Angeles, WA: Ben Simon.

Kreisman, J.J., and Straus H. 1989. *I Hate You—Don't Leave Me: Understanding the Borderline Personality.* New York: Avon Books.

Kübler-Ross, E. 1969. *On Death and Dying.* New York: Macmillan.

Leckie, D.H. 1992. Young adults—search and reunion. *AdoptNet* 4(4):21–22, 53.

Liedloff, J. 1989. *The Continuum Concept: Allowing Human Nature to Work Successfully.* Reading, MA: Addison-Wesley.

Magid, K., and McKelvey, C. 1987. *High Risk Children Without a Conscience.* New York: Bantam.

Mahler, M. 1968. *On Human Symbiosis and the Vicissitudes of Individuation.* New York: International Universities.

―――. 1972. *Rapprochement Subphase of the Separation-Individuation Process.* Psychoanalytic Quarterly, 41:487–506.

McNamera, J., and McNamera, B., eds. 1990. *Adoption and the Sexually Abused Child.* Portland, ME: Human Services Development Institute of the University of Southern Maine.

McRoy, R.G., and Zurcher, L.A. 1983. *Transracial and Inracial Adopties: The Adolescent Years.* Springfield, IL: Charles C. Thomas.

Minsky, M. 1985. *The Society of Mind.* New York: Simon & Schuster.

Moustakas, C. 1966. *The Child's Discovery of Himself.* New York: Ballantine.

Nelson, G. 1985. *Who's the Boss: How to Cope with Your Child* (previously published as *The One-Minute Scolding*). New York: Random House.

Neubauer, P.B., and Neubauer, A. 1990. *Nature's Thumbprint: The New Genetics of Personality.* Reading, MA: Addison-Wesley.

Paley, V. 1988. *Bad Guys Don't Have Birthdays: Fantasy Play at Four.* Chicago: University of Chicago Press.

Parkes, C.M., and Weiss, R.S. 1983. *Recovery from Bereavement.* New York: Basic Books.

Piaget, J. (trans. Cook, M.). 1954. *The Construction of Reality in the Child.* New York: Basic Books.

―――. (trans. Gottegno, C., and Hodgson, F.M.). 1962. *Play, Dreams, and Limitations in Childhood.* New York: W. W. Norton & Co.

―――. (trans. Seagrim, G.N.). 1969. *The Mechanics of Perception.* New York: Basic Books.

Rathbun, A. 1991. FAS and FAE children in the classroom. *Roots and Wings* 2(3):20–22.

Rando, T.A. 1984. *Grief, Dying, and Death: Clinical Interventions for Caregivers.* Champaign, IL: Research Press Company.

Register, C. 1991. *"Are Those Kids Yours?" American Families with Children Adopted from Other Countries.* New York: Free Press.

Rosenberg, M. 1989. *Growing Up Adopted.* New York: Bradbury Press.

Simon, R.J., and Altstein, H. 1977. *Transracial Adoption.* New York: John Wiley & Sons.

Stern, D. 1977. *The First Relationship: Infant and Mother.* Cambridge, MA: Harvard University Press.

Taylor, J. 1990. *Helping Your Hyperactive Child.* Rocklin, CA: Prima Publishing.

U.S. Department of Health and Human Services. 1990. *Healthy People 2000: National Health Promotion and Disease Prevention Objectives.* Washington, DC: Public Health Service, DHHS Pub #(PHS) 91–50213.

Vander Zanden, J.W. 1977. *Social Psychology.* New York: Random House.

Van Ornum, W., and Mordock, J. 1987. *Crisis Counseling with Children and Adolescents: A Guide for Non-Professional Counselors.* New York: Crossroad/Continuum.

Welch, M.G. 1988. *Holding Time.* New York: Simon & Schuster.

Wellborn, S.N. 1987. How genes shape personality. *U.S. News & World Report* 102(14):58–62.

White, B. 1990. *The First Three Years of Life.* Rev. ed. New York: Prentice-Hall.

Wilkinson, H.S.P. 1985. *Birth Is More Than Once: The Inner World of Adopted Korean Children.* Bloomfield, MI: Sunrise Ventures.

Winnicott, D.W. 1964. *The Child, the Family, and the Outside World.* Reading, MA: Addison-Wesley.

Index

Abandonment, 90, 210
  fear of, 155
  feelings of, 54–55
  and shame-based identity, 54–55
Abstract thinking, 219–20
Abused children, 225–26, 237–38,
    259–60
  and attachment, 27–28
  and reframing past traumas, 69
  and parents' suspicion of abuse, 173
ADD. *See* Attention-deficit disorder
ADHD. *See* Attention-deficit
    hyperactivity disorder
Adolescence (eleven to eighteen years),
    212–40
  alienation in, 223–24
  beginning of, 213
  and body image, 224, 227
  early, 213
  as identity crisis stage, 58
  and international adoptions, 232–35
  and interracial adoptions, 232–35
  late, 213, 214
  middle, 213, 214
  move to adoptive home during, 90,
    236–39
  parent/teen tensions in, 222–24
  pregnancy in, 225
  problem behaviors during, 238–39
  rites of passage of, 214–15

  search for birth parents in, 202–3,
    229–32
  sexuality in, 224–26, 227–29
  stages of, 213
  suggested reading, 239–40
  tasks and characteristics of, 212–14,
    219–22
  unresolved issues and, 210–11
Adoption. *See also* International
    adoption; Interracial adoption
  and bonding attachment, 19–20
  concept of, 3
  history of, 6–8
  informal, 6, 7
  as loss, 30–52
  reasons for choosing, 4–5
  types of, 8–11
Adoption laws, 259
Adoptive parents. *See* Parents, adoptive
Adulthood
  adoption issues in, 252–56
  psychosocial stages of, 252–56
  relationships with parents in, 253–54
  separation and, 217–19
Agency adoption, 9–10, 260–61
  approval processes, stress and
    powerlessness due to, 70, 71
Aggressive drives, 117
Alienation, sense of, 223–24
Ames, L. B., 107–8, 110

Anger
  at adoptive parents, 49
  at birth parents, 37, 49, 89–91, 216
  as a defense mechanism, 198
  defining acceptable outlets for, 68,
    95, 190, 199
  about loss, 32, 45–46
  in middle childhood, 198–99
  in the older infant, 149–50
  parent's response to, 90, 95
Animism, 165–66
Arrival of child, and marital
    relationship, 78–80
Asian-American orphans, 7–8
Attachment
  agency's assessment of, 260
  and bonding, 16–18, 28–29
  in early infancy, 118
  elasticity of, 18
  enhancers and inhibitors of, 89, 156
  healthy, signs of, 162–63
  in middle childhood, 205
  in older infant, 129–30, 133
  poor or anxious, 249
  and positive-interaction cycle, 21–22
  postplacement concerns about, 76
  and transition to adoptive home, 88
Attachment disorder, 27–29
Attention-deficit disorder (ADD),
    156–57, 241, 246–50
Attention-deficit hyperactivity disorder
    (ADHD), 241, 246–50
Autism stage, first-month, 112–18
  problems during, 116–18
  revisiting, 159–60

Baker, S. M., 107–8, 110
Balance theory of attitudes, in identity
    formation, 59–67
Bargaining, as defense mechanism, 43
Bedroom, child's, decorating, 75
Beliefs, of adopted children, 89–91
Belonging, sense of, 16, 22, 25, 33, 158,
    161
  in adolescence, 216

defined, 22
and family storybook activity, 82
in middle childhood, 205
Birth, adopted children's beliefs about,
    175
Birth children, 4–5
Birth parent, 36–38
  versus adoptive parents, 4–5
  alcoholic or drug-addicted, 247
  anger at, 216
  child's beliefs and feelings about,
    89–91
  closed adoption and, 9
  fantasies about, 44
  loss of, 31, 33–35, 40, 41
  overempathizing with, 37–38
  photographs of, 193, 206
  providing well-rounded picture of,
    201
  reunion with, 231–32
  searching for, 8, 45. *See also*
    Searching
  sharing difficult information about,
    203–5
  telling child about, 36–38, 203–5
Body awareness, 133, 140–41, 150–51,
    176
Body image
  adolescents and, 224, 227
  in middle childhood years, 205–6
  of preschoolers, 174–75
Bonding cycle, 13–29
  with adopted children, 18–20
  and attachment, 16–18
  completing, 18
  and daily life experiences, 27
  and day care, 121–22
  enhancers and inhibitors of, 22–27
  during first month of life, 115, 117
  healthy, signs of, 162–63
  how it works, 20–21
  newborn and, 113
  and positive-interaction cycle, 22
  postplacement concerns about, 76
  stages of, 20

Bonds
  absence of, 28–29
  and attachment, 16–18
  and daily life experiences, 27
  versus love, 18
  prenatal, 19
  primal, 19
  past, effects of, 22–23
  and trust, 17–18, 20–21
Bouchard, T., 14, 229
Bourguignon, J. P., 18–19
Bowlby, J., 47, 48, 51–52, 53–54
Brazelton, T. B., 115
Buddy Families, 73

Cain, B. S., 211
Ceremonies, and feeling of entitlement,
  81–82
Change
  in lifestyle, 76–78
  and loss, 32–33, 38–39
Checking-back behavior, 133, 135–36
Child development theory, 105. See also
  Developmental stages
Childhood, cyclical nature of, 107–9
Child's life storybook, 202
Choosing a child, 258–61
"Chosen-child" message, dichotomy of,
  54, 62, 149, 166, 194–96, 216
Claiming and belonging, 16, 25, 76,
  158, 161
  in adolescence, 216
  defined, 22
  and family storybook activity, 82
  in middle childhood, 205
Cline, F. W., 110
Closed adoption, 9–10
Coercion, by child, 138, 147
Cognitive consonance, 59–61
Cognitive dissonance, 59, 62
Communication
  of difficult information, 203–5
  about previous caregivers, 145
  timer technique for, 79–80
Conflicting messages, 55–56

Conscience development, 140
Consolidation of individuation stage,
  124, 148–57
  characteristics of, 148–51
  move to adoptive home during,
    153–55
  problems during, 155–57
Coping, during waiting period, 72–75
Core identity, 58, 62, 149
Counseling, 260. See also Professional
  help
  for stress, 82
  during transition to adoptive home,
    94–96
Crane, B., 211
Cross-cultural adoption, 55–56, 106
Cue-word technique, 48
Cultural differences. See Cross-cultural
  adoption; International adoption;
  Interracial adoption

Daily life experiences, and bonding, 27
Darting, 139
Dating, 226–27
Day care, 187
  during symbiosis, 121–22
Daydreaming, 198
Defense mechanisms
  in grief process, 41–44
  in middle childhood, 198–99
Denial, as defense mechanism, 42–43
Depression, in grief, 45
Despair, 41–42
  about loss, 45–46
Detachment. See Withdrawal
Developmental stages. See also Adoles-
  cence; Adulthood; Infancy, early;
  Infants, older; Middle childhood;
  Preschool years
  and adopted children, 105–7
  basic, 106
  effect of adoption on, 106
  and equilibrium/disequilibrium,
    108–10
  personality and, 107, 110
  suggested reading, 110–111

Differentiation stage, of separation and individuation, 124–31
  characteristics of, 125–26
  move to adoptive home during, 135
  move to new home during, 127–30
  premature, 130–31
  theme of, defined, 124
Dinkmeyer, D., Sr., 110
Dinkmeyer, J. S., 110
Disabilities, and adoption, 11
Disbelief, as defense mechanism, 42–43
Discipline, 94–95, 190. *See also* One-minute scolding technique; Timeouts
  and setting limits, 137, 138
Disclosure statements, 260
Disequilibrium. *See* Equilibrium and disequilibrium, cycles of
Disintegration, sense of, 43–44, 77–78
Distancing behaviors, 25–26, 90
Dolman, M., 78–79, 87
Derris, M., 250
Dusky, L., 240

Egan, A. B., 77, 87, 112, 114
Education. *See* School
Edward, J., 112, 155–156
Egocentrism
  movement away from, 191–92
  of preschoolers, 164–65
Emotions. *See* Feelings
Empathy, development of, 192
Empty-nest transition, 236
Entitlement to parenting, 81–82
Environment, versus genetics, 14–15
Equilibrium and disequilibrium, cycles of, 107–10
  in late infancy, 133
  in older infant, 149–50
  in preschoolers, 169–70
Erikson, E. H., 56, 58, 192, 214, 215, 220–21, 252–53, 254, 255
Expectations
  about academic capabilities, 245–46
  conflicting, 55–56

letting go of, and bonding, 26–27
  about personality traits, 183–84
  in transition to adoptive home, 93
Extended family, 5, 6
Eye contact, 158, 159

Fahlberg, V., 20, 22, 89, 142, 145, 247
Fair Labor Standards Act (1938), 7
Family
  explaining placement complications to, 73–74
  during middle childhood years, 192–93
Family history
  gathering, 97
  worksheet, 100–101
Family life cycle. *See also* Marital relationship
  adolescence and, 235–36
  in early infancy of child, 113–14
  during early infancy of child, 119–20
  during later infancy of child, 126–27, 134–35, 141, 151–52
  preschoolers and, 181–84
Family relationships
  child's awareness of, 150
  factors contributing to success of, 257–58
  preschooler's awareness of, 168–69
Family storybook, 82–87, 202
  value of creating, 82–83
  writing, 83–87
Family trees, as school projects, 243–45
Fantasy(ies), 173. *See also* Kidnapping fantasy
  of perfect parents, 193–94
Father-child relationship, 114, 119–20, 131–32
Fears, of kidnapping, 193
Feelings. *See also* Anger; Grief process; Separation anxiety
  awareness of, 73
  learning to express, 4, 50–51
Fetal alcohol effect (FAE), 247, 250

Fetal alcohol syndrome (FAS), 188, 247, 250
Finalization of adoption, wait before, 71–72
Fishel, E., 227
Fog stage, 112–18. *See also* Autism stage; Newborn
  problems during, 116–18
  revisiting, 159–60
Foos, D., 18
Foster home placement, 259
Foster parents. *See* Previous caregivers
Frasier, D., 188
Fredkove, A., 195, 197
Freeman, L., 188
Freud, A., 213
Freud, S., 253
Frustration tolerance, 137

Gabel, S., 239
Gay or lesbian adoptive parents, 5
Gender roles, 205
  in preschool years, 175–76
Generalization, 167–68
Generational conflicts, 134
Generativity versus stagnation, 254–55
Genetic endowment, child's, 4, 14, 204–5
Gerring, L., 251
Golant, M., 211
Goodbyes, importance of saying, 92–93
Gordon, S., 228
Grandparents, 134–35
  adolescents and, 237
Greenspan, N. T., 118, 123
Greenspan, S., 118, 123
Grief process, 38–41, 95, 108, 116–17. *See also* Loss(es)
  in babies, 128–29
  in children, 40
  cyclical nature of, 40
  delayed, 41
  and distancing behaviors, 25–26
  learning to express emotions in, 50–51
    and loss, 30–51
    in middle childhood, 198–200
    phases of, 38–50
    resolution of, 49–50
    resurgence of, 32, 35, 40
    suggested reading, 51–52
    unresolved, 90, 91, 249
Griffith, K. C., 230
Guilt, 45
  letting go of, 73

Hartman, C., 87
Heider, F., 59
Hirschberg, J. C., 188
History of adoption, in U.S., 6–8
Hogan, R., 56, 214, 221, 253
Holding therapy, 123
Homosexual adoptive parents, 5
Homosexuality, fears of, 225
Hopelessness, about loss, 45–46
Hopson, D., 110
Hopson, D. S., 110

Idealism, 220
Identity, 22. *See also* Identity formation; Self, sense of; Self-image
  and adopted child, 53–69
  attitudinal aspect of, 62
  changes in, 57
  core identity, 58, 62
  factors influencing, 57–58
  integration of, after loss, 46–47
  and loss, 31
  reorganization of, after loss, 46
  shame-based, risk factors for, 54–55
Identity crises, versus identity formation, 58–59
Identity formation, 57–59
  in adolescence, 212, 214–19
  balance theory applied to, 61–67
  versus identity crisis, 58–59
  inputs and outputs, 57–58
  and separation, 217–19
  theories of, 59–67
Ilg, F. L., 107–8, 110

Imaginary friends, 172–73
Imaginary play, of preschoolers, 165
Incest, conception by, 203, 204
Individuation. *See* Consolidation
  of individuation stage; Identity formation; Separation and
  individuation *headings*
Infancy, early. *See also* Autism stage;
  Symbiosis stage
  basic developmental task, 112–14
  first month of life, 112–18
  symptoms of unhealthy development
    during, 116–18
  transition to adoptive home during,
    114–18, 120–23
  two to five months, 118–23
Infant, older, 124–63
  and bonding cycle, 21
  differentiation stage, 124–31
  fifteen to twenty-two months, 124,
    137–48
  five-to-ten months, 124–31
  nine to eighteen months, 124, 131–
    37
  suggested reading, 161
  transition to adoptive home, 91,
    127–30, 135–36, 141–45, 153–55
  twenty-one to thirty-six months, 124,
    148–57
Infertility
  discovery of, 13–14
  as loss, 35–36, 71
Informal adoption, 6, 7
Integration, and completion of grief
  process, 49–50
Integrity, 255–56
Interactions, positive. *See* Positive
  interactions
International adoption, 7–8, 11, 171–
  72
  adolescents and, 232–35
  answering intrusive questions about,
    177–80
  child's beliefs about, 90–91
  issues of middle childhood, 206–8

middle childhood search in, 202
and name of child, 96
preschoolers and, 177–81
and visiting child's homeland, 92,
  202, 235
Interracial adoption, 7–8, 10–11,
  171–72
  adolescents and, 232–35
  answering intrusive questions about,
    177–80
  Heider's balance theory of attitudes
    applied to, 59–62
  issues of middle childhood, 206–8
  preschoolers and, 177–81
  social movements, 8
Intimacy, emotional, 252–53

James, J. W., 30, 38, 39, 49, 51, 52
Jewett, C., 52

Kagan, J., 148
Kasza, K., 188
Kennell, J., 18
Kidnapping fantasy, 89, 193
Klaus, M., 18
Klein, D., 78–79, 87
Koch, J., 188
Korean-American orphans, 7–8
Kranes, J. E., 251
Kreisman, J. J., 146
Kremetz, J., 239
Kübler-Ross, E., 52

Language development, 140
Learning disabilities, 245–50
  high incidence of, in adopted children,
    246–47
  suggested reading, 250–51
Lesbian adoptive parents, 5
Lifestyle of parents, change in, 76–78
Lifton, B. J., 240, 256
Logical thinking, development of, 191,
  194
Loneliness of father, postplacement,
  77–78, 119–20

Loss(es). *See also* Grief process
  adoption as, 4, 30–52
  and grief process, 30–51
  understanding experiences of, 31–33
Love. *See also* Bonding cycle
  beginning of, 114
  versus bonding, 18

McConnell, N. P., 211
McKay, G. D., 110
McNamera, B., 259
McNamera, J., 259
Macroculture(s), 55
  conflicting expectations of, 55–56
  versus microculture, 55
Magical thinking, 195, 218
  in preschool years, 166–68, 184–85,
    187–88
Mahler, M., 148
Malcolm X, 220–21
Marital relationship, 181–83. *See also*
    Family life cycle
  adolescence and, 235–36
  basic needs from, 182–83
  changes in, 36
  communication in, 79–80
  later infancy period and, 126
  postplacement period and, 78–80
  preschooler's awareness of, 168–69
Medical and family history, 258, 260
  gathering, 97
  worksheet, 98–101
Memories, child's, 4
  validating, 144–45
Mentoring programs, finding, 73
Messages
  conflicting, 55–56
  positive, and negative self-image,
    63–67
Microculture, 55
Middle childhood (six to ten years)
  beliefs about adoption during, 89
  body image in, 205–6
  developmental landmarks, 191–94
  grief in, 198–200

helping child with emotions in,
    200–202
  move to adoptive home during,
    208–10
  peer groups in, 207–8, 209
  sexuality in, 205
  unresolved problems during, 210–11
Midlife crises, parents', 236, 255
Modeling, 168
Momentos, importance of, 93–94
Moral conscience, 192
Mordock, J., 94, 95–96
Mother, adoptive
  in postplacement period, 118–20
  and separation anxiety of infant, 127
  role of, 114, 118, 152
Moving adopted children. *See*
    Transition to adoptive home

Name, of adopted child, 96–97
NBAS (neonatal behavioral assessment
    scale), 115–16
Negative behaviors, 25
Neglect, 187
Nelson, G., 154
Neonatal behavioral assessment scale
    (NBAS), 115–16
Networking, 15
Neubauer, A., 15
Neubauer, P., 15
Newborn, 112–13
Numbness, as defense mechanism,
    41–42

Object constancy, 126, 149, 155–57
  helping child with, 157
  during middle childhood, 194
  physical intimacy and, 226
  reinforcing, 154
Oedipus/Electra complexes, 169, 205
Old age, 255–56
One-minute scolding technique, 154–55
Open adoption, 8, 258–59
  versus closed adoption, 9–10
  purpose of, 9

Openness about adoption
  first move toward, 7–8
  and open placement programs, 8
Options, stressfulness of, 71
Orphans
  racially-mixed, 7–8
  wartime, 7–8
Orphan trains, 6–7
Osman, B. B., 250
Overprotection, 130, 136, 154

Parent/child fit, 117, 136, 183, 187
Parenting adopted children
  versus parenting birth children, 3–4
  preparing for, 74–75
Parents, adoptive. *See also* Family
    life cycle; Marital relationship;
    Prospective adoptive parents;
    Single adoptive parents
  challenges faced by, 4–5
  losses of, 35–36
  and special needs of adopted children,
    11
Parkes, C. M., 46, 52
Permission, 200
Pebbles technique, 200–201, 219, 223,
    262
Pediatricians, 82
Peer group
  in middle childhood, 192–93, 207–8,
    209
  minority adolescents and, 232–35
Perfect-parent fantasy, 193–94
Personality traits
  and attachments, 18
  and bonding, 23–24
  clashes in, 23–24
  and developmental stages, 107, 110
  genetics and, 14–15
  in preschool years, 183–84
  and transition to adoptive home, 88
Pets, 200
Phoning home, 147
Photographs
  of birth parents, 206

of previous caregivers, 93, 144
  in transition to adoptive home, 92
Physical traits, 25, 33
Pining, 44–45
Placement, 258–61
Placement day, recording details of, 142
Play, 140
  lack of, 187
  and modeling, 168
  preschool, 173–74
Positive interactions, 16, 158
  and attachment and bonding, 21–22,
    24–25
Postplacement period
  adjustment to new demands during,
    76
  emotional issues for parent during,
    75–82
  expectations during, 93
  parental disintegration during, 77–78
  stress in, 76–82
  suggested reading, 87
Post-traumatic stress disorder (PTSD),
    249
Powerlessness, sense of
  in children, 89, 166–67
  in prospective adoptive parents,
    70–72
Practicing stage, of separation and
    individuation, 124, 131–37
  characteristics of, 131–34
  move to adoptive home during,
    135–36
  unhealthy, 136–37
Prenatal bond, 19
Preplacement period. *See also* Arrival of
    child
  preparations during, 74–75
  stress in, 70–75
  suggested reading for, 87
  visiting child during, 92
Preschool years, 164–90
  beliefs about adoption in, 89–90
  body image in, 174–75
  common characteristics of, 164–74

gender role awareness in, 175–76
parenting tips for, 189–90
potential difficulties in, 187–88
sexuality in, 174–77
Previous caregivers, 142–45
maintaining contact with, 142–44, 185–86
transferring trust to. *See also* Transferring trust
Privacy needs, 181–82
Private adoption, 9–10
Professional help, 82, 146. *See also* Counseling
finding, 261–62
for middle childhood move, 209–10
for reparenting technique, 158
during searching, 230
seeking, 11–12
on sharing difficult information, 204
during transition to adoptive home, 94–96
Prospective adoptive parents, 10, 170–87. *See also* Choosing a child
emotional considerations of, 17
fears of, about capacity to love, 13–14, 15–16
fears of, about personality traits, 14–15
feelings about adoption process, 26
infertility of, 13–14
information needed by, 260–261
issues to consider, 17
self-exploration issues, 16

Race, and adoption. *See* Interracial adoption; Same-race adoption
Racism, 178–81, 206
Rage, 45
Rage-reduction therapy. *See* Holding therapy
Rando, T. A., 34, 40, 41, 44, 45–46, 50, 52
Rape, conception by, 203, 204
Rapprochement crisis, 138

Rapprochement stage, of separation and individuation, 124, 137–48
characteristics of, 137–41
move to adoptive home during, 141–46
problems during, 146–48
Reality, preschoolers and perceptions of, 165–66
Reparenting technique, 157–61
Replacement, in grief process, 48–50
Reunion, with birth parent, 231–32
Rituals, formal, and feeling of entitlement, 81–82
Rosenberg, M., 111
Ruskin, N., 112, 155–56

Same-race adoption, 10, 151
Schaffer, P., 188
School. *See also* Learning disabilities
and adopted child, 241–51
choice of, 241
elementary, modifying projects in, 243–45
and parent and teacher expectations, 245–46
underachievement in, 247, 249
School-age children. *See* Middle childhood
Searching, for birth parent, 44–45
in adolescence, 202–3, 229–32
in middle childhood years, 44–45, 202–3
parent-facilitated, 202–3
as part of grief process, 44–45
in preschool years, 33–34, 170–71
support groups for, 230
Self, sense of. *See also* Identity; Identity formation
false, 131
and grief process, 39, 40
in early infancy, 119
loss of, 43
Self-constancy, 149
Self-esteem, 116, 117

Self-image, 62–68, 146
  changing, 66–67
  helping child to improve, 68–69
  negative, and positive messages,
    63–67
Self-parenting, 129, 130
Self-soothing, 116, 122–23, 130,
  132–33, 150, 157
Separation and individuation, in
  adolescence, 214–19
  identity formation and, 217–19
  parent/teen tensions and, 222
Separation and individuation, in older
  infant, 23, 124–26
  consolidation of individuation stage,
    124, 148–57
  differentiation stage, 124–31
  practicing stage, 124, 131–37
  rapprochement stage, 124, 137–48
Separation anxiety, 125–26, 127, 128,
  133–34
  in older infant, 136, 138–39, 147
  and start of kindergarten, 246
Separation experience, impact of, 3–4.
  See also Loss(es)
Sexual abuse, 27–28, 225–26, 237–38,
  259–60
Sexual feelings, of parent and child,
  114, 238
Sexuality
  in adolescence, 224–27
  and adoptive parents, 113–14, 120,
    126, 225
  and birth parents, 216, 225
  in middle childhood years, 205–6
  preschoolers and, 174–77
  talking about, with adolescents,
    227–29
Shadowing and darting, 139
Shame, 45
  identity based on, 54–55, 56
  two types of, 53–54
Shock, 41–42
Sibling-group adoption, 10

Siblings, adding, during preschool years,
  184
Similarities and differences, child's
  awareness of, 150–51
Simon, N., 188
Single adoptive parents, 5, 80–81, 85
Social attitudes and opinions, 220
Social role, determination of, 221–22
Special needs adoption, 11
Stein, S., 211
Stinson, K., 211
Stranger anxiety, 125
Straus, H., 146
Stress, in adoption, 70–72
  coping with, 72–75, 82–87
  entitlement issue as, 81–82
  for married parents, 78–80
  postplacement, 76–82
  preplacement, 70–75
  for single parents, 80–81
Support groups, 15, 72–73, 230
Switzer, R. E., 188
Symbiosis stage, 118–23
  characteristics of, 118–19
  day care during, 121–22
  healthy, 118–19
  infant's perceptions during, 119
  regression to, 135
  revisiting, 159
  symptoms of unhealthy development
    during, 122–23
  transition to adoptive home during,
    120–21

Taylor, J. F., 248, 250
Teenage years. *See* Adolescence
Temper tantrums
  in older infant, 133, 137–38
  in preschoolers, 170
Timeouts, 155
Timer technique, 79–80
Transferring trust, or bond, 17, 19,
  21–26
  during symbiosis

for older infants and toddlers, 124,
127–29, 135, 142, 143, 147, 153,
156, 158
in preschool years, 185–86
Transition to adoptive home, 88–96
in adolescence, 212–13, 236–39
age as factor in, 88–89
allowing child choices during, 94
child's perceptions of reasons for,
89–91
counseling during, 94–96
during differentiation stage, 127–30
factors affecting child's reaction to,
88–89
during first month of life, 114–18
grieving as result of, 30–35
history of move, 260
during middle childhood, 208–10
optimal time for, 23
preparing child for, 91–96
during preschool years, 184–87
suggested reading, 97
Transitional care, 259
Transitional objects, 93–94, 132–33
Transracial adoption. *See* Interracial
adoption
Trauma, 31–32
and bonding, 23

Trust, 16. *See also* Bonding cycle
and age at adoption, 21
and bonding cycle, 17–18, 20–21
in symbiosis stage, 120
transference of, 22–23, 142–45, 158,
186
Turrini, P., 112, 155–56

Underachievement, 249

Validation of feelings, 35, 45, 69, 200
Van Ornum, W., 94, 95–96
Visits, to previous caregiver, 143

Waiting period
coping during, 72–75
between selection and finalization,
71–72
War orphans, 7–8
Watson, J. W., 188
Watson, K., 18–19
Weiss, R. S., 46, 52
Withdrawal, 47–48, 146–47
Wooing, 118, 121, 138, 147, 158, 159,
186
Work role, definition of, 220–21

Yearning, 44–45. *See also* Grief process